DATE DUE			

Corruption in Paradise

Corruption in Paradise

THE CHILD IN WESTERN LITERATURE

Reinhard Kuhn

Published for Brown University Press
by University Press of New England
Hanover and London, 1982

University Press of New England
Brandeis University
Brown University
Clark University
Dartmouth College
University of New Hampshire
University of Rhode Island
Tufts University
University of Vermont

809.93352054
1595c
128468
ajn 1984

LIBRARY OF CONGRESS CATALOGING IN PUBLICATION DATA

Kuhn, Reinhard Clifford.
   Corruption in paradise.

   Bibliography: p. 241.
   Includes index.
   1. Children in Literature. I. Title.
PN56.5.C48K83   1982   809'.93352054   81-43693
ISBN 0-87451-235-2

Sinon l'enfance, qu'y avait-il alors
qu'il n'y a plus? . . .

If not childhood, what was there then
that is no more? . . .

Saint-John Perse

*I dedicate this book
with gratitude and love
to two very real children,
my sons, Bernhard and Nicholas,
and to my wife, Ira,
who patiently coped with them
while I played with fictional
children.*

Contents

Preface

My expression of thanks to Brown University for the role it played in making this book possible is no mere formality. The university was generous in both its material and moral support despite the increasing economic and legalistic constraints under which it, like all other institutions of higher education, has been forced to operate. In the face of such difficulties, Brown has nonetheless succeeded in maintaining the challenging scholarly atmosphere which stimulates intellectual enterprises of this sort. Many are responsible for cultivating and preserving this fragile and precious ambience: the students who have served as willing and critical guinea pigs in the courses in which I originally developed the ideas that have culminated in this work, the friends and colleagues who have read and commented on portions of the manuscript, and the administrators who have facilitated its realization. I am equally indebted to my wife and father for their constant support and suggestions. I would also like to express my appreciation to my research assistant, Mrs. Anne Burg, whose patient and reliable help proved invaluable.

A special word of gratitude is in order for Professor Andries van Dam, the developer of FRESS (File Retrieval and Editing System), and his able staff. This system immensely facilitated the development of my work, the elaboration of my ideas, and the preparation of my manuscript. These computer specialists have provided the humanist with a tool that, by reducing frustrating drudgery, liberates the mind and that, by making it possible to view simultaneously various stages and portions of a work in progress, stimulates the creative imagination. They have known how to adapt the powers of modern technology to the needs of the writer.

The actual composition of this book occurred during the academic year 1978–1979 in what is still virtually an uncorrupted paradise: Cassis, France. There, thanks to a residential fellowship from the Camargo Foundation, I was able to spend an extended period under nearly ideal working conditions, uninterrupted by the distractions of academic life. I found the same atmosphere the following year at the Institute for Advanced Study, at Princeton, where I completed the final revisions.

Portions of the first chapter of this book appeared in very different form under the title "Traces in the Sand: Gide and Novalis with the Enigmatic Child," in *Intertextuality: New Perspectives in Criticism*, the second volume of the *New York Literary Forum* ([1978], pp. 77–86), whose editor graciously extended permission to republish this material. An early version of parts of the fifth chapter was published by the *Michigan Quarterly Review* ([Spring, 1980], pp. 171–92), as "The Massacre of the Innocents: Mortality among Fictional Children." I am grateful to the editor for having allowed me to use this material again.

Except where otherwise noted, all translations of quotations in foreign languages are my own. I have included the originals only for poetry and in those cases when it seemed helpful for the understanding of the issues under discussion.

R.K.

Reinhard Kuhn died on November 6, 1980, before Brown University had recommended his completed manuscript for publication to the University Press of New England.

In editing *Corruption in Paradise* I have tried to represent my husband's intentions as closely as possible and to limit the number of substantive editorial changes. I have left the primary sources in the bibliography in their original form, and I have respected his belief that the bibliography should contain only works that deal specifically with the theme of the child and those that might assist the reader interested in pursuing the subject. Works are included that are not mentioned in the text, and many footnote citations have been omitted. I have documented the work to the best of my ability, and I would like to take this opportunity to thank the friends and colleagues who helped me trace the many familiar, yet elusive references.

Whenever possible, official translations of titles have been supplied. When not available, my own translation appears in parentheses. The titles of poems are given both in the original language and in English.

Ira Kuhn

Corruption in Paradise

Introduction

It is with a kind of fear that I touch upon the enigma of my
impressions of the beginning of life,—uncertain if I really
experienced them myself or if they were not mysteriously
transmitted recollections. I have something like religious
scruples about sounding this abyss.

Pierre Loti

"We do not know childhood." With this confession of universal
ignorance concerning the initial period of human development
Rousseau introduces *Emile*, the treatise which consecrates what
Ariès has designated as the centuries of childhood[1] and which
ushers in the age of the cult of the child. Two centuries and hundreds of books later, we are as ignorant as ever and can only agree
with George Bernard Shaw's bemused confession that "on the subject of children we are very deeply confused"[2] as well as with Alain's
admission that "all our ideas concerning childhood are false."[3] It is
my intention to take a modest step toward a better comprehension
of the real child by proposing a phenomenological description of
his fictional counterpart. In the following study I do not pretend to
attempt the impossible task of disengaging the essential nature of
the child from the literary context which simultaneously emprisons
and reveals him. To try to seize this protean figure and force him
to expose his authentic identity would be a vain enterprise, for it
would lead us to question, as does Leslie Fiedler, the legitimacy of
the child as a representative of a preexisting reality: "So ubiq-
uitous and symbolic a figure is, of course, no mere reproduction
of a fact of existence; he is a cultural invention, a product of
the imagination."[4] The psychologist Daniel Lagache, as quoted by
Jacques Lacan, goes even further by negating, at least in his early
stages, the independent existence of the child: "Before existing
in himself, by himself and for himself, the child exists for and

3

through others; he is already a pole of expectations, projects, attributes."[5]

And yet, despite Fiedler's brilliant argument, the child is more than an aesthetic invention leaping *ex nihilo* into a fictive existence; despite Lagache's dogmatic assertions, he is more than a mere surrogate for our unconscious, impulsive lives. He does exist in, by, and for himself, and his very autonomy gives him a transformative power which influences not only the image we have of children, but also the image we have of ourselves as adults. In view of these complexities, it would be tempting to resign myself to the relatively simple task of writing a straightforward history of the appearance of the child in literature while tracing the development of this image throughout the ages. Such a scholarly exercise could easily be justified and would supply an important tool for further research. But it would also imply the indifference expressed in Hugo von Hofmannsthal's "Ballade des äusseren Lebens," a poem which eloquently expresses the distance that separates the adult from the child:

> Und Kinder wachsen auf mit tiefen Augen,
> Die von nichts wissen, wachsen auf und sterben,
> Und alle Menschen gehen ihre Wege . . .
> . . . .
> Was frommt das alles uns und diese Spiele,
> Die wir doch gross und ewig einsam sind
> Und wandernd immer suchen irgend Ziele. . . .[6]

> And children grow up with deep eyes,
> Which know of nothing, grow up and die,
> And all people go their way . . .
> . . . .
> What matters all of that, and these games, to us,
> We who are after all big and eternally alone
> And wander never looking for any goals. . . .

In contrast to this attitude of aimless detachment, there is the impassioned commitment to childhood expressed in the verses of Paul Eluard:

> Les flammes de l'enfance immenses tournoyaient
> Eclairant dévorant un monde sans rupture . . .[7]

Immense, the flames of childhood wheeled about
Lighting up, devouring a world without rupture . . .

Because this conviction concerning the immense significance of the child is the one to which I subscribe, I have tried to go beyond literary history, but without succumbing to the temptation of establishing an ideologically oriented and abstract construct of childhood. Therefore, the following chapters are reflections on the inscrutability of the child, on its paradoxical nature, in which I attempt not to resolve the enigma, but to ask questions that will lead to an understanding of why this enigma must exist. To come to terms with this puzzle I have adopted Claude Lévi-Strauss's model of the enigma as "a question to which one postulates that there will be no response."[8] To elucidate its elements I have found it necessary to study the formative interactions among literary children rather than the literary child in isolation. This task requires an intertextual rather than a chronological approach and implies that literature is a syntagmatic whole in a state of constant transformation. Thus I make no attempt at historical coverage of a hypothetical field, and anyone looking for a comprehensive survey will be disappointed by obvious gaps. I can only hope that the inherent logic of my enterprise will make it self-evident why, for example, I neglect Mark Twain, one of the major celebrants of boyhood (as distinct from childhood). The desire to avoid needless duplication must serve to justify the passing over of many poets like Traherne whom one naturally associates with the theme of childhood. Intertextuality poses far more serious dangers than those of possible omissions. By abstracting a work from its cultural and temporal matrix an intertextual critic runs the risk of doing violence to history. The lack of constraints can lead to misreadings which totally distort the literary map. However, the intertextual approach need not be an anachronistic one. It is perfectly legitimate to juxtapose a medieval text with a modern one as long as the identity of each text is scrupulously respected. The juxtaposition of Chrétien de Troyes and Henry James, for example, might strike a traditionalist as irresponsible, but it is precisely by making possible such a collision of distinctive codes that intertextuality can facilitate new readings of familiar texts.

Such a mode of investigation must presume that the reality of its object can emerge only during the course of the work and thus precludes an overly restrictive a priori definition. To establish age limits and proclaim any human figure falling within them a child would be too arbitrary. My reluctance to do so has made it possible to take examples ranging from Blake's innocent two-day-old infant to the not-so-dutiful daughter well past her adolescence portrayed in Proust's "Confession of a Girl." The lack of a common definitional feature leads to the danger of indiscriminate choice and leaves me exposed to the charge that the apparently amorphous and open-ended nature of my subject has made it possible to include anything which I choose to call *child* (with the consequence that the term itself, being all embracing, would lose all meaning). I have attempted to obviate this difficulty by limiting my selection to representatives who do have a common quality: the children I deal with have not yet experienced what Yves Bonnefoy calls "the feeling of this incessant loss of self."[9] They have not yet sensed the irreversible and ineluctable impoverishment which leads to adulthood.

There is a positive aspect to this negative definition. Children can be considered as incomplete beings who in their very lack of completion possess gifts that are lost in the finished product. They are both more and less than "specula naturae," the mirrors of nature as Cicero defines them:[10] less, because they do not faithfully reflect all of human nature; more, because their function is not limited to a mimetic one. For the child is the inarticulate bearer of tremendously significant but undecipherable tidings. Although he seems to move toward us to deliver his message, he remains within a separate sphere whose puzzling nature cannot fail to tantalize the potential but never actual recipient. Although it is contiguous with the adult world, the autonomy of this realm lends it an air of mystery that surpasses anything the most exotic countries have to offer. Despite its foreignness, this world is a continuous presence. It is this dynamic combination of strangeness and familiarity that has determined the structure of this book. The initial chapter examines the nature of the enigma posed by the fictitious child. Using this analysis as the point of departure, the second chapter explores the topography of the universe in which he moves. I then derive from this description a structure of the corruption of the child's world through Eros and Thanatos, the forces of sex and death. In this first part of the book I hope also to indicate the centrality of childhood to our own existence, in other words, to explain why Bachelard could claim, "A part of us, still a part of us, forever a part of us, childhood is a state of the soul."[11] Proceeding from this base, I go on to analyze the inevitability and yet impossibility of the death of the child, in an attempt to illuminate the shocking nature of the paradox of the mortal *puer aeternus.* Finally, through speculating about the song of the child, I attempt to indicate how this paradox can be transcended. This book, then, is both more and less than another exercise in traditional literary scholarship: less, because it does not emphasize or attempt to prove the historical assumptions upon which any considerations of the child in literature must be based (such as the obvious fact that the eighteenth century is the critical period in the total re-evaluation of the status of the child); more, because of the very nature of my speculations on a subject that lends itself naturally to philosophical considerations. For inherent in the child are all the possibilities of the man, some of which have been realized in his ultimate form while most have been discarded. Just as the acquisition of speech is a process of elimination and choice among the infinite number of sounds the child is capable of articulating, so the whole epistemological and emotive development of the human being is a reductive one. Thus the literature dealing with the child as a creature of infinite potential represents a confrontation between the fully formed adult writer and his earlier incarnation, between an avatar and his preexisting persona, both of whom are in a state of perpetual development. "The easiest thing of all," according to Hegel, "is to judge what has content and solidity; it is harder to grasp it; most difficult of all is its representation, which is a combination of both processes."[12] The task of representing childhood, already complex because of the dual state of flux within which both authors and their subjects exist, is all the more difficult because it is "the becoming of itself, the circle whose end presupposes its purpose which is its beginning, and which achieves its reality only through its execution and its end."[13] The following study of what is and what might have been, of the interaction of two states of becoming, while utilizing the appropriate techniques of literary criticism and especially intertextual analysis based on close readings as well as those of historiography, is designed as a dialectical demonstration oriented toward the discovery of some of the foundations of a nonstructural anthropology.

The scope of such an enterprise is of necessity broad; the

child's persistent will to survive through the ages is symbolized by the graceful arm, holding onto a rein, which emerges from the ruins of Delphi.[14] Although the exaggerated worship of the child may be a modern phenomenon, man has been intrigued by those earliest phases in his own development which can be classified under the general rubric of childhood. From time immemorial he has stood in awe of the enigmatic figure of his primitive form. In the *Iliad* (6. 466–86) Homer depicts the terror of Astyanax when he sees his father in battle regalia. Hector immediately divests himself of his helmet (which in the child's eyes is a menacing object) and kisses and comforts his son, then hands the child to the mother, who fondles him against her breast. Astyanax's fright is ominous, and the adults demonstrate their respect for him in their solicitous attempts to assuage it. The removal of the headgear is more than an effort to allay fear; it is a gesture that has always denoted obeisance. Hector's respect becomes manifest in his prayer to the gods that one day someone will say of Astyanax that he was a far better man than his father. Thus this celebrated farewell scene between Hector and Andromache actually centers on their concern for their child. This example from archaic times prefigures the far later institutionalization of child worship. The privileged status of Roman children was made manifest by their symbolic garment, the purple and white *toga praetexta* with all its sacerdotal implications,[15] and the satirist Juvenal proclaimed their entitlement to the greatest reverence ("Maxima debetur puero reverentia"). As for medieval society, Ariès is simply wrong when he denies the child any significant role within it. Le Roy Ladurie, in a meticulous study of an Occitanian village, comes to the opposite conclusion, namely that at this time "there existed in the depths of the soul very lively, very spontaneous and very pronounced feelings for childhood and even for earliest childhood."[16] There is certainly sufficient evidence to back up this contention. Der Wilde Alexander's astonishing poem "Hie bevorn dô wir kinder wâren" (c. 1250) is a nostalgic evocation of childhood joys undermined by childhood terrors which anticipates many modern treatments of this subject. This elegy is no exception. The extent of the attachment of parents to their young children is reflected in the emotional outburst of the wife of Richard in *L'Escoufle, roman d'aventure* (c. 1200):

—je l'aim plus que nule rien
K'il n'est rien plus bele de lui,
Mautalens, corous ne anui
Ne puis avoir tant que jel voie:
C'est m'esperance, c'est ma joie,
C'est mes jouiaus, c'est mes soulas.[17]
                              (lines 1858–63)

—I love him more than anything else
For there is nothing more beautiful than he,
Neither to irritation, anger, nor care
Can I be subject as long as I see him:
He is my hope, he is my joy,
He is my delight, he is my solace.

Just as the presence of the child can be a cause for joy, so its loss can be a tragic experience. In the medieval French romance *Jordains de Blaivies*, Oriabel is distraught when she learns of the death of her daughter:

—si se pasme souvine,
Detort ses poins et debat sa poitrine,
Ses chevex tire et desrompt sa poitrine.[18]
                              (lines 3240–42)

—she faints often
She wrings her hands and beats her breast
She pulls her hair and tears her bosom.

The child has always been more or less central to human concerns.

Despite the child's ubiquity, writers in general have displayed a peculiar hesitancy in their attempts to come to terms with him. This reticence can be attributed in part at least to a certain unease which the adult feels when faced with his diminutive counterpart. One of the many minor but revelatory incidents which Rousseau recounts in his *Confessions* illustrates this discomfiture and simultaneously hints at its causes and implications. It also sheds light on the ambiguous comportment of later devotees of children like Lewis Carroll. During the course of Rousseau's sojourn at Montmorency, Mme. de Luxembourg, his protectress, invites her granddaughter, Amélie, for a visit. The forty-seven-year-old Jean-Jacques is enchanted by the girl, not yet eleven years old, whom he describes with a veiled sensuousness that would delight the pre-Raphaelites: "She was a charming person. Her countenance, her gentleness and her timidity were really virginal. Nothing more kindly and intriguing than her face, nothing more tender and more chaste than the feelings which she inspired."[19] In the presence of the grandmother, Rousseau is encouraged to kiss the child, but, abashed, does so only with his habitual peevishness ("ma maussaderie ordinaire"). As he stands in front of her, speechless and taken aback ("muet et interdit"), he wonders which of them feels more shame. On the following day he is even more confounded when unexpectedly he runs into her on the staircase. Not knowing what to say to her, he offers her a kiss, which in her innocence she accepts. In his recital of this brief encounter Rousseau desperately tries to justify his impulsive act and vehemently asserts the innocence of the furtive kiss, an innocence which nobody would have thought to question but which Rousseau's own defense renders suspect. Twice within a few lines he repeats the phrase "I can swear" in maintaining the purity of his intentions and the asexual nature of an embrace which, nonetheless, he qualifies as "reprehensible." The guilt-ridden aggressor concludes his reflections with a question: "How is it that a very child can intimidate a man who is unafraid of the power of kings?" (p. 536). The answer to this rhetorical query can be deduced from his own description of the episode. Like so many who have attempted to delve into the mystery of childhood, he is both disconcerted and intrigued by its enigma and terrified lest its essential nature be destroyed by an attempt at possession. This frustration is enhanced by his awareness that the ethereal creature (who shares his shyness) is an incarnation of his own irretrievable and unrecognizable childhood, the purity of which is lost and forgotten.

It is this oblivion, this total forgetfulness of a universally shared condition, that makes it so difficult, if not impossible, to come to terms with the reality of childhood. The phenomenon, known by modern psychologists as childhood amnesia,[20] is attributed by Freud to the progressive repression of infantile sexuality, a process which leaves in its wake only undecipherable and fragmentary *Deckerinerrungen*, which are screens subconsciously designed to conceal the reality of childhood.[21] The same censor who deletes what is essential in dreams[22] is at work making it impossible to recall any material which might, because of its disruptive nature, be objectionable. In other words, childhood amnesia, according to Freud, is the result of a traumatic experience. Despite the convincing quality of its simple argument, there is something suspect about this thesis. If it were based on reality, a resolution of the traumatic state should immediately make the suppressed data available to the conscious memory, a result which has never been achieved. I would prefer to consider childhood amnesia as the natural consequence of the discontinuous progression that leads to the transformation of the child into the adult. At some point there is a radical change in conceptual codes which marks the progression from the prerational stage of childhood to the intellectual stage of adulthood. Coleridge, in his critique of Wordsworth in the *Biographia Literaria*, complains about the impossibility of recapturing the child's vision: "Children . . . give us no . . . information of themselves; and at what time were we dipped in the Lethe, which has produced such utter oblivion of a state so godlike?"[23] Coleridge thus posits a radical rupture that obliterates what is essential in the past; he goes on to mourn the tragic loss which such a divorce entails:

There are many of us that still possess some remembrances, more or less distinct, respecting themselves at six years old; pity that the worthless straws only should float, while treasures, compared with which all the mines of Golconda and Mexico were but straws, should be absorbed by some unknown gulf into some unknown abyss. (p. 482)

In this powerful image Coleridge, well before Freud, describes the relationship of the *Deckerinerrungen* with the profundities of the subconscious. The insignificant flotsam survives the cataclysm that engulfs the inestimable wonders of the early years. The question remains as to whether a poet can plunge into the depths to retrieve this treasure. The intellectual structure of adult cognitive functions does not contain categories within which the childhood world can be subsumed or experienced. It simply is incompatible with the experiences of a previous age. While in our normal state and operating in an experiential realm that makes constant practical demands on us, we employ a linguistic system which is perfectly suitable for survival but which does not enable us to cope with matter foreign to it, whether this material comes to us from the domain of childhood or that of dreams. That is not to say that the past is irrevocable. The conjuring up of a lost time is, after all, not a rare experience. As long as the adult can recover, through the intellect, the imagination, or the involuntary memory, the mental set of the child and appropriate for himself the schemata within which the child orders the elements of his experiences, then he can relive the profound reality of his erstwhile condition and can even retranslate it into terms comprehensible to other adults. Such transmission, however, requires more than mere transcription. It is possible only through a process of reeducation in which the others are forced to assume, even though only temporarily, the mental structure of a child. Since the utilitarian nature of language itself poses a barrier to a form of expression which must transcend articulation, it is not surprising that some of the most impressive successes have been achieved in the realm of the nonverbal arts. In music the *Kinderszenen* (*Scenes from Childhood*) of Robert Schumann and the *Kindertotenlieder* (*Children's Death Songs*) of Gustav Mahler and in the pictorial arts the paintings of Henri Rousseau and Franz Marc create the immediately accessible magical world of childhood. But writers, too, have succeeded in overcoming the rationalistic nature of language by exploiting its affective aspects and symbolic resonances. While some, like Hugh Walpole, have contented themselves with a sentimental ideal of childhood that is merely an expression of adult wish-fulfillment, others, like Proust, have adopted "this creative doubt of the child, this fecund aporia of his language."[24] Thanks to Freud, the former vision is no longer a tenable one. It is, of course, he who did more than anyone else to demolish the myth of an innocent childhood paradise and to focus attention on the earliest stages of life as the crucial period in human development. The fact remains, however, that he actually tells us very little about childhood and devotes only a few pages of his extensive works to its description. Childish traits he deems as obstacles to the development of the mature adult, for the child is nothing more than a homunculus, a primitive form of the more complex and higher being represented by man. In *The Interpretation of Dreams* Freud states unambiguously that they are of interest only as underdeveloped subjects:

The most simple dreams of all, I suppose, are to be expected in the case of children, whose psychic activities are certainly less complicated than those of adults. The psychology of children, in my opinion, is to be called upon for services similar to those which a study of the anatomy and development of the lower animals renders to the investigation of the structure of the highest classes of animals.[25]

Even in his detailed depiction of the phobia of five-year-old Hans, Freud casts little light on the condition of the child as child. Rarely does he go beyond insisting, as in *Leonardo da Vinci and a Memory of his Childhood*, that ". . . childhood is not the blissful idyll into which we distort it in retrospect."[26] Feminist criticism has recently attacked Freud for considering woman merely as an incomplete male; one could apply the same objection to his presentation of the child. In one important sense such a critique is unfair, for Freud never pretends to develop a morphology of the child (or of the woman). He does something much more important, in that he provides us with the insights that make such a project possible. At the same time, Freud also discovers the essential link between the fictional and the real child: "Thus the 'childhood reminiscences' of individuals altogether advance to the signification of 'concealing memories,' and thereby form a noteworthy analogy to the childhood reminiscences as laid down in the legends and myths of nations."[27] It is this analogy which needs to be explored more extensively.

The child has attracted a great deal of attention in the recent past, and a few of the studies devoted to him have indeed investigated the Freudian analogy in a creative fashion. This is particularly true of the significant books of the anthropologist George Boas, the psychologist Serge Leclaire, and the literary historian Peter Coveney, all of which have influenced my own thoughts on this subject. The majority of the studies by literary and art historians are of a more limited value. However, as more or less stimulating illustrated catalogues of the theme they have an undeniable utility. Many of the studies by the psychologists have gained a wide audience but ultimately prove disappointing. As brilliant as Erik H. Erikson's probings of the childhoods of Gandhi and Luther may be, they remain psychobiographic fictions. Jean Piaget's meticulous delineations of stages within childhood are intellectually provocative but artificial constructs, even when based on direct observation. They illustrate the limitations of what Hegel calls "tabular reasoning," which is incapable of revealing "the necessity and the concept of the contents" that alone constitute reality.[28] Although the more objective contemporary historians like Ariès have made significant contributions to understanding the situation of the child within a given society, they have not attempted to draw conclusions concerning the nature of the child. There have, of course, been innumerable pedagogical treatises which deal with the child. Many of them, most notably those of John Dewey and Maria Montessori, have had a profound impact in their practical applications, but the systems they promulgate are designed for a hypothetical child which may or may not have any relationship with a real one. Whatever their faults, the studies of anthropologists, historians, psychologists, and philosophers of education are useful and often even stimulating. This cannot be said of the efforts of the sociologists. When their righteous wrath concerning abused children is based on carefully compiled data,[29] it rarely transcends the emotionalism of polemics and is often falsified by a commitment to a radical political vision in which the family structure, on which the ills of the child-victim are blamed, is destined for abolition.[30]

The model of the child constructed and dissected by scientific discourse is an artificial one, less convincing in reality than is its literary counterpart. It is for this reason and in order to avoid the unnecessary confusion endemic to attempts to bring together categories as incompatible as those of aesthetics and of the social sciences that I exclude from this study the findings of historians, sociologists, psychologists, and philosophers of education and limit myself strictly to literary manifestations of childhood. During a period of heightened social awareness, an approach that resolutely asserts the primacy of literature as a cognitive tool might be considered a facile evasion of responsibility. It may be true that a study of Lord Shaftesbury's efforts on behalf of legislation designed to eliminate the child abuse attached to the trade of chimney sweeps can help us understand the social position of children in Victorian England. However, it is only through a reading of Blake's poem "The Chimney Sweeper" that we can gain intimations of the inner condition of those diminutive victims. As Wordsworth said in *The Prelude*, only poets can "almost make remotest infancy / A visible scene, on which the sun is shining" (1. 634–35). So the task I have set for myself is simply to illuminate the fictional child, and if such an illumination simultaneously casts some light on the flesh-and-blood child living in the real world, so much the better.

The child, containing as it does our past which we have forgotten and a future which we shall never know, is indeed a fascinating personage who perhaps deserves the silence which Michel Butor wants to accord him: "The new apparition of the child who sleeps within the depths of ourselves, covered over by such a thick blanket of deceit and oblivion, demands attention and silence."[31] But the child is also an assertive presence who challenges us to come to terms with him and simultaneously with ourselves as adults through speech. Such is his dominance that even attempts to misuse him as an instrument or an object fail to reify him. When he is employed as a symbol (as in Hawthorne's *The Scarlet Letter*) he is not emptied of his real content but maintains his personality as a child, and when he is used for polemical purposes (as in Dickens's *Oliver Twist*) he transcends his functionality. In any delimited society, the ideas and images concerning the child emerge from their representations in works of art and coalesce into a dynamic pattern. By looking at these representations not individually but as a kinetic and yet coherent corpus, we can discern a specific system with its own language. In similar fashion, within the totality of Western societies, the multiplicity of literary works in which the child is represented, varied as they are, also forms a complex system with various levels of significance, but also with a common language in which it is no longer possible or desirable to distinguish the dialect spoken by the child from the dialect used to represent it. By analyzing certain specific themes sounded in literature, it may be possible to make audible some of the accents of a composite language which is the retrospective creation of adults who have sought to become like unto children.

CHAPTER ONE

The Enigmatic Child

What manner of child shall this be!
Luke 1:66

Traces in the Sand

Riddle of destiny, who can show
What thy short visit meant, or know
What thy errand here below?
Charles Lamb

André Gide's *The Voyage of Urien* (1893) is a tale of such apparent transparency that the commentator is constantly tempted to provide simple interpretations that then prove to be so simplistic as to miss the point. The novella is cast in the familiar form of the imaginary voyage that is the reflection of an inner odyssey. The symbols are equally traditional. Consequently, one can hardly fail to equate the algae-choked Sargasso Sea in which the boat is becalmed with the concept of ennui, or the icebound arctic landscape that the travelers eventually find with the notion of sterility. Nor does it require much perspicacity to see in Eric, the brutal killer of birds, the personification of the Nietzschean superman. Yet such explanations remain unsatisfactory. At best, they are descriptive of external events in terms of subcutaneous phenomena. Such substitutions of an underlying symbolic system for a narrative one never rise above their inherent inconsequentiality, for the random replacement of one code by another is an exercise incapable of transcending itself. Paul Valéry, in "Propos me concernant," wrote, "Events are the foam of things. It is the ocean that interests me."[1] In examining Gide's fiction the critic must explore the level below the events and their analogical reflections in order to sound the depths that the reader senses underneath the limpid surface of the narration.

One of the most mysterious of the seemingly clear events during the voyage is Urien's encounter with a young boy on a beach. After having drunk from the icy waters of a glacial spring, Urien and his companions are delighted by a sensation of beatitude. They rediscover one of the miracles of childhood, for they become capable of marveling at everything ("nous nous étonnions de toute chose"). At noon they descend toward the shore, and it is there that the meeting with the young child takes place:

On the edge of the sea we met a mysterious child seated on the sand who was dreaming. He had large eyes as blue as a glacial sea; his skin shone like lilies and his hair was like a cloud tinted by the rising sun. He was trying to understand the words that he had traced on the sand. He spoke; from his lips his voice sprung forth in the same way a matinal bird while shaking off the dew soars away; we would have gladly given him our shells, our insects, and our stones. His enchanting voice was so sweet that we would have happily given him everything we had. He smiled, and his smile was one of infinite sorrow. We would have liked to have taken him away with us to the boat, but, poring over the sand, he had resumed his tranquil meditation.[2]

It would be easy to see in this episode a prefiguration of the many other youths who appear in Gide's later works and to interpret it as an early translation into symbolic terms of the longing after palingenesis, the expression the author himself used frequently to define his obsessive desire for rebirth.[3] It is equally obvious (and equally unenlightening) that this is an early manifestation of Gide's pedophilic tendencies.[4] There is more to this incident, however, than such Freudian readings reveal.

This episode represents the discovery by the adult of the child as pure enigma. The significance of the encounter is indicated by the extraordinary nature of its triviality, and its true dimensions can be apprehended only within an intertextual framework. It is more than an echo of the miraculous heralding of the birth of the child, of the Vergilian exclamation of wonderment, "Puer natus est!" that resounds throughout the ages. The Gidian incident is one of the most effective of the many sporadic manifestations of an archetypal theme. What gives the Gidian variation on this topos its peculiar quality is its author's conscious exploitation of one of the earlier incarnations of the enigmatic child, which he had found in Novalis's *The Novices of Sais* (1798). The textual parallels cannot be attributed to mere coincidence. Gide even mentions Novalis in a footnote to his text (though he does not indicate the source), and in a letter to Valéry written during the period of composition of *The Voyage of Urien* he sends his friend a few freely translated lines from *The Novices of Sais* (again without revealing their provenance). The physical traits of Gide's child are similar in many but not all respects to those of his model. Both have large blue eyes, but whereas Novalis describes them as dark with an azure background, thus emphasizing the depth of the mystery, Gide depicts them as being as blue as the glacial sea, thus reducing their dimensionality and introducing a new attribute suggesting an inhuman chill. Both children's skins shine like lilies (symbolic of death and purity). But whereas the hair of the Novalis child is like a cloud glowing with the reflections of the setting sun, connoting warmth and softness, the hair of the other is like a cloud tinted by the dawning sun. Aside from the obvious intimations of matinal freshness and purity, Gide's simile also has sacramental implications because of the secondary meaning of the French word for dawn. *L'aube* is also the white ecclesiastical vestment worn over the cassock by the priest celebrating mass. The import of the color symbolism and the emphasis placed on the eyes, concomitant with the images of freshness, can be appreciated in the light of a later development of this complex of ideas in *The Fruits of the Earth*:

Oh, how I would like to recreate a new vision for my eyes, to wash them clean of the filth of books, to make them more like unto the azure sky which they are contemplating and which today has been completely purified by the recent rains. . . . (p. 161)

In this Mallarméan passage is contained a summary of the encounter on the beach.

The impact of the two children on their elders is also grounded in a basic similitude with subtle variations in the details. The confrontation with what is the essence of inscrutability has an immediate effect on the explorers. They approach the child as a god and are ready to offer to the newly discovered divinity any and all of their possessions. In coming close to him, they themselves become childlike, as is indicated by the nugatory and yet portentous nature of their proposed offerings (shells, insects, and stones). In the Novalis novel the apprentices are prepared to render unto the child their flowers, stones, and feathers, products of the fields as opposed to those of the shore. The child, though unknowable, elicits and causes childlike behavior in those who perceive him. And yet the child refuses this homage and ignores the willingness of the sailors in one case and of the apprentices in the other to sacrifice to him. The voyagers return alone to their vessel, but the influence of the child's presence makes itself felt long after the travelers in search of truth have left him. Previously, Urien and his companions had sought solace in the waters and had taken a sensual delight in swimming. After they leave the shore this time, however, the narrator soberly states, "On this day we did not go into the water" (p. 31). And, indeed, they never do again. After meeting the young boy, there is no further need for ablutions or for sensual pleasures. The eyes of the voyagers are now forever fixed upon the azure. So, after this first encounter, the child vanishes, never to appear on the scene again. There is no further need for his continuous presence or for his return. Novalis's child also disappears after his brief appearance, but the teacher of the students of Sais predicts that he will come again and that then the lessons will come to an end. But even his one visitation has produced an effect, for his proximity has reduced the opacity of being. His gaze has revealed to the apprentices their spiritual essence.

In brief, these two emblematic figures, never named, separated in time by almost a century, are the same children and yet different. They are both evanescent enigmas, peripheral and unchanging personages who transform those who cross their paths. Nevertheless, the implications of these two enigmas are different. The earlier one is clearly rooted in the Christian mystical tradition, and his advent is the prefiguration of the second coming. The more modern one performs the function of exorcizing the sensual, but the consequent purification does not necessarily lead the explorers to salvation.

Despite their different symbolic functions, both children are manifestations of the same archetype. The child as presented by both Gide and Novalis is an unfathomable being, a stranger with whom adults cannot communicate although they are irresistibly attracted to him. The child speaks, but Urien and his companions do not hear the words; instead they are struck by the soaring beauty of his voice. In *The Novices of Sais* the child's voice penetrates the hearts of his auditors, but he speaks not a word. The Gidian child does speak, and the tone of the sounds he emits is "charming" and "gentle"; however, it is a voice but not words that emerges from his mouth. Speech for children is not an instrument of communication, but the very essence of their jubilant nature.

In *The Voyage of Urien* the aura of incomprehensibility is enhanced by the fact that even the child himself cannot decipher the mysterious symbols he traces in the sand, a method of transcription that suggests the evanescent nature of the signs. Here again we have one of those obsessive images that seem to haunt writers. It can even assume sinister undertones, as in Kafka's depiction of the normally reassuring scene of children playing in a Parisian park:

sitting on two chairs facing each other in the park of the Champs-Elysées. Children who had stayed up much too late were still playing in the half-dark, unable to discern clearly the lines they had traced in the sand.[5]

In *The Novices of Sais* there is an incident similar to the one in Gide and in Kafka. The old teacher frequently tells his disciples how, as a child, he had often sat on the shore searching for shells and how he had observed the stars and imitated their configurations in the sand. What Gide has done is to amalgamate the teacher as child and the child as future teacher, which may well have been the intent of Novalis. In any case, Gide's fictional interpretation leads us retrospectively to a new level of understanding of the Novalis text.

In all their works Gide and Novalis were obsessed by the tantalizing figure of the child. Lovingly they cultivated him with premonitions and wandered with him through fabulous and sometimes fearful zones. Their composite boy is the dreamer, living in his own world of the imagination. His existence represents a closed system, but one that exerts an extraordinary attraction on the adults who are transformed by its impact. Using modern terminology, one might say that he is the forever undecodable signifier. His appearance is transparent, but in its inexplicability forever opaque.

The child as an enigma that no amount of speculation can resolve is a recurrent theme in contemporary literature. The examples abound; we need think only of Miles and Flora in James's *The Turn of the Screw* (1898). They remain as inscrutable to the narrator and to the reader as to their governess. An even more striking instance is that presented by the same author in *What Maisie Knew* (1897). The child-heroine finds herself in the center of a chaotic world of divorced parents, step-parents, and lovers whose relations to one another are constantly changing and who all compete for her affection, not out of love but in order to use her. In their attempts to maintain the fiction of her innocence, they pretend to shield her from the truth of their adulterous affairs. While the kaleidoscopic patterns of their relationships are portrayed through the eyes of Maisie, she herself, in her very stability, represents a puzzle for her elders as well as for the reader. She remains inscrutable and apparently uninvolved emotionally in the various events of which she is the focal point. Her personal reactions to what goes on around her seem transparent but are, in fact, unfathomable. Her consciousness appears as objective in its recording of experience as the lens of a camera. If Maisie knows everything, the reader is left wondering whether she understands anything. And even the extent of her knowledge remains in doubt as the novel comes to its ambiguous end:

Maisie waited a moment; then "He wasn't there" she simply said again.

Mrs. Wix was also silent a while. "He went to *her*," she finally observed.

"Oh I know!" the child replied.

Mrs. Wix gave a sidelong look. She still had room for wonder at what Maisie knew.[6]

This wonder that Mrs. Wix experiences is related to the astonishment that overwhelmed Gide's voyagers when they contemplated the youth on the beach. The enigmatic child can be the incarnation of a miracle that awakens the sense of the marvelous in those who encounter him.

The theme of the puzzling child is a recurrent one in Virginia Woolf's *The Years* (1937) and provides an important clue for understanding this troubling and rich novel. In the opening pages, the death of a little boy haunts the mind of the moribund Mrs. Pargiter, but she never reveals to her own family what little boy it is who has died. The aura of mystery surrounding the role of the child is enhanced by the fact that the seven children who surround her deathbed remain as incomprehensible to her as she to them. As these children and their cousins grow older, they themselves are excluded from a childhood world that in its inscrutability seems vaguely inimical. The reaction of a couple of children to Kitty, who had come to take tea with their mother, is typical of the encounters between grown-ups and children portrayed throughout the novel:

Two children were already eating. Slices of bread and butter were in their hands, but they stayed the bread and butter and stared at Kitty as she sat down. . . . The children kept their eyes fixed upon her with a look of solemn amazement. Their owl-like stare went up and down over her uncompromisingly.[7]

The taciturnity of children seems to express a fundamental hostility toward the adults, and, when they do speak, their words are empty of meaning, for they are but the accurate reflections of what the grown-ups want to hear. This is depicted in a scene in which Abel Pargiter offers a birthday present to his niece:

He was very fond of children. "Many happy returns of the day to you, Maggie!" He felt in his pocket for the necklace that Crosby had done up in a cardboard box. Maggie came up to him to take it. Her hair had been brushed, and she was dressed in a stiff clean frock. She took the parcel and undid it; she held the blue-and-gold necklace dangling in her hand. And she was silent. Her mother at once supplied the words she should have spoken.
    "How lovely, Maggie! How perfectly lovely!" Maggie held the beads in her hand and said nothing.
    "Thank Uncle Abel for the lovely necklace," her mother prompted her.
    "Thank you for the necklace, Uncle Abel," said Maggie. She spoke directly and accurately, but the Colonel felt another twinge of doubt. A pang of disappointment came over him out of all proportion to its object. (p. 121)

Such vignettes are woven into the fabric of the narrative, and it is they perhaps that form the pattern that Eleanor momentarily senses under the meaningless surface of her social existence: "a theme, recurring, like music; half remembered, half foreseen? . . . a gigantic pattern, momentarily perceptible?" (p. 369).

The finale of *The Years* is a brilliant fantasia whose predominant theme is the hollowness of existence as revealed through the passage of time. Woolf uses a device similar to that of Proust in *The Past Recaptured*. She brings together all the surviving characters of the Pargiter family and their friends years later at a reception to which members of the younger generations had also been invited. It is a sad and disillusioned feast. The constantly interrupted clichés of these unreal shadows interdict any real communication and serve only to remind them of the fact that their longing for communication has never been realized. These false dialogues are occasionally interrupted in brutal fashion by outbursts of truth, such as Delia's exclamation that even their idealized childhood had been nothing but hell. And she might have added that from this hell they had never emerged. The climax of this *danse macabre* comes at dawn, when the party is about to break up. Two children are led into the room, and no one knows who they really are, though there is speculation that they belong to the caretaker. They are given cake, which they accept in sullen silence, staring at the guests with "a curious fixed stare as if they were fierce" (p. 428). When ordered to eat, "they began to munch slowly, gazing around them" (p. 429). When ordered to speak, they shake their heads from side to side, and when asked direct questions they respond with gestures. This ominous silence is at last broken when Martin asks them to sing a song, but the ensuing incomprehensible sounds are more terrifying than their muteness:

They stared but remained silent. They had stopped eating. They were a centre of a little group. They swept their eyes over the grown-up people for a moment, then, each giving the other a little nudge, they burst into song

> Etho passo tanno hai
> Fai donk to tu do,
> Mai to, kai to, lai to see
> Toh dom to tuh do—

That was what it sounded like. Not a word was recognizable. The distorted sounds rose and sank as if they followed a tune. (p. 429)

They go on with the second stanza of gibberish, which they sing more fiercely than the first: "The rhythm seemed to rock and the unintelligible words ran themselves together almost into a shriek" (p. 430). Their voices are harsh, their accents hideous, and the adults do not know whether to laugh or cry; they, who throughout the novel have been able to respond to any situation in standard fashion, do not know how to react in their encounter with the enigmatic children. Suddenly, in the middle of the third stanza, the children break off unexpectedly: "They stood there grinning, silent, looking at the floor. Nobody knew what to say. There was something horrible in the noise they made. It was so shrill, so discordant, and so meaningless" (p. 430). As soon as this disruptive pair has departed, there is felt the sense of relief that usually accompanies the restoration of normalcy. The grown-ups again can have recourse to their comforting clichés, which are more meaningless than the children's language. They comment on their performance by saying how nice it was and explain away the incomprehensibility of the song by the supposition of a cockney accent. Only Eleanor, the eldest of the Pargiters, who has sensed the existence of a mysterious pattern, is astonished and finds their hideous noise beautiful. Only the chosen few are sensitive to the charm of the enigmatic child.

Notwithstanding the plethora of examples in twentieth-century fiction, the figure of the enigmatic child is not a modern invention. In fact, in the guise of the *puer senex*, the cryptic child, old beyond its years, was a commonplace topos in the Latin literature of late antiquity and retained its popularity in the Middle Ages, when it was employed as one of the clichés of hagiography.[8] Before becoming a current theme in modern literature, it was used by Chaucer as the object of caricature in *The Canterbury Tales* (1387–1400). It is the mawkishly sentimental prioress who recounts the martyrdom of a seven-year-old child in a tale that seems in many respects to occupy a place apart in the universe of Chaucer. Although the narrator, as portrayed in the "General Prologue," is so sensitive that she weeps at the sight of a dog being beaten or of a mouse maimed by a trap, the tale she recounts is a harrowingly brutal one. She tells of a pious schoolboy who is so entranced by the *Alma redemptoris* that, with the help of an older companion, he learns the hymn by heart. He understands not a word of it, but nonetheless sings it "wel and boldely." Unfortunately for the little "clergeoun," it is every day on the way to and from school as he is passing through the Jewish quarter, that he prefers to intone this song of praise to the Virgin Mary. Feeling provoked and insulted, the Jews find an assassin who slits the child's throat and throws the body into a privy. Yet piteously the child continues to chant his hymn until a monk removes the cardamom seed that the mother of God had placed on his tongue. And so at last the tormented child is allowed to find peace in death. What emerges clearly from this otherwise murky story is that the child, who is at the center of the narration, is the incarnation of simplicity and innocence. As such, he remains from beginning to end inscrutable. He is a puzzle to his own mother, who discovers the singing corpse; to the monk who buries him; to the prioress herself, who recounts his brief life; and to the reader who attempts to discover the meaning of this strange existence. The child appears on the stage briefly; his transitory presence and his disappearance are in fact inconsequential and yet seem portentous, fraught with a significance that passes our understanding.

The fate of the enigmatic child is often a tragic one, for his puzzling nature evokes fear in adults, especially those whose existence is assured by an armature of reason. For them the irrationality which he embodies is a threat. This is the menace represented by the seven-year-old Meretlein, whose pathetic story interrupts the narrative of Gottfried Keller's *Der Grüne Heinrich* (1854–55). Despite its clumsiness, this intercalation provides a contrast between the enigmatic and the logically motivated child. Lee, the child-narrator of his own story, had been punished but subsequently forgiven by his mother for his refusal to say grace before meals. Although too shy to justify his apparently unreasonable behavior to his mother, he does analyze for the reader this inability and ascribes it to certain psychologically convincing factors which determined the child's behavior. Immediately after this episode, the now all-too-comprehensible child finds the simply inscribed gravestone of a girl who had died a century earlier and then discovers a portrait of her holding in her hands the skull of a child. Finally he comes across the diary of the pastor who had been responsible for the death of this strange creature. The notations in this document tell the story of the last months of Meretlein. She, too, had been incapable of saying her prayers aloud or of participating in devotions. In her case, however, no explanation for such an incapacity is offered. The parents send her off to live with a pastor reputed for his piety and severity, in the hope that the instruction he will provide will exorcize the evil spirits by which they believe their daughter is possessed. The pastor is a self-centered and unimaginative rationalist who, like the parents, sees in his charge a witch child, a menace to his own stability. The simple village folk, on the contrary, and especially their children are enchanted by the ethereal child and even make efforts to protect her from the minister. The pastor, however, prevails. His self-serving journal is a depressing recital of the punishments he inflicts on her for her own good. He isolates her in her chamber, whips her, deprives her of food, and forces her to wear as her only garment a hair shirt. When this physical maltreatment threatens the health of the girl, he refuses to let the doctor care for her. Finally, he breaks her spiritually by denying her instruction or any other kind of intellectual stimulation. Weakened in body and lapsing into imbecility, Meretlein, after having been placed prematurely into her coffin, finally expires. The pastor has eliminated the child whom he could never understand.

The most tantalizing of these creatures with whom adults find it so difficult to come to terms is to be found in Adalbert Stifter's little-known masterpiece, *Abdias* (1842). This novella, a parable without a comprehensible lesson, provides a perfect framework for the presentation of an insoluble puzzle. As in Roussel's *Impressions d'Afrique*, the sober facticity of the recital is at odds with the exotic and violent nature of the events recounted. At the same time, a bourgeois realism is constantly undermined by the intrusion of the marvelous, a technique which anticipates the experiments of the surrealists. Equally baffling is the sudden shift in setting from the arid Sahara to a fertile mountain valley in Europe. The startling juxtaposition of caravans traversing the Atlas Mountains and Austrians tilling their fields, of a nomadic people and a village folk, drains both locales of their reality. The individual scenes retain nothing more than the precision of mirages. The resultant atmosphere of hallucination is heightened by the obsessive emphasis that Stifter placed on multitudinous objects which he describes in such minute detail that, as in the novels of Robbe-Grillet, they are deprived of their substantiality. This disorienting tale, replete with violent adventures that seem to lead nowhere, might have been the product of a collaboration between Scheherazade and an Austrian *Heimatsdichter* as rewritten by a *nouveau romancier*.

The first part of what is essentially the fictitious biography of Abdias is set in an oasis in the midst of the wasteland of the North African desert, the site of an ancient Roman town fallen into ruin. In this debris of a destroyed culture the adherents of a Jewish sect have established their secret place of habitation. The wealthiest member of this community is the merchant Abdias, who has amassed his wealth by traveling and trading throughout the Near East. On his return from one of his long expeditions he finds the town and his home pillaged by an Arab chieftain. In the ransacked inner sanctum of his dwelling lies his wife, Deborah, suckling the new-born Ditha. Abdias is overwhelmed by the presence of this infant:

It seemed to him, in the midst of destruction, as if he had encountered the greatest fortune on earth, and, as he sat next to the mother on the bare floor and as he touched the whimpering little worm with his hands, he felt in his heart the beginning of that salvation which had never come and for which he had never even known where to begin to look. It was there now, and infinitely sweeter and milder than he had ever imagined.[9]

Like Abdias, the reader is led to believe that Ditha will play the traditional Christian role of the redemptive child. And this initial interpretation is reinforced by the fact that, thanks to the existence of the baby, there is an immediate reconciliation between Abdias and Deborah, who had become estranged from each other. But this salutary effect of the child as intermediary is only momentary: a few hours later Deborah dies because of the unstanched flow of blood that followed Ditha's birth.

From then on, Abdias devotes himself entirely to the restoration of his lost goods and to the care of Ditha. By dint of hard work, he gradually replaces his plundered fortune, and, as soon as his wealth is sufficient, he sets off to resettle with Ditha in Europe, where she will be sheltered from the looting and rapine to which he had been constantly exposed in the desert. He finds an Alpine retreat far from the nearest village and builds a solid house in whose center he installs the four-year-old child as if she were an odalisque. Once again there is a hint that, though enigmatic, she is a child of promise: "She lay there before him, a sacred puzzle, having emerged from his being and in expectation of an unknown revelation" (p. 642). Like the preceding one, this promise is deceptive. Abdias notices that his girl is not like other children, that she cannot walk and that her blue eyes are empty and lifeless. Most troubling of all is her inability to learn to speak intelligibly: "Her tongue could not yet form words, but, when everything was going well, she lisped strange tones which had no resemblance to the sounds of any human language and which no one could comprehend" (p. 644). Abdias cannot but believe that his daughter is an idiot, a conviction which only makes him redouble his attentions to her.

The inability of the enigmatic child to communicate is a trait we have already perceived in Gide's boy on the beach, in Virginia Woolf's menacing children, and in Chaucer's little victim, and it is a characteristic we shall note in many other children. In this particular case, however, this incapacity actually leads to a higher level of understanding and to a deeper intimacy between father and daughter:

Abdias taught her to say words whose meaning she did not possess—she said the words after him and invented others, which she found in the depths of her inner being and which he did not understand, and which he in turn learned. So they spoke for hours on end with each other, and each knew what the other wanted. (p. 649)

Abdias has succeeded in the seemingly impossible enterprise of communicating with the enigmatic child, of creating with Ditha a private mode of discourse which enables them to live together in perfect harmony and in a reality separated from the ordinary world.

A turning point comes in their lives when Abdias discovers that Ditha is not an imbecile, but that she is blind and that her learning disabilities can all be traced to her lack of sight. His subsequent efforts to find physicians to heal her are of no avail, but he is successful in bringing her up and in teaching her. It is when she is almost fully grown, when she is approaching the age of puberty, that a miracle occurs. In the middle of the night a violent storm breaks out, and a bolt of lightning strikes Ditha's chamber. It passed through the floor and ceiling, and its heat melted even the iron grating of the bird cage; but it left the girl unharmed—and capable of seeing for the first time in her life. The lightning bolt as a miraculous instrument has literary resonances. Whether Stifter was thinking of Vergil or not, the fact remains that this scene in *Abdias* is remarkably similar to a crucial episode in the *Aeneid* (2. 665–99). During a family council, Aeneas and his father, Anchises, refuse to desert Troy despite the pleas of the others. At a critical point in the argument, lightning strikes and plays around the head of Ascanius, the young son of Aeneas. Although his cap catches fire and the bright flames actually lick his hair, it leaves the child unscathed. This is manifestly a sign from Jupiter, and father and grandfather realize that their prime mission is to save Ascanius, to flee the sack of Troy so that the city may be reconstructed by a younger generation. The symbol of lightning is apt indeed, for, though all its effects can easily be attributed to natural phenomena, its impression is a supernatural one. The burning but unconsumed head of the child is a symbol of the permanence of Troy, even though the city be in flames. The lightning that strikes Ditha's room also brings illumination, but no real change in her way of life. As before, a promising event proves to be inconsequential. She and her father, who is now farming the formerly sterile lands he has acquired, still live together, separated from the rest of mankind in a tranquil existence which Abdias would like to eternalize. But this cannot be, for Ditha inevitably attains physical maturity. At the harvest season, another storm builds up. As a woman Ditha no longer enjoys the same protection as before, and this time, when lightning strikes, it kills her. Abdias lives on for more than thirty years, a Beckettian figure sitting passively on a bench, oblivious of everything, while others supervise the cultivation of his fields. His existence had turned about the enigmatic child, and her disappearance leaves a void which paralyses him.

There are other instances in literature of a somewhat different sort in which the child, while still an emblematic abstraction, does have a direct and crucial effect on the course of the narrative. This is the case in a little work by Goethe, *The Novella* (1827). The story is a simple one. While the countess is out for a ride with her retinue, a conflagration breaks out in the village, where a country fair is taking place. The flimsy stands go up in flames, and a tiger and a lion escape from their cage. One of the courtiers believes the life of the countess to be in danger and after one unsuccessful attempt manages to shoot the tiger. The owners of the menagerie, a couple and their young child, discover the corpse of the animal and are distraught. It appears that the wild beasts were perfectly tame. Their distress becomes even greater when the count proposes to hunt down the lion as well. They plead with him and promise that their child will bring the lion back to his cage without any danger to anyone. The count agrees, and, while he is explaining the precautions he plans to take in order to avert a possible tragedy, the child, who has not spoken a word, begins to play on his flute:

The child pursued its melody, which was not a melody at all but a series of tones without structure, and perhaps for that very reason so over-whelmingly moving; the people standing around seemed as if entranced by the movement of a songlike mode.[10]

As in the case of the martyred child, his only means of expression is music. The boy proceeds to the cave in which the lion has sought refuge, alternately playing his flute and singing triumphantly. His song consists of three stanzas whose verses are constantly altered, again without apparent reason. However, from these variations there emerges a clear theme:

> Und so geht mit guten Kindern
> Sel'ger Engel gern zu Rat,
> Böses Wollen zu verhindern,
> Zu befördern schöne That. (p. 195)

> Blessed angels gladly counsel
> And accompany good children,
> In order to prevent evil will
> And to encourage beautiful deeds.

The lion limps out of the cave after the child, who, in a reenact-ment of the story of Daniel, removes a thorn from the tamed beast's paw. The story ends with the child still playing his flute and sing-ing, constantly transforming the order of the verses.

Within the framework of *The Novella* there is a striking con-trast between the child and the young courtier, Honorio, who had slain the tiger. The latter had acted sensibly, as a young man, and could hardly be blamed for the fact that his deed was based on a false assumption. Yet he is disgraced; the last we see of him, he is looking toward the setting sun, toward the evening of his life. The innocent child, on the other hand, continues to inhabit his autono-mous sphere, a tonal construct whose durability is assured by the eternal nature of music.

The Menacing Child

> je n'entends pas votre langage
> je refuse un autre cerveau
> dit l'enfant
> L'enfant sauvage

I do not understand your language
I refuse another brain
says the child
The wild child
                    Jacques Prévert

The insoluble conundrum posed by the presence of an uncommunicative child is not always as reassuring a symbol as it is in *The Novella*. It is true that in William Blake's *Songs of Innocence* (1789) the vision of childhood is still an apparently untroubled one, but under the clear surface of even these early lyrics there are disturbing undercurrents. In "Infant Joy," for example, the nameless baby is the incarnation and future recipient of joy:

"I have no name:
I am but two days old."
What shall I call thee?
"I happy am,
Joy is my name."
Sweet joy befall thee!
                    (lines 1–6)

The function of this brief poem is a sacramental one, that of baptism. But the feeling of unease caused by the presentation of this rite in its simplest and at the same time most significant terms may be due to the suspicion that this act of naming is an incantatory one, carried out to ward off the unvoiced dangers of joylessness.

In the much later (and much more difficult to interpret) "The Mental Traveller" (1803), the subdued threat is made explicit; the infant becomes a symbol of terror. The narrator-voyager of the poem had, in his travels through the land of men and women, seen "such dreadful things / As cold Earth wanderers never knew" (lines 3–4). But of all the horrors imaginable, the most frightening is the encounter with a frowning baby:

But when they find the frowning Babe,
Terror strikes thro' the region wide:
They cry "The Babe! the Babe is Born!"
And flee away on Every side.

For who dare touch the frowning form,
His arm is wither'd to its root;

> Lions, Boars, Wolves, all howling flee,
> And every Tree does shed its fruit.
>
> (lines 93–100)

The presence of this child is so menacing that it causes people to panic, is destructive of the individual, and is an awesome threat even to nature. The child as an enigmatic figure assumes the same rhetorical dimension as in *The Voyage of Urien*: it precipitates in the adults a childlike reaction that, in the poem as well as in the story, is reinforced by the primitivism of the imagery and syntax.

That the apparently defenseless innocence of a quiet child can actually present a menace for the adult world is a concept by no means unique to Blake. It is also the case of the strange little being who one evening appears unexpectedly at the door of Jude and Sue in Thomas Hardy's *Jude the Obscure* (1895). His very origins are shrouded in mystery. Born in far-off Australia, he is the son of Jude's first wife, Arabella, but he does not know his father, who might be Jude himself. He is unbaptized and nameless, and is simply called Little Father Time. As this appellation indicates, he is another incarnation of the *puer senex*: "He was Age masquerading as Juvenility."[11] From the outset Hardy describes this unwanted offspring as separated from the rest of mankind. In the railroad carriage taking him to the home of his putative father, all the other travelers make themselves comfortable and eventually close their eyes. To accentuate this feeling of general well-being, the author even describes a kitten curling itself up in a basket. Not so the child, who does not have the same confidence in the security of the train compartment as do his companions and thus "remained just as before . . . doubly awake" (pp. 217–18). This other-worldly creature, who knows more than the others and perceives reality in a different fashion from them, is suspicious and constantly on his guard. Not only is he set apart from the adult world, but he is separated from his peers as well, in fact from all of nature. This feeling of total estrangement is underlined in the description of the boy's lonely walk from the station to the house where he is to take up residence:

The child fell into a steady mechanical creep which had in it an impersonal quality. He followed his directions literally, without an inquiring gaze at anything. It could have been seen that the boy's ideas of life were different from those of the local boys. Children begin with detail, and learn up to the general; they begin with the contiguous, and gradually comprehend the universal. The boy seemed to have begun with the generals of life, and never to have concerned himself with the particulars. To him the houses, the willows, the obscure fields beyond, were apparently regarded not as brick residences, pollards, meadows; but as human dwellings in the abstract, vegetation and the wide dark world. (pp. 218–19)

The arrival of this singular child transforms the lives of Jude and Sue and eventually brings about the melodramatic catastrophe that destroys their existence.

Initially, the unexpected apparition of the child does not disturb their domestic arrangements as much as they had feared. His taciturnity makes it possible at first almost to ignore him. They find him "to be in the habit of sitting silent, his quaint and weird face set, and his eyes resting on things they did not see in the substantial world" (p. 220). Thus, at the beginning they are hardly conscious of his presence and seem insensitive to a certain portentous quality which Matthew Arnold has expressed in "To a Gypsy Child by the Sea-Shore":

> Who taught this pleading to unpractis'd eyes?
> Who hid such import in an infant's gloom?
> Who lent thee, child, this meditative guise?
> What clouds thy forehead and fore-dates thy doom?

Occasionally, however, when they have practically forgotten him, his small, slow voice emerges from what seem to be subterranean depths, and a brief remark makes them realize that he had absorbed everything they had said and, worse yet, seen through everything. Such instances naturally provoke in them an acute sense of discomfort. Then, too, because of the child's yearning look, Jude and Sue sense in him a desperate need to be loved, and yet they are frustrated in all their attempts to demonstrate their affection toward him. All their efforts at making him happy fail, and they find themselves faced with the unsatisfying task of dealing with a boy "singularly deficient in all the usual hopes of childhood" (p. 227). Thus he acts as a constraining factor that to some degree spoils their happy-go-lucky relationship. When they set forth on an outing, they take Little Father Time with them, but the shadow of his company casts a spell over their excursion:

. . . they had taken care to bring Father Time, to try every means of making him kindle and laugh like other boys, though he was to some extent a hindrance to the delightfully unreserved intercourse in their pilgrimages which they so much enjoyed. (p. 229)

This inability to disturb the child's fundamental indifference troubles and saddens them. But most frightening of all is the child's own awareness of the effect he has on others, coupled with his frank admission of this awareness:

"I feel we have returned to Greek joyousness. . . . There is one immediate shadow, however—only one." And she [Sue] looked at the aged child, whom, though they had taken him to everything likely to attract a young intelligence, they had utterly failed to interest. He knew what they were saying and thinking. "I am very, very sorry, Father and Mother," he said. "But please don't mind!—I can't help it." (p. 234)

The two adults are thwarted in their attempts to deal with the preternaturally aged child, they are disturbed by his lucid intuition, and this combination of frustration and fear sours their own relationship.

The effect of the child's presence on the inner life of the couple is insidious and subtle, but the impact on their social existence is dramatic and obvious. For it is the child, by the mere fact of his position in the household, who forces upon them a crucial decision regarding their own intercourse. Until his arrival, the two cousins had lived together, but maintained a platonic relationship. They are still too fastidious and intellectually honest to overcome their aversion to the institution of marriage and thus refuse to go through the ceremony of legalizing their union. However, they do decide to live together as husband and wife. Furthermore, in order to give their union a semblance of respectability that might make the child's life easier, they pretend that they had indeed been joined in wedlock. Thus the presence of Little Father Time has forced on them the very hypocrisy typical of the Victorian age which they had always condemned. The results of their cohabitation are two children, a boy and a girl, whose existence places additional constraints on the already restricted life-style of the family. Compelled to move to another city (ironically Christminster, the goal of Jude's original aspirations and where he had first met Sue), they seek lodgings but find only a temporary refuge for the mother and children. Before putting the young ones to sleep in a narrow closet,

Sue speaks openly to Little Father Time of the problems they face, problems exacerbated by the fact that she is again pregnant. His responses, as usual, are laconic. The next morning, when Sue opens the closet door to awaken the children, she finds all three with cords tied around their necks, hanging strangled from the garment hooks. Near the elder boy the bereaved mother sees an overturned chair. The following evening the child Sue was carrying is stillborn.

This climactic catastrophe results in a dénouement in which the relationship between Jude and Sue disintegrates completely and both Jude and Sue as individuals are destroyed. The lurid disaster seems in one sense unprecipitated, and it is easy to reproach the author for presenting an unprepared and melodramatic climax. Yet it is the very unexpected nature of the double murder and suicide that gives the reader an insight into the nature of the enigmatic child. Because he is unable to communicate and because his inner existence remains impenetrable to the adult intelligence, his actions are totally unpredictable. Although the motivation of the child remains unclear, his unexpected crime is no *acte gratuit*. Nor does it suffice to say that the carnage he wreaks represents simply a revolt either against the human condition or against a society that is based on injustice. The doctor who had attempted unsuccessfully to resuscitate the three little corpses does make an effort at a reasonable explanation:

The doctor says there are such boys springing up amongst us—boys of a sort unknown in the last generation—the outcome of new views of life. They seem to see all its terrors before they are old enough to have staying power to resist them. He says it is the beginning of the coming universal wish not to live. (p. 264)

Hardy himself offers yet another interpretation:

On that little shape had converged all the inauspiciousness and shadow which had darkened the first union of Jude, and all the accidents, mistakes, fears, errors of the last. He was their nodal point, their focus, their expression in a single term. For the rashness of those parents he had groaned, for their ill assortment he had quaked, and for the misfortunes of these he had died. (p. 264)

Perhaps Little Father Time's own poignant justification is, in its brevity and simplicity, closest to the truth. Before hanging himself, he had scrawled in pencil on a piece of paper: "Done because we are too menny" (p. 264). This statement should not be construed in narrowly defined economic terms, for it is no mere complaint concerning the overpopulation of which he is indeed a victim. It is the philosophic dimension of this phrase that is striking. Little Father Time, like Sartre's Roquentin, is conscious of the superfluity of man's presence on earth. His own existence, as well as that of others, is *de trop*, and thus the simplest expedient is to rid the world of some of these excessive and suffering beings.

Despite all these attempts at rationalization, the fact remains that the enigmatic child as portrayed by Hardy represents a menace to human life and to human institutions, because his is a perception of them that is radically different, and thus his reactions to them appear unmotivated, but only because they are for adults unpredictable. The enigmatic child has the uncanny knack of seeing life as it is, stripped of all human pretenses and conventions. Since man cannot stand too much reality, the unwavering stare of the child which reveals it in a stark and unadorned fashion is a serious threat. It is Sue who sensed all of this when she first saw Little Father Time and compared his face to the mask of Melpomene, the muse of tragedy.

The fictive universe of Kafka, like that of Hardy, is not one usually associated with children, and the very atmosphere of sordid inns and wretched tenements that serve as thresholds to labyrinthine bureaucracies seems hostile to the innocence normally associated with childhood. And yet the youngster, he claims in a letter to his sister Elli (autumn 1921), is "the only incorruptible searcher after truth and relentless mediator." [12] Indeed, children abound in the fragmentary novels and short stories of Kafka. [13] The apartments of the buildings in which the offices of the tribunal are lodged teem with them, and they are omnipresent in the hovels of the village that lies at the foot of the castle. Because of its complexity, the symbolic import of these children is extremely difficult to assess. At the very least, they represent an annoying intrusion upon personal life: their presence makes it impossible, in *The Castle* (1927), for the land surveyor and Frieda to settle down to a domestic life in the schoolhouse. As for K.'s two assistants (who are repeatedly portrayed as children), their destructive and irresponsible pranks are a constant hindrance. At the same time, children represent something far more difficult to define. When K. initially attempts to communicate with the castle, the receiver of the telephone emits a buzzing of a type K. has never heard before. The eerie hum is compounded of the echoes of children singing at an infinite distance, and K. is literally entranced by their incomprehensible voices and is enraged when the sound is interrupted by the comprehensible words of adults. The children's murmuring is here equated with the song of sirens, a song that is perhaps responsible for luring him into a continuation of his hopeless quest. All these children, whether seductive or inimical, are, thanks to their hermetic nature, seemingly sinister forces.

Even more difficult to interpret is the moribund little boy in the short story "A Country Doctor" (1919). In this parable, as in the Gidian fable, the perceptive Freudian critic is faced with the temptation of saying the obvious. Nothing seems more evident than that the doctor, called in the middle of the night to visit a patient, has actually been summoned to try to heal the ills of mankind. The curer of physical ailments presumes to become a universal healer of souls. The loneliness of the task is underlined by the unwillingness of anyone to lend him the horse he needs for his journey. The steeds led forth from the pigsty by a sinister groom clearly represent the darker forces that have always been lying in wait. They carry him off as if by magic to the home of the patient, while Rosa, the serving girl who has been left behind, is raped by the groom. She is the sacrificial victim of the doctor's good intentions. In the meanwhile, the physician is unable to find anything wrong with the sick boy and considers him a malingerer, until the horses look through the windows and whinny. Then, suddenly, he discovers a wound as large as the palm of his hand. In a repetition of a common hagiographic topos, the doctor, like Saint Julien the Hospitaller, removes his clothes and lies down by the ailing child. But, unlike his illustrious predecessor, the physician is not successful; in fact he is rebuffed by the child, who complains of his taking up too much of his own room. In other words, the healer may be using the boy in a vain attempt to cure himself. The doctor leaves, but he is now a broken and embittered old man who will never be able to return to his practice and is condemned to roam forever aimlessly through the snow-swept countryside, drawn on by the now slowly plodding steeds who have themselves lost their force. Having succumbed to the temptation of playing the role of savior and having discovered his own impotence, he will never be able to resume his ordinary life. And yet there is more to be said than what is revealed by such a logical summation. The allegory in its crystalline opacity is a troubling one precisely because a straight-forward interpretation seems to obscure even further the enig-matic kernel of the narration. This core is to be found in the en-counter between the child and the man. When at first the physician is incapable of diagnosing any ill, the patient wants only to die. Then, when the doctor finds the source of his pain, he wants to be saved, only to reject the doctor when he tries to do so. The gaping and loathsome wound is alive with writhing worms: it is an un-answerable challenge to the doctor's healing powers. The youthful victim is a threat to the doctor's very existence. As the defeated physician leaves, the mocking song intoned by a children's choir conducted by a schoolmaster rings in his ears: "Rejoice all you pa-tients, / The doctor has been laid in your bed!"[14] The adult, de-ceived by a false and treacherous call, has been destroyed by the encounter with the enigmatic child.

In *The Trial* (1925) we find the same basic hostility between the child and the adult world of accepted social conventions as in *Jude the Obscure*, only in this instance the resultant conflict is stripped of all melodrama and presented with a stark realism that accentuates the nightmare that Kafka's thirty-year-old protagonist attempts unsuccessfully to elucidate. The initial encounter between Joseph K. and a group of children takes place during his first at-tempt to obtain a hearing before the tribunal. He has located the building in which the courtroom is presumably situated and where the interrogation is scheduled to take place, but he is at a loss as to which of the many entries of the complex structure might lead him to the proper room. He picks a door at random and begins to go up the staircase. His way is temporarily blocked by a horde of chil-dren who say nothing to him:

In going up, he disturbed a lot of children who were playing on the stairs and who looked up at him with anger as he strode through their ranks. He said to himself, "The next time I come here again, I must bring with me either candy to win them over or a cane to beat them with." Just be-fore reaching the second floor he even had to wait a moment, until a roll-ing marble had completed its course; in the meanwhile two little boys with the queer faces of grown-up vagabonds held him fast by the legs of his trousers; had he wanted to shake them off, he would have had to hurt them, and he was afraid of their cries.[15]

Here again we have taciturn boys, older than their years, and they inspire fear in Joseph K. as they hinder his progress. They seem to be sinister agents of obstruction, the sullen guardians of the portals to the antechambers of the law.

Joseph K.'s other encounter with children also takes place on a staircase. This time he is looking for the studio of the painter Titorelli, who, he hopes, might give him some useful information concerning the minor judges whose portraits he paints. There are obvious similarities between the group of girls he meets this time and the boys who hindered his passage earlier. The girls, too, are an unprepossessing lot. Their leader is slightly hunchbacked, and they are all described as being corrupted despite their youth: "All their faces represented a blend of childishness and depravity" (p. 171). They, too, are intially taciturn, and when K. asks them whether they know where the painter Titorelli lives, they stare at him "with a piercing, provocative gaze" (p. 170). But, in an apparent paradox typical of Kafka, the subsequent attitude of the girls toward K. is very different from that of the boys. Instead of making it difficult for him to proceed, it is really only thanks to them that he finds his way. As he is about to take a wrong turn, their leader points out the right corridor to him. In fact, as he approaches, they make a concerted effort to speed him on his way: "The hunchbacked girl clapped her hands, and the rest of them crowded behind K. in order to push him forward more quickly" (p. 172). It is as if these strange girls were intent on propelling him more rapidly toward his doom. Titorelli, during his interview with K., had to lock them out of his atelier. Nonetheless their presence is constantly felt, and their ceaseless chatter behind the door accompanies the conversation of the two men. Furthermore, they seek to attract the attention of the interlocutors by all sorts of distracting means; one of them, for example, pushes a straw through the crevice between the door and the sill and moves it back and forth with maddening regularity. Such shameless flaunting of premature sexuality is disorienting to the extreme. K., who is already having trouble concentrating on the intricate meanderings of Titorelli, becomes even more bewildered because of their obscenely suggestive antics. But when K. inquires about the girls, Titorelli leaves no doubt concerning their allegiance. They belong to the tribunal, he informs him, and this revelation serves to make K. even more uneasy. In fact, he is so afraid of encountering them again that he finally asks his host to be allowed to leave by a different door in the back of the room. As he passes through the back entrance, he finds himself in the corridors of the offices of the tribunal—and at once runs into the same bevy of girls whom he had hoped to avoid. The conclusion is clear. The enigmatic children in *The Trial* represent a menace; they belong to the tribunal. If they seek to hinder the progress of the protagonist, it is in order to make his existence more difficult. If they seek to further his progress, it is to help him on the way to his execution. Whichever of these two courses they pursue, their mere presence, whether in its sinister taciturnity or in its irritating loquacity, is a constant mockery and torment.

In his portrayal of children (as in so many other more obvious respects), Kafka both epitomized certain trends and served as a precursor. His children are contemporaries of the little monstrosities engendered by the surrealists. The nameless child in Jean Cocteau's *Wedding Party on the Eiffel Tower* (1921) disrupts the marriage feast by bombarding the guests; Victor, in Roger Vitrac's *Victor or Children to Power* (1928), celebrates his seventh birthday by precipitating a triple suicide. Perhaps closest in spirit to Kafka's children are those of Fernando Arrabal. They represent a disquieting blend of innocence and corruption that leads to the worst of perversions. When they are not victimized, they become victimizers, but in either case they are the instruments of a higher and sinister force. Today, their innumerable progeny have captured the popular imagination and continue to multiply.[16] Since the success of William March's *The Bad Seed* (1951), in which a ten-year-old murderess triumphantly survives her mother's attempt to rid the world of her, authors have cynically exploited the demonic child, in whom they have found an almost certain vehicle for instant success. Despite March's simplistic genetic thesis and his heavy-handed treatment of a subtle moral issue, his sweetly vicious protagonist is an original contribution to the literature dealing with a very specific type of menacing child, the cursed youngster who by the fact of his childhood is by definition evil.

Not all damned children are as unabashedly evil as March's juvenile compulsive killer, and some borderline cases seem to be the fruit of two contradictory heritages. Ever since Rousseau, one popular conception of the child is that, as a personage living in the state of nature, he is basically good until the forces of civilization corrupt his naive essence. A far more somber tradition, usually associated with Calvinism, holds that the unformed child, as a being deprived of divine grace, is given over entirely to the satanic forces of nature and is redeemable only through a training designed to eliminate all spontaneity. Only by becoming an adult can such a child be saved. Nathaniel Hawthorne, in *The Scarlet Letter* (1850), presents Pearl, the illegitimate child of Hester Prynne, in such ambiguous terms that initially the reader is unable to place this novel in either of the two traditions. In any case, the girl is certainly an enigmatic figure, a living hieroglyph endowed with a strange remoteness and intangibility. But whether the nature of this enigma is good or evil is a question left in suspense. On the one hand, Hawthorne over and over again refers to this girl, brought up by her mother in a state of nature, as an "elf-child" and insists on her "airy charm." She is constantly associated with light, and, during the course of a walk through the forest with her mother, she does try to capture the sunlight and actually succeeds:

Pearl set forth, at a great pace, and, as Hester smiled to perceive, did actually catch the sunshine, and stood laughing in the midst of it, all brightened by its splendor, and scintillating with the vivacity excited by rapid motion. The light lingered about the lonely child, as if glad of such a playmate, until her mother had drawn almost nigh enough to step into the magic circle.[17]

Pearl proceeds to explain that she can catch the light because she is but a child, not yet marked by a scarlet letter. At such a point one might well wonder whether the *A* glowing on her mother's bosom and which so fascinates the child stands not merely for "Adulteress" but for "Adult." So impressed is Hester with these bright qualities of the child that at one point she is even tempted to consider her as a beneficent spirit:

If little Pearl were entertained with faith and trust, as a spirit-messenger no less than an earthly child, might it not be her errand to soothe away the sorrow that lay cold in her mother's heart, and converted it into a tomb?—and to help her to overcome the passion, once so wild, and even yet neither dead nor asleep, but only imprisoned within the same tomb-like heart? (pp. 238–39)

The interpretation of Pearl as an agent of redemption is contradicted and overshadowed by Hester's realization that the child actually plays a far more unpleasant role, that of "messenger of anguish" (p. 336). While, as we have noted, Hawthorne often refers to Pearl's elfin qualities, he emphasizes her dark nature even more, an evilness with which she had been endowed at birth:

The child's own nature had something wrong in it, which continually betokened that she had been born amiss,—the effluence of her mother's lawless passion,—and often impelled Hester to ask, in bitterness of heart, whether it were for good or ill that the poor little creature had been born at all. (p. 218)

Throughout the novel she is referred to harshly as "an imp of evil," a "demon offspring," and an "infant pestilence." At times her very expression has something inhuman about it: "It was a look so intelligent, yet inexplicable, so perverse, sometimes so malicious, but generally accompanied by a wild flow of spirits, that Hester could not help questioning, at such moments, whether Pearl was a human child" (p. 125). Pearl's actions indicate more clearly than such descriptions her function as a tormentor. Incessantly she teases her mother with her constant and insistent references to the scarlet letter, to the point where the reader begins to wonder about the extent of knowledge of this seven-year-old who seems as precocious as Maisie.

The fundamental maliciousness of Pearl is clearly demonstrated when this uncommonly articulate child refuses to speak comprehensibly at a critical moment. Arthur Dimmesdale has a nameless horror of Roger Chillingworth though he does not know that he is the husband of Hester whom he had cuckolded. The pastor does have an urgent need to know the latter's real identity, and Pearl assures him that she can reveal it. The minister eagerly bends his ear to her lips:

Pearl mumbled something into his ear, that sounded, indeed, like human language, but was only such gibberish as children may be heard amusing themselves with, by the hour together. At all events, if it involved any secret information in regard to old Roger Chillingworth, it was in a tongue unknown to the erudite clergyman, and did but increase the bewilderment of his mind. The elvish child then laughed aloud. (p. 207)

There is something monstrous about this gratuitous mockery of her progenitor. Less gratuitous is the ultimate temptation into which Pearl leads the pastor. In their first encounter on the scaffold where her mother had been put to shame, she taunts him for not daring to appear in public with them. Later on, when Hester and Dimmesdale decide to flee together, Pearl reproaches him for the same reason, only this time her words seem more portentous. Reflected in the brook which separates her from the couple, her frowning image and imperious gesture are doubled and reemphasized. Her words have the desired effect: the minister, after his ultimate triumphal sermon, steps onto the scaffold with Pearl and Hester to make his public confession and to expire. The demon offspring has triumphed and fulfilled her punitive role.

The protagonist of *The Bad Seed* is a less ambiguous figure than Pearl. However, her very unidimensionality gives her a demonic fascination which is impressive. Equally enthralling for the same reason are some of the child demons spawned by science fiction, such as the telepathic creatures in Wyndham's *The Midwich Cuckoos*. Nothing need be said about Pearl's many other reincarnations in such lurid and poorly written best-sellers as Dean R. Koonz's *The Demon Seed* (1976). The origin of these monsters, who in their very lack of psychological depth have the force of caricatural representations, can be traced back to the German *Schauerromantik*, and their prototype is to be found in Achim von Arnim's *Pope Joan* (1812). In this aberrant drama the child is described as one:

Das böses Blut in allen Adern trägt,
In dessen Herzen keine Liebe schlägt,
In dessen Blick kein frommer Segen liegt,
Auf dessen Mund kein reiner Kuss sich fügt,
Durch dessen Schrei die Muttersorg verwirrt
In Angst und Gram zum Fluche sich verirrt![18]

Who carries evil blood in all its veins,
In whose heart pulses no love,
In whose eyes lies no pious blessing,
On whose mouth no pure kiss is formed,
Through whose scream the mother's care becomes
    confused,
And in fear and grief loses itself in a curse!

The reading public has demonstrated an insatiable appetite for even the most vulgar of such menacing children, and the viewing public has assured a similar success for the many films dealing with the same topic. The result has been a proliferation of evil children on such a scale that one might well fear that it is they who will inherit the earth.

The Redemptive Child

> Et la voix des enfants est plus pure que la voix du vent dans le calme de la vallée.
>
> And the voices of children are purer than the voice of the wind in the calm of the valley.
>
> Charles Péguy

Fortunately, the enigmatic child appears as a beneficent force just as frequently as in the guise of a menacing presence. The concept of the child as a symbol of resurrection predates Christianity and is found in the famous prophecy of the birth of Immanuel, the child nourished on butter and honey who will reject evil in order to choose the good (Isaiah 7:15). According to Ovid, in the *Metamorphoses*, Iacchus was a child-god in the Eleusinian mysteries, a redemptive *puer aeternus*. For Vergil, Ascanius, the son of Aeneas, is the subject of a miracle when lightning plays harmlessly around his head, presaging the salutory role he will play. And in his messianic fourth eclogue Vergil sees in the figure of a baby boy the herald of a golden age. The child as savior is firmly established at the very core of the Christian and classical traditions.

One of the most striking modern portraits of the enigmatic child as a redeemer is that of Joas (or Eliacin, as he is called until his identity is revealed) in Racine's biblical tragedy, *Athalie* (1691). Upon the death of her son, Athalie, in order to assure herself of the throne, follows the bloodthirsty tradition of her family and stabs all of her grandchildren. Unknown to her, one of the infants survived this carnage and was raised by Joad, the high priest, and his wife, Josabet. The first encounter—a silent one—between the murderous queen, now a worshipper of Baal, and Joas takes place when he is nine years old. She sees him by chance in the temple that she has entered in order to confront the high priest. The aging queen recognizes him, but not as her offspring. For her he is the incarnation of the apparition of the gentle and modest boy who, in a dream, has come to assassinate her. The sight of the real child seems to paralyze her. Although her mouth is open to speak, she can utter not a sound; her wild and terrified eyes cannot turn away from the child. From this mute scene there emanates a sense of horror that can be attributed to the chilling presence of the incomprehensible child.

Although words are exchanged during the entire course of their second meeting, the effect is equally disorienting for Athalie. Hoping to elucidate the mystery represented by Eliacin, she has summoned him in order to interrogate him. She is convinced that the child cannot help but reveal the truth:

> This age is innocent: its ingenuousness
> Does not yet alter simple truth.
> Let him explain himself concerning everything.
> (act 2, scene 7, lines 629–31)

Indeed, Joas's curt and simple responses provide answers to everything; at the same time they reveal nothing. Just a few examples of these questions and answers suffice to demonstrate how candor only deepens the mystery:

> ATHALIE: What are you called?
> JOAS: My name is Eliacin.
> ATHALIE: Your father?
> JOAS: I am, so they say, an orphan.
> ATHALIE: You have no parents?
> JOAS: They abandoned me.
> ATHALIE: How and since when?
> JOAS: Since I was born.
> (act 2, scene 7, lines 633–40)

As Athalie probes deeper into his existence, his replies, while losing nothing in simplicity, become more ambiguous, and all seem designed to wound her. For example, when she wishes to know what he is learning, he paraphrases the law—but precisely that part of it that deals with the punishment of homicides. Whether such parries are the result of the calculated cruelty of a child seeking to draw the blood of an aging woman or of the ingenuous spontaneity of an innocent boy who does not know what he is saying is a question that remains forever unanswered. Joas is as much an enigma for us as for Athalie.

From the beginning Joas represents a menace for Athalie. His mere presence suffices to sap the will power of the queen and to transform her from a calculating and decisive tyrant into a wavering and sentimental old woman. There is a further tragic dimension to the downfall of Athalie. The child elicits from the normally harsh queen a feeling of true tenderness, and it is this feeling that makes her vulnerable. Here again there is the fundamental double effect of children: their vulnerability can make those who encounter them equally vulnerable. And so Joas is her nemesis, and when, at the end of the play, his pathetic and broken grandmother is taken away to be executed, he stands by, inscrutable and silent. Although an obvious menace for Athalie, this child is the symbol of salvation for the Hebrews. When the play opens, they have practically deserted the temple and have given up all hope. They are a "broken people" (act 1, scene 1, line 93) who have lost their faith and no longer have the courage to oppose the military might of Athalie. In the last act, when the true identity of the child Joas is revealed to them, and he is crowned their king, the children of Israel are immediately reanimated; they find their former zeal and put the armies of Baal to rout.

The redemptive quality of the child is a favorite theme of the romantics and recurs in authors as dissimilar as Novalis, Wordsworth, and Hugo. In the *Hymns to the Night* (1799) Novalis's carefully cultivated child figure assumes the dimensions of a savior. The supernatural quality of the "miraculous child" is made clear from the outset:

With divine fervor the prophetic eyes of the blossoming child looked toward the days of the future . . . without concern over the days of his earthly fate. Soon the most simple people gathered around him, marvelously overwhelmed by a deep love.[19]

This child, who has such an immediate impact upon the existence of those who surround him while himself remaining indifferent to his own existence, inspires a passing bard to devote his entire heart to him. This minstrel is inspired to song by the presence of the strange child:

> You are the youth who since time immemorial
> Sunk in deep reflection has been standing on our graves;
> A comforting sign in the darkness—
> The joyful commencement of a higher humanity.

In death eternal life becomes manifest,
You are death and make us well. (p. 408)

Shortly after the departure of the singer, the youth, who strad-
dles life and death, himself passes away. However, the initial
deep mourning of his family and of the entire land is quickly replaced by tears of joy and thanksgiving. For there is a miraculous
resurrection:

Angels—gently formed out of his dreams—sat by the slumbering youth.
Awakened into a new divine magnificence he scaled the heights of the
new-born world—with his own hand he buried the old corpse in the
abandoned hollow and with an all-mighty hand laid upon it the stone
that no force may raise. (p. 409)

First his mother, and in the ensuing years thousands of others,
abandon the life of pain and torment. Imbued with faith and longing they follow the tantalizing child into the "kingdom of love,"
which is also the "temple of celestial death." Thus the enigmatic
youth presented by Novalis is the herald of eternal life in death.

Although some of the sources of Clemens Brentano's mysti-
cism are as ancient as those of Novalis, they are for the most part
highly suspect, and the poetic products they inspired, though often
seductive, are of a dubious quality. It is in the apocryphal *Evan-
gelium infantiae* that he found the model for the disquieting figure
of Agnuscastus, who plays a central role in the never completed
Romanzen vom Rosenkranz (1801–12).[20] He is the *puer aeternus*,
condemned to remain his age forever because, though he had
saved the infant Jesus on the Holy Family's flight to Egypt, he is
culpable.[21] His function throughout the long poem is a redemptive
one, and he intervenes efficaciously at every turn of the excessively
complex narrative. And yet the message with which he converts his
auditors is an incomprehensible one; for, though his voice is clear,
his words are dark, and only in an unspecified future and in an
unspecified location will he be able to enunciate his tidings:

Einst werd' ich am rechten Orte
Wunderbare Dinge sagen.
                                    (12.965–66)

Once I shall at the right place
Say marvelous things.

The child whose life is one of expiation and who saves himself by saving others is a recurrent figure in Brentano's works and reappears in his late *Blätter aus dem Tagebuch der Ahnfrau* (*Pages from an Ancestor's Diary*) (1838) in the guise of a boy who must make endless reparation to atone for the crime he had been tempted to commit. Whereas the savior of Novalis has retained his innocence, and his ascension in death is a triumphal one, the more complex redemptive child of Brentano is guilty, and his eternal life is not a blessing but a curse.

Whereas the eternity announced by the child in *Hymns to the Night* lies in the future and that of Brentano in the present, Wordsworth (like Proust in this respect) looks to the past. His children, though existing in the present, are fragile beings constantly threatened by an uncertain future. So the six-year-old H. C., the "faery voyager," exists on the verge of extinction, and the poet expresses his concern for her:

> O blessèd vision! happy child!
> Thou art so exquisitely wild,
> I think of thee with many fears
> For what may be thy lot in future years.[22]

At the slightest instigation she could slip out of existence without forewarning and without anyone's noticing her passage into the nothingness of death, for she is:

> A gem that glitters while it lives,
> And no forewarning gives;
> But, at the touch of wrong, without a strife
> Slips in a moment out of life.
> (lines 30–33)

The evanescent nature of childhood can be overcome by memory. But it is not merely a recollection of the unclouded joys of childhood that suffices for the poet. He is certainly not insensitive to the ordinary charms of the age of innocence that the memory evokes, but they are simply insufficient to justify his jubilation. This he states clearly in the "Ode on Intimations of Immortality":

> The thought of our past years in me doth breed
> Perpetual benediction: not indeed
> For that which is most worthy to be blest;

> Delight and liberty, the simple creed
> Of Childhood, whether busy or at rest,
> With new-fledged hope still fluttering in his breast:—
>> Not for these I raise
>> The song of thanks and praise
>
>> (lines 134–41)

What does inspire Wordsworth to intone his paean are certain immutable values which he retrospectively perceives in childhood and which are immune to the vicissitudes of passing time:

> Those shadowy recollections,
>> Which, be they what they may,
> Are yet the fountain-light of all our day,
> Are yet a master-light of all our seeing;
> Uphold us, cherish, and have power to make
> Our noisy years seem moments in the being
> Of the eternal Silence: truths that wake,
>> To perish never
>
>> (lines 150–57)

This conclusion to the ode presents a platonic vision in which the child is the bearer of eternal verities. Remembrance of things past makes possible eternal benediction. And still the blessed and exquisitely wild child who makes all of this possible remains a puzzling figure whose words, as in the case of H. C., are "fittest to unutterable thought."

Victor Hugo is known above all as the poet of childhood. He is also its novelist. In *Les Misérables* (1862) the intervention of the enigmatic child in human affairs is a recurrent theme. In fact, nearly every critical turning point in the story is marked by the appearance of such a child. There are many significant episodes besides the ones involving the famous Parisian gamin Gavroche or the mistreated and then cherished Cosette. For example, when M. Madeleine is on the verge of resuming his identity as Jean Valjean in order to save an old man who has been falsely accused of a crime, he cannot find a conveyance that will take him to the court in time. He is relieved because, through no fault of his own, a man will be condemned and he himself will be forever saved from the clutches of Javert and from the galleys. Fate has intervened to make his sacrifice impossible, and he will be able to continue a good and comfortable existence as before. In extremis a nameless young boy, to whom no one had previously paid any attention, offers his services and finds a carriage. It is because of this child, who never reappears, that Jean Valjean assumes his guilt and takes up again his life of penal servitude. It is thanks to him that he takes a significant step on the road toward sainthood. This anonymous apparition is but one of the many incarnations of the archetypal child redeemer who is responsible for the sinner's initial conversion and for his eventual salvation. Shortly after he has stolen the silver candlesticks of the bishop and fled from his home, Jean Valjean, who hardly knows what he is doing, encounters a ten-year-old Savoyard boy roaming through the countryside singing and playing with some loose change. Little Gervais drops one of his coins and Jean Valjean, in an almost trancelike state, places his foot on it and remains impervious to the child's pleadings. The diminutive creature, terrified by the ex-convict's imposing physical presence, takes to his heels. As soon as he has disappeared, Jean Valjean returns to his senses and realizes that he is holding the child's coin. In the nearest village, he asks a priest to identify the boy for him, but all the information the curate can give him is that little Gervais is a foreigner whom they do not know in their town. Jean Valjean gives the priest money for the poor, and this first act of charity will be followed by many others. In one sense, the rest of his life is devoted to making restitution to the unknown child. What Hugo calls "the mystery of the luminous innocence of children"[23] is the agent of salvation for Jean Valjean.

The revolutionary impact that the appearance of a child can have on the life of an adult is perhaps best dramatized in George Eliot's *Silas Marner* (1861). The story is a familiar one. After being falsely accused by his best friend and condemned by his church for a theft he has not committed and after losing his fiancée to his treacherous companion, the disgraced Silas Marner leaves the city and moves to Raveloe, where for fifteen years he leads the life of an eccentric recluse. During this extended nadir in his existence, the weaver, in a Kafka-like metamorphosis, is deprived of most of his human attributes and is transformed into a functional bug: "He seemed to weave, like the spider, from pure impulse, without reflection."[24] As if to reemphasize the point, the author goes on to explain that "his life [became] the unquestioning activity of a spinning insect." The only interruptions in this monotonous production are provided by the calls of hunger and by sleep. Shortly after his arrival in the village, there is an event that "might have been the beginning of his rescue from the insect-like existence into which his nature had shrunk" (p. 19). In a movement of pity, Marner cares for and relieves the suffering of a sick woman. But this charitable impulse is both exploited and misunderstood by the villagers:

Thus it came to pass that his movement of pity towards Sally Oates, which had given him a transient sense of brotherhood, heightened the repulsion between him and his neighbors, and made his isolation more complete. (p. 20)

Consequently, the weaver resigns himself to a meaningless form of life in which only one pleasure, and a sterile one at that, replaces all former feelings, namely the love of gold:

So, year after year, Silas Marner had lived in this solitude, his guineas rising in the iron pot, and his life narrowing and hardening itself more and more into a mere pulsation of desire and satisfaction that had no relation to any other being. His life had reduced itself to the mere functions of weaving and hoarding, without any contemplation of an end towards which the functions tended. (pp. 21–22)

Even the solace he finds in hoarding is finally denied him through the inexplicable theft of his bags of money.

It is the unexpected appearance of an orphaned child that saves Silas Marner. That such an act of redemption cannot be the work of just any child is indicated by the fact that Marner had encountered one youngster earlier without any results. The previous meeting, with his neighbor's seven-year-old son, had proved totally inefficacious: "Marner, on the other side of the hearth, saw the neat-featured rosy face as a mere dim round, with two dark spots in it" (p. 87). In contrast, the appearance of the half-frozen Eppie has an immediate impact: "In utter amazement, Silas fell on his knees and bent his head low to examine the marvel: it was a sleeping child" (p. 115). He knows at once and instinctively "that this child was somehow a message come to him from that far-off life," and his imagination is unable to extricate itself from a vague, dreamy state that is marked by "the sense of mystery in the child's sudden presence" (p. 115). Thus Silas Marner is saved by the advent of a child whom he could cherish, by a young being who has been sent to him out of the darkness. Thanks to her, he can resume his life among his fellow men. She had awakened him from a long nightmare into an existence marked by normalcy.

George Eliot comes closer than any of her predecessors to defining what element it is in the child that makes such a redemption possible. Because of her resemblance to a younger sister Marner had lost early in life, Eppie's presence unlocks the doors of the past to "a hurrying influx of memories." She liberates Silas Marner from the prison cell of the present: "As the child's mind was growing into knowledge, his mind was growing into memory: as her life unfolded, his soul, long stupefied in a cold, narrow prison, was unfolding too, and trembling gradually into full consciousness" (p. 131). As in the powerful conclusion to Proust's *The Past Recaptured*, there is a magnificent reconciliation between past and present:

. . . with reawakening sensibilities, memory also reawakened, he had begun to ponder over the elements of his old faith, and blend them with his new impressions, till he recovered a consciousness of unity between his past and present. (p. 145)

The child can certainly put an end to that condition defined by C. S. Lewis as "the great divorce," but it can do even more by infusing the condition of reunification with jubilation. Thus Eppie transforms ordinary existence into a feast that she and Marner can celebrate. While she broadens the scope of her adoptive father's life by reestablishing communication between him and the others, she fills that newly opened space with joy:

. . . Eppie called him away from his weaving, and made him think all its pauses a holiday, reawakening his senses with her fresh life, even to the old winter flies that came crawling forth in the early spring sunshine, and warming him into joy because *she* had joy. (p. 130)

This rejoicing may not be the *gaudium spirituale* of Saint Thomas Aquinas, but it is at the very least its secularized form:

In the old days there were angels who came and took men by the hand and led them away from the city of destruction. We see no white-winged angels now. But yet men are led away from threatening destruction; a hand is put into theirs, which leads them forth gently towards a calm and bright land, so that they look no more backward; and the hand may be a little child's. (pp. 136–37)

With this moving profession of faith George Eliot summarizes all the possibilities inherent in the child that the romantics had sought to express.

In the pseudo-romantic literature of the twentieth century the motif of the child-savior becomes debased and sentimentalized. There are, of course, exceptions, like the child Aubain, who brings about the impressive reconciliation between heaven and earth with which Paul Claudel's drama *Tidings Brought to Mary* (1912) ends. This profound reenactment of the Christian myth has its secular counterpart in Jean Giraudoux's *Adventures of Jérôme Bardini* (1930). The protagonist's successful evasion of his bourgeois marriage and of his bureaucratic existence as a tax collector fails to give substance to his life, and he becomes a platonic shadow without identity roaming aimlessly in an oneiric world of ideal forms. Even his liaison with Stéphy remains an unsuccessful attempt to merge two dreams. It is at Niagara Falls, the banal setting of countless honeymoons, that Bardini encounters the nameless vagabond child, divested of all ties to humanity, to whom he will devote himself. Like all enigmatic children, this one lives secretively in a world apart, and the rhythm of his existence is not in synchronization with that of the real world: "He had a secret plan, a secret rhythm. . . . It seemed as if for him there was another geography, another history, another tree of poetry and painting, reserved for his race alone and of which he never spoke."[25] Whether from the point of view of a child or an adult, his activities are as uninterpretable as the traces in the sand drawn by his earlier incarnations: "The child did not play. He kept himself occupied only with those simple and blessed activities which in themselves signify nothing" (pp. 154–55).

At first Bardini is suspicious of this child whose very lack of any status in society might be a trap. Furthermore, a social worker who wants to rehabilitate this runaway warns Bardini of the dangers inherent in keeping company with such a creature, whose frequentation inspires a taste for revolt and nothingness in those who come in contact with him. But instead, this child, who had never been in complicity with humanity, proves to be the surrogate who can carry his burden for him. And so he is ready to follow "his precise footsteps on an uncertain itinerary" (p. 136). Eventually he must lose the child, but in the meantime his life has acquired meaning. Although Bardini finally returns to his ordinary life as a functionary of the state, Giraudoux can conclude, "Such is the story of Bardini, saved by a child messiah" (p. 160).

More typical of contemporary literature than Giraudoux's sensitive and subtle treatment is the exploitation of a secularized version of this figure by Jean Anouilh, in whose plays the enigmatic child-redeemer becomes a cliché. In *The Voyager without Baggage* (1936) the adult Gaston has become hopelessly enmeshed in the sordid financial and sexual affairs of his family, and there seems no way for him to extricate himself or to escape from the consequences of his own wretched past. However at the end of the play he is saved by a *deus ex machina* in the form of an orphaned boy who asks him where he might find "the little place where one can be tranquil" (the bathroom). With this child, who seems to have come from nowhere, Gaston will embark on a new and unencumbered life. Equally typical though less cloying is the ending of Anouilh's version of *Antigone* (1944). Creon's decision to have Antigone executed has resulted not only in her death but in the suicides of his son and of his wife as well. He is, as the chorus proclaims, all alone now. Nonetheless, as the aging ruler leaves to attend to the business of state, a little page boy is there to support him. What occasionally gives these maudlin scenes a tragic dimension is Anouilh's bitter awareness of the illusory nature of this symbol. The playwright knows that the only hope he proffers, the purity of the innocent child, is a transient phenomenon without any real redemptive powers. The child searching for the tranquility of the lavatory will grow up all too soon, and his candor will be replaced by the cynicism against which Gaston has revolted. The little page boy whose presence is the only comfort Creon can find is in a great hurry to become a man and will pay no heed to Creon's admonition never to grow up if he can help it. And in *Romeo and Juliette* (1946) Anouilh goes so far as to deny the existence of the ideal of childhood while simultaneously demonstrating the impossibility of life without that ideal. Lucien's last words before plunging himself into eternal darkness are "There are no more children, now. Good-by."

There is indeed something suspect about the child-redeemer, and it is one of the ironies of Henry de Montherlant's *Queen after Death* (1942) that the otherwise astute monarch, Ferrante, completely misinterprets the enigma that his twelve-year-old page boy, Dino del Moro, represents. Although portrayed as being extremely suspicious, Ferrante has an implicit trust in the young Andalusian, who, unknown to him, dislikes him intensely and listens at the doors. Dino is actually a creature of the infanta, who employs him as a spy; the lad's facility at dissimulation makes of him an ideal informer. Unaware of his recent betrayal, Ferrante, as he is dying, draws Dino, whom he calls his "little brother," close to him and then, holding him tightly, utters his penultimate words: "Let the innocence of this child serve as my protection when I appear before my Judge" (act 3, scene 7). And then the king gives his last order to his page: "Remain by my side, whatever might happen . . . even if I die." The faithless child disobeys and, when the king expires, commits his final act of treason. After some hesitation, he turns away from the body and follows the other courtiers to kneel by the bier of Inès, the "queen after death" whom Ferrante had ordered executed. Abandoned at last by the child, the corpse of the king remains alone.

In a very different cultural and religious tradition, Philip Roth, in "The Conversion of the Jews" (1958), also questions the redemptive ability of the child. The young protagonist, Ozzie, in a simultaneously dramatic and hilarious revolt against the traditional religious instruction of his rabbi, must use the threat of suicide to force the Jews to their knees in the Gentile posture of prayer. Only when he has compelled his coreligionists to promise to practice tolerance can he jump from the roof of the synagogue "right into the center of the yellow net that glowed in the evening's edge like an overgrown halo."[26] Despite the religious symbolism of this concluding phrase of the story, Ozzie is not a savior but merely the caricature of a martyr. Once the threat of self-immolation has been removed, it is doubtful that the conversion the child has brought about will last.

Whereas Roth is merely skeptical of the salutary effect of the child, J. D. Salinger takes as one of his major themes the inability of the young to influence the fate of others. His children are all as impotent as they are enigmatic. This is a recurrent topos in the most important of his *Nine Stories* (1948). In "Teddy" the clairvoyant prodigy does not even have the will to save himself from the death he had foretold and lets his little sister push him head-first into the deep end of a drained pool. In "Uncle Wiggly in Connecticut" little Ramona, who creates her invisible companions to accompany her in her own imaginary world, cannot serve as an intercessor for her alcoholic mother. The child's visions and the mother's intoxicated reminiscences are but two futile means of trying to escape from the boredom of suburbia. While a letter from an inscrutable thirteen-year-old girl may or may not help keep intact the faculties of the battle-weary soldier of "For Esmé—With Love and Squalor," it is certain that the intervention of an even younger and equally puzzling girl in "A Perfect Day for Bananafish" cannot help the shell-shocked veteran who attempts to have her enter his own fantasy world. After his brief encounter with her, Seymour Glass commits suicide. With Salinger, the enigmatic child's potential for good or evil can never be actualized.

The Complexity of the Enigmatic Child

> What sort of secret is a child?
> Clemens Brentano

> Nobody can keep a secret better
> than a child.
> Victor Hugo

The theme of the unknowable child (whether as redeemer, threat, or pure enigma) is a complex one, and if there is any writer who has done full justice to its richness it is Thomas Mann. His early novella, *Tristan* (1903), already contains all the later elements of his masterpieces: the interrelationship of art and disease, the dangers of music, and the confrontation between the practical world and the aesthetic one. Even the locale of the story, the sanatorium, is one that Mann was to develop later in *The Magic Mountain*. The realm of art in *Tristan* is represented by the novelist Spinell, who persuades his fellow inmate Gabriele Klöterjahn, the ailing wife of a businessman, to play the piano for him. She yields to this temptation, and her desperate plunge into the world of romantic music is the equivalent of an act of treason against the world of commerce personified by her husband. More than that, it represents an act of adultery and finally suicide, a sort of Wagnerian love-death. Her betrayal has profound consequences not only on the symbolic but on the realistic plane: the emotional upheaval caused by the intensity of the music is too much for her frail constitution. It leads to a serious deterioration of her already fragile health and eventually to her death. And just prior to her passing away, it results in a violent clash between two antithetical ideologies. This confrontation takes the form of a bitter debate between her husband and Spinell, an argument between an ineffectual visionary and a materialistic activist that is interrupted by the announcement of the demise of Gabriele Klöterjahn and thus left temporarily in suspension. The resolution comes only at the end of the story, in a dramatic encounter between Spinell and the now motherless Klöterjahn baby who is being wheeled in his pram by his nurse. There is something insolent in the appearance of this extraordinarily healthy infant, who is described as "plump . . . with chubby cheeks, superb and well-proportioned."[27] And the eyes of the child that meet those of the novelist are "cheerful and infallible." As Spinell is about to avert his gaze, something "horrendous" occurs. The child begins to laugh triumphantly, and this inexplicable, jubilant screeching is sinister. Spinell becomes even more uneasy when young Anton Klöterjahn shakes his rattle and his pacifier at him as if he wanted to mock him and to drive him off. It is then that Spinell turns on his heels and walks off "with the powerfully hesitant steps of someone who wants to hide the fact that inwardly he is running away" (p. 262). It is with these words, describing the controlled panic of flight, that *Tristan* ends. Spinell, whose aestheticism is allied with sickness and death, has encountered the future in the form of a grotesquely healthy and incomprehensible child.

Gustav Aschenbach, the author-protagonist of *Death in Venice* (1912), is the very antithesis of Spinell, just as the child who tempts him is the very opposite of young Klöterjahn. Aschenbach is a successful writer, and his prose is "lucid and powerful" (p. 450). His "sober conscientiousness" had brought into check the "darker, fiery impulses." His is an art that has by force of will overcome any decadent tendencies. It reflects the constant tensions between the intellect and the passions. The highly disciplined Aschenbach never lets himself go. Thus he is not, like Spinell, a tempter; he is the one who is tempted and succumbs. The story of the last months of his life is the recital of his progressive awareness of the real nature of beauty. Simultaneously, it is the account of a progressive self-abandonment, the degenerative movement from a Spartan existence to the disintegration caused by self-indulgence. His salutary nemesis is Tadzio, the Polish boy whom he encounters but never meets in Venice. The youth is the incarnation of physical perfection, of godlike beauty. There is something supernatural in his "expression of fair and divine earnestness" (p. 469). He is clearly a being apart and is treated differently from his three sisters even by his mother and governess. From the very first, when Tadzio turns to gaze at him in the lobby of their hotel, Aschenbach is fascinated. Already in the early stages of his infatuation, the presence of the child makes Aschenbach conscious of his own decline. As he looks in the mirror, only moments after his initial encounter with Tadzio, he for the first time becomes aware of his gray hair, of his flabby and tired face. The more his mind is occupied by the vision of Tadzio, the more a mortal lethargy seems to overome the once vigorous writer. Simultaneously his thoughts turn to illness and he seems to detect in Tadzio a sickly element, an unnatural, ivorylike pallor. It is at this time, too, that he realizes how deleterious the stagnant air of Venice is for his own health. However, his one half-hearted attempt at flight is aborted, more because of his own lack of volition than because of the misdispatched trunk that he uses as convenient excuse to prolong his stay indefinitely. Several weeks later, Aschenbach is irremediably overcome, when the child secretively looks at him with a mysterious smile that the aging writer accepts as a "fearful gift." It is immediately thereafter that Aschenbach obtains the first intimations of the mortal sickness that is infecting all of Venice. But the potential cholera epidemic that frightens off most of the tourists exerts a dreadful fascination on him, a fascination that is closely linked with the seductive influence of Tadzio's existence. Aschenbach's obsession is a compound of "fear and ecstasy and a terrified curiosity" (p. 516). This unhealthy preoccupation with sickness and love leads to Aschenbach's desperate attempt to make himself more attractive through a pathetic recourse to cosmetics.[28] On the day of Tadzio's planned departure, Aschenbach, seated in his chair on the beach, watches Tadzio for the last time as he wades into the sea. He thinks that Tadzio is beckoning to him, and he wants to follow him toward the "awful region full of promise" (p. 525) that the boy's graceful gesture indicates. But it is during this vision, as he gives himself over completely to the enchantment that Tadzio exercises over him, that death overtakes him. The encounter with the enigmatic Tadzio has been a fleeting one, with not a word ever exchanged. It is the encounter with Eros that had come too late, or perhaps the revenge of Eros on the writer who had tried to deny him.

Like all Mann's texts, this one is too ambiguous to be treated in a formulaic fashion, and there is more to the mortal confrontation at its center than is suggested above. Whereas Anton Klöterjahn is the frightful harbinger of a new world order inimical to aesthetic values, Tadzio is the homoerotic incarnation of the type of child who in *Hymns to the Night* promised salvation through beauty and through death. But the promise of an authentic eternity with which Tadzio tantalizes his victim may be as illusory as the hair dye with which Aschenbach counterfeits youth. So this novella holds out a somber warning. As Fiedler has pointed out,[29] the nostalgia for innocence, as represented by the yearning for the child, may well be suicidal.

Whereas Mann indicates the possibilities and dangers inherent in any attempt at interpreting the enigmatic child, Samuel Beckett demonstrates the impossibility of such an enterprise. The timid boy who appears at the end of each of the two acts of *Waiting for Godot* (1955) may or may not be the same person, may or may not be an emissary of Godot, may or may not have come before, may or may not come again, and may or may not be an agent of salvation. What seems certain is that he represents that tiny element of hope which makes it impossible for Vladimir and Estragon to put an end to their misery, and which impels them to go on day after day. At the same time it is more than possible that the hope the child represents here may be the cruelest delusion of all. The presence of the small boy in *Endgame* (1957) is even more troubling. At Hamm's request his servant Clov has countless times scanned the horizon with his telescope and seen nothing. There are no signs of life, not even seagulls over the waveless ocean; there is no sun in the sky, and yet not even darkness. But once when Clov peers at the gray wasteland he espies, to his horror, a sign of life: a small boy sitting on the ground, leaning against something, and staring at his navel.[30] Hamm's immediate reaction to this startling news is to utter, "The stone that has been rolled away." This is a direct reference to the discovery by Mary Magdalene and the other Mary of Christ's empty sepulcher, from which the tombstone had been rolled away (Matthew 28:1). In other words, Hamm initially interprets this presence as an indication of the miracle of the resurrection. Clov, on the contrary, feels menaced by this existence, for he sees in the child "a potential procreator." But Hamm, through his subsequent diffidence, dissuades Clov from going out to exterminate the boy: "If he exists he'll come here or he'll die there, and if he doesn't. . . ." This inconclusive response, trailing off into silence, indicates that the ultimate rejection of the possibly redemptive child is the passionless unconcern of the indifferent, for whom there is no place even in hell. And the child in limbo is powerless to help the denizens of the antechamber of the infernal regions. Beckett's despairing portrayal is, in some sense, the end-vision of the child.

Conclusion

> And look upon us, angels of young children, with regards not quite estranged, when the swift river bears us to the ocean!
>
> Charles Dickens

The enigmatic child, as he appears in literature from antiquity to modern times, assumes a multiplicity of forms. His presence may be threatening or beneficent or neither of these. He may, like Joas in *Athalie*, play the role of intercessor or, like Little Father Time in *Jude the Obscure*, of destroyer; or, as in Stifter's *Abdias* and Gide's *The Voyage of Urien*, he may play no real role at all. He may, as in the poetry of Hugo, assume a comforting stance, or, as in Novalis's *Hymns to the Night*, may represent a metaphysical concept. Despite all the seemingly disparate incarnations of this protean figure, the various personages have so many traits in common that it is possible to speak of the enigmatic child in generic terms. First of all, this child's universe represents a self-enclosed, nonreferential system. Both Chaucer's child and Mann's Tadzio are strangers to the world and are independent of it. Second, communication between the child and the adult is virtually impossible. This is symbolized by the linguistic deficiency of so many of these children. The boy in "The Prioress's Tale" does not even comprehend the words he sings; the one in Goethe's *The Novella* must have recourse to the flute; Tadzio, in *Death in Venice*, speaks a language incomprehensible to Aschenbach; and the children in *The Waves* intone lyrics that to the adults are gibberish. Third, despite his taciturnity, the enigmatic child has a message to deliver; in this respect the boy in *Waiting for Godot* is typical. He is an emissary, even if we do not know from where or from whom. It is here that we see the fundamental paradox of the enigmatic child: though a message-bearer, he is inarticulate, or at least incapable of making himself understood, or, occasionally, as in the case of Hawthorne's Pearl, perversely unwilling to reveal the truth. Fourth, these children, of whom James's Maisie is a prototype, are all wise beyond their years even though their wisdom may be more apparent than real. Thus they present a combination of youth and age that adds to their mystery. Finally, these children are all doomed, for though their being is atemporal, they are subject to the vicissitudes of time. Like Creon's page boy they must deny their essence by accepting the fact that they will grow up, or, like Wordsworth's child, they must depart from this world. In summary, the enigmatic child is a stranger to this world, sufficient unto himself, incapable of communication and yet the bearer of important tidings. Thus it is his presence that is significant, even if we can never decipher its meaning.

It is the enigmatic child's evanescence that makes him such a haunting, elusive character. It is this transience that explains why, despite his importance, he is rarely to be found center stage, but remains a peripheral figure, relegated to the function of an unanalyzable catalyst that precipitates an analyzable transformation. The writer dares not dwell too long on the child himself, because at best he can recapture only the disappearing echo of his faint voice. Georges Bernanos, in a moving passage, expressed this basic dilemma when he confessed his frustration at being unable to write the child's language:

After all, I should have the right to speak in his [the child's] name. But that's precisely the trouble, no one speaks in the name of childhood; to do so, it would be necessary to speak its language. And it is this forgotten language, this language that, imbecile that I am, I seek in book after book, as if such a language could be or had ever been written. Never mind! Sometimes I do succeed in recapturing a trace of its accent.[31]

Faced with this elusive language, the writer is forced to focus his attention not directly on the child but on the reaction to him, and that is why we must resign ourselves to being satisfied with the adult perception of the child without giving up the hope of some day gaining an insight into his reality, or an approximation thereof.

Bernanos himself looked forward to such a time: "The deadest of the dead is the little boy I used to be. And yet, when the time comes, it is he who will resume his place at the head of my life." (p. 8). And Bernanos concludes with the prophecy that it is the child who, like a young officer at the head of his troops, will lead the way into the house of the Father.

It is only by indirection that we can come to terms with the enigmatic child. Günter Grass in *The Tin Drum* (1959) suggests a tentative resolution of the difficulties of a task considered practically impossible by Bernanos. As a newborn infant, Oskar, the narrator, is already painfully aware of the inability of adults to understand him; while his parents, leaning over the crib, are speculating about his future, the precocious baby thinks to itself that they "did not have the organ to comprehend my objections and decisions and thus to respect them."[32] But years later, Oskar, now a professional drummer in a cabaret, does succeed in bringing about communication between adult and child, for he has discovered the secret of evoking the language that Bernanos searched for in vain. The little boy resumes his rightful place at the head of the twenty-one-year old Oskar's life. Having forgotten all the routine pieces normally performed by and for adults in a nightclub and having no preconceived project, he begins to improvise:

. . . I did not play what I could, but what I knew from the depths of my heart. Oskar succeeded in pressing the drumsticks into the fists of a once three-year-old Oskar. . . . I revealed the world from the point of view of a three-year-old. (p. 445)

The habitués of the cabaret themselves have a childish vision of Oskar: they see him as the Pied Piper of Hamelin and are ready to follow him anywhere. And Oskar gradually transforms them into children. They take each other by the hands and join in singing the children's songs that Oskar's drum-playing inspires in them. He awakens all the childhood fears in them, and, when they become too terrified, he again reassures them. Accompanying their games on his drum, he "led on the whole group, which was now shouting with glee, giggling and foolishly babbling with the voices of children" (p. 446). Oskar continues his performance until the adults no longer can resist a childish urge and all wet their pants. His success is indisputable: "Every evening the guests all called for Oskar, for his tin drum, for the one person who was able to evoke the childhood of every patron, no matter how old he might be" (p. 447). Like the sailors in *The Voyage of Urien*, the beholders of the child themselves become children, and the transformation takes place because Oskar had been able to hand over the drumsticks to the three-year-old he once was.

The climactic episode in *The Tin Drum* is a variation on a favorite theme of the German romantics. The reversion to childhood as the goal of the artist-magician is a problem central to Tieck's satiric play within a play, *Puss in Boots* (1797), in which the audience is outraged at the fictitious author's attempt to subject them to a staged fairy tale. One of the irate spectators finally cries out, "But for God's sake, you must think we're children!" The author responds, ". . . I only wanted to make the attempt to transport you back into the distant sensations of your childhood years." The attempt is a spectacular failure, and the stage performance ends in a brilliant debacle. Unlike Tieck's mistreated playwright, the narrator of Brentano's structurally complex, late version of the fairy tale *Gockel, Hinkel, and Gackeleia* (1838) is witness to and participant in his heroine's successful realization of just such a transformation. After Gackeleia has recovered the magic ring of Solomon, she immediately fulfills all her desires: the castle of her forefathers is restored, her friends and parents rewarded, and she herself is wedded in pomp and circumstance to the prince she loves. Nevertheless, during the magnificent marriage feast she is melancholy, for instantaneous satisfaction deprives her of anything to long for. All that is left is a nostalgia for an anterior existence and the never expressed but omnipresent fear of sex. So Gackeleia turns the ring for the last time and makes the ultimate wish, namely that she and all of her companions (including the narrator) might be changed into little children. The consummation of the nuptials is forever postponed. The feast and the story, merged into one, conclude with all the personages, now children, listening entranced to the recital of the fairy tale in which they had lived. This is the transposition which Oskar realizes so brilliantly, and it is the most powerful effect the enigmatic child can produce.

The constant reemergence of the enigmatic child in literatures of various periods, nations, and genres indicates that it is an archetypal theme deeply embedded in the psyche of the human race. Seeming to slumber in the human consciousness, the child awakens periodically to make his appearance in works of art and literature.

Like a somnambulist, he traverses our horizon briefly to disappear again in the void from which he emerged. His transient appearance is a disturbing one because the enigmatic child is uncomfortably similar to all children, even the most ordinary. He is a composite of the elements which define the essence of all those who have not yet reached maturity. For to a certain degree all children are autonomous universes; to some extent all of them speak their own language and seem to have a message to convey that they forget just as soon as they are old enough to transmit it.

Without overemphasizing the Jungian implications of the preceding interpretation, one could say that the theme of the enigmatic child seems to respond to a deeply felt universal need that is indefinable in anything but symbolic or poetic terms. It is possible to see in this theme the expression of a combination of nostalgia for the past, as in Wordsworth, and a longing for a new and transcendental future, as in Novalis. Out of this rich amalgam there emerges the verbalization of a far more complex aspiration, the desire to suspend time, that implacable enemy of childhood. And so there is inherent in the existence of the enigmatic child a profound tragedy, for on the one hand he is eternal and on the other hand constanly menaced by extinction. Like Saint-Exupéry's Little Prince, he cannot prolong for too long his sojourn in a world that is not his natural habitat. He must return to the celestial regions whence he came, his message unspoken or misunderstood, leaving behind the adults to their hopeless yearning after innocence.

CHAPTER TWO

The Heaven and Hell of Childhood

Childhood, the plain-dealer: nothing
approached it but upon intimate terms.
It's the shades of experience that afford
shadows of fear, but the black-and-white of
childhood discovers the intimacy of terror.
William Gaddis

The Childhood Domain

Children have neither past nor future and, what hardly
ever happens to us, they revel in the present.
La Bruyère

The child, enigmatic or otherwise, moves in a realm whose
nature has tantalized many writers. Although this domain is contiguous with that of the adult, its autonomy lends it an air of mystery, a secretiveness that represents a constant challenge to the
writer. The descriptions of this strange continent are myriad, comprising both heaven and hell and ranging from the willfully naive
representation of the home that contains the swarm of jubilant
children surrounding Lotte in Goethe's *Werther* to the sophisticated portrait of Bly, the haunted estate inhabited by the joyless
Flora and Miles in James's *The Turn of the Screw*. Yet the car-
tographers of these fictional countries are of necessity adults, and
thus there is always a residue of doubt in the reader's mind concerning the authenticity of their geographies. Without impugning
the validity of such works as art, some difficult questions must be
asked as to what they really represent. An effort must be made to
determine to what extent (if any) they reflect the reality of the
childhood experience.

In general, books dealing with childhood may be divided into
two broad categories. In one are those works whose central purpose

is to recapture the essence of a lost past. The means of achieving this end are diverse, and various authors employ widely differing techniques to reach it. Proust attempts a rigorous exploitation of the techniques of the voluntary and involuntary memory, whereas Zola's reconstruction is at least partially based on thorough documentation and is realized by the recording of meticulous observations. Other writers, like Hesse and Mauriac, have recourse to psychological analyses. The most audacious attempts are those of James Joyce in his depiction of the childhood of Stephen Dedalus in *A Portrait of the Artist as a Young Man*, of William Faulkner in the opening chapter of *The Sound and the Fury*, and of Monique Wittig in *L'Opoponax*. They are among the rare authors who have dared to exploit the device of a mimetic stream of consciousness to reproduce the childhood vision. Whatever the tools employed, the practitioners of this art subscribe to the proposition that childhood is an eternal element in our existence. If this is the case, then methodological attempts to resurrect it can be successful and can be expected to produce at least approximations of the real world of childhood.

The second category contains those works in which the construction of a childhood world is not an end in itself but a pretext. Such creations may serve as an outlet for the nostalgia of the adult, for the fulfillment of the yearning after a long-lost paradise that may never have existed. The child as a prelapsarian Adam in his own garden of Eden is the tempting vision proffered by Bernardin de Saint-Pierre in *Paul and Virginia* that many later romantics succumbed to. Nonmimetic realms are thus created that represent wish fulfillment in the domain of the imaginary. The establishment of artificial children's worlds may also be a response to other needs. They can serve as convenient repositories for certain values and ideologies. Often the representation of an idyllic domestic world as the natural habitat of the child is an expression of the bourgeois infatuation with the family as the perfect social unit. Still another purpose that may be served by the establishment of a fictitious childhood universe is that of providing a convenient allegorical framework for the expression of certain philosophical viewpoints. Such fables are as often as not woven into the fabric of a world that is as sinister as that of Bernardin de Saint-Pierre is reassuring. Among the latter, there are some extreme cases, like William Golding's *Lord of the Flies*, in which a childhood hell becomes the abstract paradigm of the human condition.

In considering these two categories, it appears that the works that make up the first would be very useful in any attempt to determine the nature of the childhood world, whereas those in the second grouping have aims so foreign to a realistic depiction that their vision is almost inevitably deformed. Nonetheless the latter cannot simply be dismissed as irrelevant. The best among them are not mere falsifications, and even the most exaggerated examples occasionally contain insights into the reality of the childhood universe. As in the case of caricatures, certain truths, through their very distortion, become visible that might pass unperceived when presented with a greater degree of verisimilitude. Furthermore, in at least one essential respect there is a striking similarity between the universes depicted by those who attempt to reconstitute the world of the child and those who use it as a framework for their own retrospective concerns. In both, the childhood universe is usually portrayed as an extreme one. The child as described in literature does not live in a mediocre world. He inhabits either heaven or hell, and in some cases moves from one to the other, often without transition. Because this is a characteristic common to many works of all types in both categories, it is the trait that will serve as the basis for an analysis of the literary portrait of the childhood universe.

Shuttling between Heaven and Hell

Anfance est li fondemanz de vie.

Childhood is the foundation of life.
Philippe de Navarre

It is Charles Dickens who most dramatically and extensively depicted both the heaven and hell of the world of the child in their extreme manifestations. In *Oliver Twist* (1838) the young protagonist's early existence, first in a pauper's hospital, then in the workhouse to which he was farmed out, is reduced to a struggle for survival in a monstrous and, to him, incomprehensible world in which the reality of death is omnipresent. During this period "Oliver was the victim of a systematic course of treachery and deception."[1] This stage of his existence culminates when, only nine years old, he is indentured to the parochial undertaker; in his new place of employment the bed he sleeps in is as narrow as the half-finished coffins that clutter the room. Oliver's world is one unmitigated physical horror; it is characterized by brutality, pain, and famine. Oliver and his fellow inmates at the workhouse are starved and beaten, and their lives are constantly dominated by the ferocious pangs of hunger. Precariously they hover on the threshold between life and death, and there are enough who do not survive to keep the coffin maker occupied.

Oliver takes flight and makes his way to London, where he is taken in by one of Dickens's most notorious villains, Fagin. The urban hell that Oliver unwittingly moves into is very different from the parochial one, and, if conceivable, even more dreadful. A hiatus signals that this is no mere continuation but rather a new chapter in Oliver's life. A glass of warm gin and water which he is forced to drink upon his arrival immediately plunges him into a long, deep slumber. Dickens employs a period of unconsciousness almost as a formal device to separate each stage of his protagonist's existence. Oliver awakens to find himself in an alcohol-soaked nightmare, in the world of thieves, cutthroats, prostitutes, and pimps. It is a world that his past experience in a different circle of hell does not help him to comprehend. In his anterior existence, the parish authorities had tried to starve the boy; Fagin attempts to poison him with liquor. The undertaker and his vicious apprentice had abused Oliver physically, but even their most violent thrashings were of little consequence compared with Fagin's merciless campaign to corrupt Oliver spiritually. The games Fagin plays with Oliver and the instruction he provides him are determined by the systematic application of the techniques of brainwashing. Fagin is not content merely with implicating him in crime or with perverting the innocence of the child. He tries to transform his mind, to twist a naive and good mentality into a criminal one.

An all-too-brief interlude presents a striking contrast with the physical and spiritual hells that are all Oliver has previously known. Broken and ill and accused of theft, Oliver is sheltered and cared for by Mr. Brownlow, an amiable eccentric, and by his kindhearted housekeeper, Mrs. Bedwin. His entry into this world is also preceded by a long, deep sleep, and upon awakening he discovers a new mode of existence: "They were happy days. . . . Everything was so quiet, and neat, and orderly; everybody was kind and gentle; that after the noise and turbulence in the midst of which he had always lived, it seemed like Heaven itself" (p. 94). The following days are ones of physical restoration and also of initiation into the world of the intellect as Oliver is introduced to Mr. Brownlow's extensive library.

This happy interval comes to an abrupt conclusion. While out on an errand for Mr. Brownlow, Oliver is abducted by Fagin's accomplices, and the monstrous games begin again. Dickens now makes Fagin's design explicit in a brief summary:

In short, the wily Jew had the boy in his toils. Having prepared his mind, by solitude and gloom, to prefer any society to the companionship of his own sad thoughts in such a dreary place, he was now slowly instilling into his soul the poison which he hoped would blacken it, and change its hue for ever. (p. 134)

This episode is brought to a violent end with an abortive housebreaking. Oliver, wounded by a gunshot, is taken into the very home he had been forced to try to burglarize. Once again, he must pass through a period of somnolence before gaining admittance to paradise. Here, as before, Oliver finds an atmosphere that is the opposite of what he had known previously. The gentleness and compassion that reign in the home of Mrs. Maylie are indicated from the outset by an act of generosity. The same servant who has fired upon Oliver bends over the unconscious child and helps to carry him upstairs "with the care and solicitude of a woman" (p. 211). As before, the orphan's physical strength is restored and his moral and intellectual education taken up where it had been interrupted. His life is now a sheltered one, and, in the country with his benefactress, Oliver learns to love nature and to read the Bible. A sense of menace still hovers over this Eden, which is threatened by the powers of evil that almost destroyed Oliver. On two occasions these malignant forces intrude and momentarily cast a shadow over an idyllic existence. The first of these episodes is a reenactment of the one that led to Oliver's forcible return to the world of Fagin. Like Mr. Brownlow before her, Mrs. Maylie sends Oliver on a commission and entrusts him with her purse. Once again, there is a terrifying encounter with the past. When he finds the inn where he is supposed to deliver the letter, Oliver stumbles against an emissary from Fagin's world who recognizes him—Monks, the very person responsible for Oliver's past woes. He curses the child incoherently and advances upon him with clenched fists. But as he is about to strike the child, he falls writhing and foaming to the ground, seized by an apoplectic fit. Oliver seeks help for the stranger whom he considers a madman and returns home. The unpleasant event completely passes out of his mind. A second ominous intrusion takes place a few days later, while Oliver is sleeping. In his state of unconsciousness he feels himself moving back into another world: ". . .the scene changed; the air became close and confined; and he thought, with a glow of terror, that he was in the Jew's house again" (p. 256). He seems to hear the voice of his former tormentor, and there is such hatred in his tone that Oliver awakens with a start. To his horror, the dream does not fade away entirely, for at the window of his room he sees the frightful countenances of Fagin and Monks and even thinks he hears them conversing. The apparition is momentary, and the two figures vanish. But Oliver is convinced of their reality, even though no trace can be found of the two criminals. This is the last intrusion of the nightmare world. Shortly afterward Mrs. Maylie and Mr. Brownlow join forces to destroy, once and for all, the evil powers represented by Fagin and Monks. When Oliver is adopted by Mr. Brownlow, he is firmly ensconced in paradise.

Oliver Twist is a work of protest, a scathing condemnation of the child abuse so prevalent in England at the time. As a teleological fiction, it is, to a certain degree, impersonal. The partially autobiographic *David Copperfield* (1849–50), on the other hand, is a work of reminiscence. As an evocation of the reality of childhood, it is no longer a pretext but an end in itself. Nonetheless, the similarities between the two works are striking. The same rhythm, the alternation between heaven and hell, also forms the underlying structure of Dickens's most personal novel. David Copperfield's idyllic existence with his widowed mother is brutally destroyed by the intrusion of Mr. Murdstone and his sister, who transform his childhood life of blissful domesticity into one dominated by cruelty. David finds a temporary refuge in the home of Peggotty, where the quality of his sojourn is symbolized by the very house he lives in, a beached ship, a child's dream come true. But he is ejected from this heaven into another hell, that of a mediocre boarding school. After another brief interlude at Peggotty's, the child is sent to London to work in the warehouse of Murdstone and Grimby. He is totally dependent on himself, and his life is reduced to a struggle for survival in the urban jungle. The dangers he meets are less physical than spiritual. In his loneliness he is tempted by the gin mills, and the work he is hired to do gives no promise of future promotion. Divorced from any intellectual stimulation, he is faced with the threat of stultification. He is menaced by the possibility of being forever crushed, of becoming a mindless automaton. Finally he decides to escape from his servitude and seek out his only hope, an aunt who had seen him only once, at his birth, and who had rejected him because she had wanted a niece and not a nephew. He sets out on foot from London to Dover, and before he is even outside the city is robbed of his little money and meager possessions. The ensuing journey represents a passage through hell. He is cheated by the used-clothes merchants to whom he tries to sell his jacket, he is footsore and close to starvation, and he is menaced constantly by the unemployed vagabonds who roam the countryside in hordes. Half dead from fatigue and hunger, he arrives at his aunt's home, is taken in and accepted by her, and, like Oliver Twist, eventually finds a childhood paradise in which he can live.

The physical mistreatment of children is almost totally absent from *Great Expectations* (1861). At the worst, it can be said that young Pip was "brought up by hand." Although neither Pip nor Estella is subject to starvation or brutality, they come to know a subtler form of torture that transforms what should have been a childhood paradise into a spiritual hell within which they run the risk of succumbing to a moral rather than mental sclerosis. Pip is raised by his sister and her kindhearted husband, the blacksmith Joe Gargery. In its absolute simplicity the life that the sensitive child shares with the illiterate Joe is an idyllic one, only occasionally disrupted by the tantrums of Mrs. Joe. It centers on the forge where Pip often lends a hand, the marshes through which he walks, and the public house to which he accompanies Joe. He receives little or no instruction from Mr. Wopsle's great-aunt, who keeps both a general store and a schoolhouse. But there he meets the ingenuous Biddy, with whom he shares all his adventures, aspirations, and disappointments. This prelapsarian state is corrupted and ultimately destroyed by the eccentric Miss Havisham, an embittered recluse who has asked for a boy to come and visit her occasionally in order to distract her from a lonely life. Pip is the victim chosen to fulfill this function. Pip's first encounter with Miss Havisham is a chilling one. She orders him to play, and the timid child is paralyzed. Miss Havisham employs as her agent of corruption her orphaned ward, Estella. Just as Miss Havisham had planned, Pip is overwhelmed by the beauty of the young girl and immediately enamored of her. Estella, however, has been raised to be proud. She taunts Pip, whom she treats disdainfully as a "working boy." So Pip becomes dissatisfied with his condition as a future apprentice to a blacksmith and ashamed not only of his own simplicity but also of the ignorance of his good friend Joe. The aspirations awakened in him by Estella make him discontent with his station in life, and, realizing that his future is blocked by his lack of education, he falls into despondency. Totally insensitive to the hurt he does her through his confidences, he confesses all this to Biddy. The unexpected announcement that he is a legatee and is to live in London at his anonymous benefactor's expense before coming into his fortune seems to make possible the fulfillment of Pip's great expectations. This miracle also reinforces the corrupt instincts awakened by Miss Havisham. He leaves for London and does not even want Joe to see him off: he is ashamed of the blacksmith's coarseness. He demonstrates a similar lack of gratitude toward Biddy. Later on, when he returns to the village to call on Miss Havisham and Estella, he does not even stay in the humble abode of the blacksmith but instead takes a room in the best inn in town. When he does see Joe again, the latter is so intimidated by the presence of the young gentleman that he cannot help addressing him as "sir." At the same time, Pip, conscious of his own ingratitude, is plagued by conscience. But no matter how hard he tries to resume his old familiarity with Joe, his attempts are so artificial that they only make him feel more remorseful and Joe more constrained. Miss Havisham has succeeded. With the help of Estella she has transformed the innocent paradise of Pip's childhood into a place of remorse and guilt, and her victim has become a vain and superficial gentleman. The damage is not irremediable and the boy's good heart reasserts itself. His disinterested and generous friendship for Herbert, the compassion he displays toward the convict Provis, and finally the forgiveness he asks of Joe and Biddy all serve to redeem the corrupted child. He has lost the innocence of the childhood paradise, but he has gained entrance to a new world of generosity and manliness.

Miss Havisham eventually failed with Pip, but for her he was only a secondary victim. The spinster, whose heart had been forever broken when she was deserted on her wedding day, had originally taken in Estella in order to prevent at least one girl from knowing a similar fate. Consequently, however, she does to the orphan what had been done to her. Pip eventually becomes aware of Miss Havisham's crime and of the punishment she herself has to suffer in retribution:

That she had done a grievous thing in taking an impressionable child to mould into the form that her wild resentment, spurned affection, and wounded pride found vengeance in, I knew full well. But that, in shutting out the light of day, she had shut out infinitely more; that, in seclusion, she had secluded herself from a thousand natural and healing influences; that her mind, brooding solitary, had grown diseased . . . , I knew equally well.[2]

Just as Fagin brainwashes the young boys he takes in, so Miss Havisham twists the mind of her young ward. As she herself admits, "I stole her heart away and put ice in its place" (p. 378). Miss Havisham finally induces the totally indifferent Estella to marry the wretched Drummle (known as "the Spider"). But it is the very suffering that Estella is subjected to in this union that makes it possible for her to regain her stolen heart, to find again the ability to feel human sentiments that had been extirpated by Miss Havisham. The childhood paradise of Pip and Estella has been demolished, but they emerge from hell into a richer existence. The original version of the novel concludes with the statement that ". . . suffering had been stronger than Miss Havisham's teaching, and had given her [Estella] a heart to understand what my heart used to be" (p. 461).[3]

As children, the protagonists of the major novels of Dickens pass through incalculable physical and psychological horrors. The nightmare of their existence is only occasionally and briefly interrupted by Edenic interludes. And yet, despite the abuses they endure, they have an inner toughness that enables them to survive mental manipulation and torture; they emerge from their childhood hell unscathed into a world of innocence and joy. But these heroes are the exceptions. Most of the children of Dickens never emerge from their inferno except through death. In most cases they are irremediably corrupted by their milieu. Unlike Hugo's Gavroche, that incarnation of the Parisian gamin, the London urchins of Dickens lack any moral or heroic dimension. They may, like the Artful Dodger, have a certain city wit and charm, but they are destined to become hardened and heartless criminals. Unlike Oliver, they are not immune to the brainwashing of Fagin. Those who can neither remain impervious to the childhood hell nor adapt themselves to it are doomed to be destroyed. In *Oliver Twist* this latter type is represented by Little Dick, whom Oliver Twist had known in the orphanage. He is the only person from whom he takes leave before setting out for London. At the moment of their separation the child who is condemned to stay blesses the one about to depart. It is the first benediction bestowed on Oliver, and he is never to forget it. When Oliver is finally ensconced in his own childhood paradise, he returns to his native town with plans to take care of Little Dick and to restore him to health and happiness. His aim is to gain entrance for his diminutive friend into his own paradise. But it is too late. Little Dick has suffered too much at the hands of his tormentors and has escaped into death. Samuel Butler's contention that "Young people have a marvellous faculty of either dying or adapting themselves to circumstances"[4] could serve as a cynical but illuminating commentary on this episode.

For those maltreated children who lack the resilience necessary to pass through hell unaffected and who at the same time refuse to serve the forces of evil, it is always too late. This is a major theme in *Nicholas Nickleby* (1838–39), Dickens's most virulent exposé of the people and institutions that corrupt the innocence of childhood. The young inmates of Dotheboys Hall are described in poignant terms:

Pale and haggard faces, lank and bony figures, children with the countenances of old men, deformities with irons upon their limbs, boys of stunted growth, and others whose long meagre legs would hardly bear their stooping bodies, all crowded on the view together; . . . There were little faces which should have been handsome, darkened with the scowl of sullen, dogged suffering; there was childhood with the light of its eye quenched, its beauty gone, and its helplessness alone remaining; . . . With every kindly sympathy and affection blasted in its birth, with every young and healthy feeling flogged and starved down, with every revengeful passion that can fester in swollen hearts eating its evil way to their core in silence, what an incipient Hell was breeding here.[5]

The theme of the *puer senex* that emerges in this passage is reinforced in the description of the school as "a den where sordid cruelty . . . runs wanton, and youthful misery stalks precocious; where the lightness of childhood shrinks into the heaviness of age, and its every promise blights, and withers as it grows" (p. 251). Like Oliver, Nicholas Nickleby makes a desperate attempt to save one of the victims. When he himself leaves Dotheboys Hall, he takes with him Smike, a half-starved boy whose mind has been destroyed by the sadistic schoolmaster Wackford Squeers. Nicholas shares his own tribulations with the retarded but kindhearted Smike, and, having succeeded in creating his own paradise with the help of the Cheeryble brothers, he adopts him and shares his happiness with the former companion of his misery. But again it is too late. Weakened in body and in mind, brutally shocked by Squeers's attempt to abduct him, he is not strong enough to survive. Dickens insists on the hopelessness of his case in his description of the half-wit's spiritual condition:

To prepare the mind for such a heavy sleep, its growth must be stopped by rigour and cruelty in childhood; there must be years of misery and suffering lightened by no ray of hope; the chords of the heart, which beat a quick response to the voice of gentleness and affection, must have rusted and broken in their secret places, and bear the lingering echo of no word of love or kindness. Gloomy, indeed, must have been the short day, and dull the long, long twilight, preceding such a night of intellect as his. (p. 500)

The voice of kindness and compassion cannot penetrate the dark night of the mind. Despite all Nicholas's efforts, Smike remains "the same listless, hopeless, blighted creature, that Nicholas had first found him at the Yorkshire school" (p. 500). Smike is the child condemned to live forever in hell. The exceptional heroes of Dickens eventually regain a childhood paradise from which they can make a relatively painless transition to an adult world that retains many of the juvenile features of their anterior Eden. But the majority of the children he depicts are trapped in a childhood hell from which there is no escape but death.

The Hell of Childhood

> One single celebration in the whole
> life of a child is indeed very little.
> Jules Michelet

The vision of childhood as a period of unmitigated suffering is by no means unique to Dickens. Hugo, in "Melancholia" (from *The Contemplations*), vigorously condemns an urban economy which is based on the exploitation of children:

> Evil work which takes the tender youngsters in its claws,
> Which produces wealth while creating wretchedness,
> Which uses a child like a tool.

In *Germinal* Zola portrays in detail the fate of children condemned to toil in the coal mines, where they are imprisoned in the depths of the earth and deprived of sunlight. It is only natural to associate the Europe of the Industrial Revolution with the brutal exploitation of the young, and to consider this period as one when minors were tormented as never before. But the young have always suffered, and the childhood hell has existed since the earliest days of mankind. One of the most eloquent to bear witness to this infernal condition is Saint Jerome. In a letter to her father (418) he depicts the brief life of Pactula, who, as a young girl, had been exposed to the battles that preceded Alaric's sack of Rome. Children who manage to survive after having witnessed the physical horrors of warfare can know nothing of the joys usually associated with the innocence of early years:

Such are the times, then, into which your Pactula has been born. Slaughter and death are the toys of her childhood. She will know tears before laughter, sorrow before joy. Scarcely arrived on the stage of this world, soon she must exit. That the world was always like this—what else can she believe? Of the past she knows nothing; from the present she flies; she longs only for the future.[6]

The child, in the Dark Ages, is the victim of social and political turmoil which surpasses in horror the conditions that so shocked Dickens and his contemporaries.

Throughout the ages the child has been caught up in the nightmare of warfare. From the pathetic creatures who set forth on the Children's Crusade to Anne Frank, the slaughter of the innocents has been a recurrent historical phenomenon which has been exploited by numerous authors. In *The Inferno* Dante recounts the history of Count Ugolino, the leader of one of the factions of the Guelfs, who for his punishment had been frozen in a hole in the last circle of hell together with his enemy, the Archbishop Ruggieri, whose head he is condemned eternally to devour. His last days on earth, as he tells Dante, had been fearful ones. Ruggieri, the leader of the Ghibellines, had imprisoned him in a tower together with two of his sons and two of his grandsons. After they had been confined for a number of months, the key to their dungeon was thrown away and they were left to die of hunger. Hearing the boys weep and ask for bread, the father gives vent to his horror and concludes: ". . . I perceived in their four faces my own countenance" (33.56–57). The suffering children serve as his mirror image, and the traitor, in his turn betrayed, bites on both his hands with grief. The last words of the first child to succumb are touching in their simplicity, in their biblical resonance, and in the utter impotence they reveal: "My father, why do you not help me?" (30.69). After the last of them has perished, Ugolino mourns for three days, and when "fasting overpowered grief" he presumably consumed the corpses (33.75).[7] The innocent children suffered the agonies of starvation because of the senseless strife between two warring factions, because of the obduracy of two traitors.

In book 3 of his *Chronicles* (1390) Jean Froissart recounts an equally harrowing incident. Instead of the metaphysical framework and spiritual overtones of the Ugolino episode, there is a sinister starkness evoked by gratuitous violence. Gaston de Foix suspects his only legitimate son, who had just returned from a visit to his mother at the court of the king of Navarre, of having willfully attempted to poison him. In actuality, the child's host has given him a lethal powder to sprinkle on his father's viands, but has told the boy it is a magic compound that will influence Gaston de Foix to reconcile himself with the boy's mother. During dinner, Gaston de Foix discovers on the boy's body the sachet containing a suspicious powder. In a highly dramatic scene, the father gives some of it to his greyhound, who at once falls dead. In a rage he attempts to stab the child, but is restrained by his entourage. The count is finally convinced to imprison his beloved son temporarily rather than execute him. In his cell the young Gaston, moved by despair, refuses to touch the meat placed before him. When the father discovers his heir on the verge of starvation, he misinterprets the child's abstinence and puts the knife with which he had been paring his nails to his throat. The child is the victim of his father's temper and of the king of Navarre's vicious machinations.

Of the early accounts of the violent and unjustifiable death of children, the most affecting is Antoine de la Salle's *Concerning the Consolation of Madame du Fresne* (c. 1458). In this letter the author attempts to inspire Mme. du Fresne, who has lost her first-born, with courage and resignation by providing historical examples of stoicism. The most impressive of these is an episode that allegedly took place during the Hundred Years' War.[8] The prince of Wales had been laying siege to Brest, which was defended by the French captain du Chastel. A truce was negotiated, and du Chastel agreed to turn over to the Black Prince his only child, a thirteen-year-old boy, as a hostage, with the understanding that, if he adhered scrupulously to the terms of the cessation of hostilities, the child would be returned to his parents. Although du Chastel kept his side of the bargain, his British counterpart tried to extort new terms that would dishonor his adversary. Du Chastel refused and the child was executed.

The distress of parents when confronted with the death of their offspring was the focus of the accounts of both Dante and Froissart. It is a topos that Shakespeare later exploited in the lamentation of Queen Elizabeth when she learns of the slaughter of her babes by the bloodthirsty Richard (*Richard III*, act 3, scene 4). But in these powerful scenes, it is through the reactions of the adults, and hence only indirectly, that the horror of the child's suffering is conveyed. Although Antoine de la Salle also depicts the distress of the parents, what imparts to his recital its unique force is that he gives direct expression to the terror of a child confronted with his own destruction. When the boy is first thrown into irons, he weeps bitterly but is consoled by Thomas, the head guard, who tries to reassure him. The following day the hostage realizes that he is indeed being led to his execution and breaks forth in his plaint, calling not only to his guard, but to his absent parents:

Oh! Thomas, my friend, you are leading me to die, you are leading me to to die; Alas! You are leading me to die! Thomas, you are leading me to die! Alas! My father, I am going to die! Alas! My mother, I am going to die, I am going to die! Alas, alas, alas, I am going to die, to die, to die, to die![9]

In these simple words, repeated over and over again, is found all the pathos of the child faced with his own annihilation.

The theme of the martyred child has nowhere been exploited more strikingly than in the picaresque novel. Although their protagonists often survive physically because, like the Artful Dodger, they adapt themselves to the circumstances in which they find themselves, they are usually destroyed spiritually. This is the case of the protagonist of the anonymous *Lazarillo de Tormes* (1554). The first eight years of Lázaro's life are devoid of joy, and he is exposed to hunger and physical abuse. His father, caught stealing, is sent on an expedition against the Moors, and his mother takes up with a Negro, who tells the innocent child bluntly that his mother is a whore. Lázaro's submission to events ends with dramatic suddenness. His mother has entrusted him to a blind man whom he was to serve. The first lesson he learns from his master is the existence and meaning of gratuitous evil. The blind man shows the young boy a statue of a bull and tells him to put his ear to it, promising him that he will hear a loud noise. The gullible child obeys:

I was so simple that I did just that, and when he [the blind man] felt that my head was against the stone, he straightened his arm and gave me such a blow that my head crashed against that blasted bull so hard that it hurt me for three days and more.[10]

This blow actually brings Lázaro to his senses. As the blind man cackles with glee, Lázaro's innocent illusions are forever shattered: "At that moment I felt as if I had woken up and my eyes were opened. I said to myself: 'What he says is true; I must keep awake because I'm on my own and I've got to look after myself'" (pp. 27–28). The destruction of simplicity brings an awakening, and the loss of innocence makes possible an awareness of reality as it is. Lázaro will be able to cope in the nightmare world because he will stay awake in order to fulfill what is now his one goal in life: survival in hell. The simpleton becomes a cynic.

The wild child's battle for survival is a ferocious one, and he knows "that if I hadn't used all my cunning and the tricks I knew, I would have died of hunger more than once" (p. 20). Fortunately, he has learned the blind man's lesson well and succeeds in outwitting his master, stealing from him often enough to save himself from utter starvation. Eventually, however, Lázaro is found out and punished. With all his strength the blind man smashes a heavy wine jug against Lázaro's gaping mouth. All the child's teeth are demolished and his face badly cut up. As his master continues alternately to brutalize him and to treat him kindly by carefully bandaging the wounds he had inflicted, Lázaro becomes aware of the perverse enjoyment his master derives from maltreating him. This sadism is infectious, and Lázaro no longer limits his trickery of the blind man to acts dictated by the exigencies of survival. He begins to take pleasure in inflicting pain on his master even at the cost of augmenting his own suffering. The corrupted child has become a practitioner of gratuitous evil and, before deserting his first master, induces him to hurl himself into a post. Jeering he leaves him with his head split open.

Lázaro's second master, an avaricious priest, is even more cruel and, because he can see, more difficult to outwit. Again the child faces starvation, but this time sees no solution but in death. His will to live enables him to triumph over this crisis of despair, and, through a combination of luck and cunning, he manages to find a means of stealing from the breadbox, which the priest keeps carefully locked. As before, he is discovered and this time barely survives the cudgeling he receives.

A new theme is introduced along with Lázaro's third master. The impoverished gentleman upon whom the child waits is not only incapable of providing nourishment for his servant, but even for himself. So Lázaro finds himself forced to beg food for their mutual sustenance. Strangely enough, he does not resent a relationship which requires on his part a high degree of altruism. No matter how hungry he himself may be, he admits to feeling not even half as sorry for himself as for his poor gentleman. "I'm right to take pity on this one here," (p. 58) he explains to himself. As long as he can still feel compassion, the corruption of the child is not total. As if in recognition of this residual purity which is again combined with simplicity, his neighbors assert to the officers who are interrogating him concerning the disappearance of his debt-ridden master that ". . . this boy is quite innocent" (p. 65).

This residual innocence is gradually eroded during what remains of his apprenticeship in life. With his subsequent masters his initial lesson of cynicism is reinforced. When he obtains his first job, that of water carrier, he no longer needs to fear starvation. His subsequent self-satisfaction signals the total destruction of the child. "That was my first step towards becoming a respectable citizen because now my hunger was satisfied," (p. 76) he admits. He becomes a town crier and soon all the merchants are dependent on him: "If anybody anywhere in Toledo has wine to sell or anything else, he won't get very far in his business unless Lázaro has a finger in the pie" (p. 77). He crowns his success by marrying the maid of a high priest: knowing full well what the situation is, he willingly serves as a cover so that the ecclesiastic can keep his mistress without danger of scandal. His patron explains the situation to Lázaro in unambiguous terms:

Lázaro de Tormes, you'll never get on in life if you take any notice of what people say about you. I'm telling you this so you should not be surprised if someone says he sees your wife going into my house and leaving it. . . . Neither of you need be ashamed of what she does; this I can promise you. So, don't pay any attention to what anybody says; just think about your own affairs, I mean, what's best for you. (p. 78)

Lázaro follows the priest's advice scrupulously and attains the height of his good fortune. He has survived the hell of his childhood at the price of his integrity. The respectable people with whom he now takes up succeed where the villains who were his former masters had failed. They have totally destroyed his innocence and made of him a self-serving and hypocritical adult.

The early life of Pablos, the protagonist of Quevedo's *The Swindler* (*La Vida del Buscón*) (1626), is just as unpleasant as that of Lázaro, and there are many similarities in their sufferings. In both novels, the early revelation of the mother's degraded status serves as an initiation. When a school comrade taunts him by referring to his mother as a whore, Pablos's natural reaction is to smash his tormentor's head in with a stone. His mother laughs when she learns of the incident and calmly informs her child that he did well even though the accusation was an accurate one. Pablos feels as if he had received a kick in the stomach. The obsessive fear of hunger underlies the similarity of many of the subsequent episodes. Pablos, too, has a close brush with death by starvation. He and his friend, Don Diego, are sent to the boarding school of Dr. Goat, whose refectory makes that of Dickens's Yorkshire schoolmaster seem lavish by comparison. They are saved at the last moment by Diego's father, who takes them home just before their hunger-rotted bones begin to crumble. Pablos had been reduced to an animal-like state: "My teeth were yellow, desperate fangs, rotten with tartar." [11] Both children had "jaws which were black and twisted" and they "looked like shadows of other men and as yellow and thin as the descendants of desert hermits" (p. 100).

Pablos is slower than Lázaro to awaken to the need for survival. It takes a series of incidents of the utmost cruelty to bring about the end of his state of simplicity. These occur during the first twenty-four hours of Pablos's stay at a boarding house in Alcalá, where he has accompanied Don Diego as a servant-companion. First it is the students who torment Pablos by spitting on him until he is slimy from head to toe with their phlegm. He escapes to his room, but not before being savagely beaten. When Don Diego finds him in his befouled and bruised condition, crying with rage and sorrow, he gives him the same advice that the blind man had offered Lázaro: "Pablos, you've got to wake up. Watch out for yourself" (p. 108). Instead, the simpleton goes to bed and falls asleep, comforted by the apparent solicitude of his fellow servants. As soon as he is unconscious they set about beating him savagely with a thick rope. Pablos finally manages to hide under the cot, but while he is doing so, one of the servants defecates into his bed. He regains consciousness the next morning battered, sick, and stinking. But this time he really awakens. He urges himself to watch out and claims, "I determined to change my outlook" (p. 111). And indeed he does. When he was very young, his parents had proposed a choice of careers to him: he could either follow in his father's footsteps and become a thief or emulate his mother by becoming a male witch. He had declined these offers and asked to be allowed to go to school so that he could learn to become an honest man. Now that the brutality of the servants and students has demonstrated to him what the fruits of knowledge and honesty are, the simple child transforms himself into the swindler. He embraces criminality with gusto and revels in it. He will never attain the respectability that Lázaro achieved and that he himself set as his initial goal.

The horror of Pablos's childhood world is summarized in one episode from which all of his future woes seem to spring. As a schoolboy, during the carnival, Pablos has drawn the lot that made him boy king for the day. Dressed in his royal regalia, he climbs on a skinny old horse provided as the royal mount. When the procession celebrating the child-king passes through the vegetable market the half-starved nag snatches a cabbage. At once the market women begin to pelt the rider and his steed with turnips. The horse rears and throws Pablos into a pile of excrement. The celebration of the child-king ends in the disgrace of a stinking urchin. This incident, representative of the derision of all that is sacred in childhood, haunts Pablos for the rest of his life. Years later, when he disrupts the respectable life of a town by making a mockery of its authorities, he notes, "I never forgot how they treated me when I was boy king" (p. 119). It is this initial scene that structures his existence and that recurs in somewhat different form when he is about to succeed in life. Having assumed the guise of a wealthy nobleman, he is on the point of winning the hand of a woman with a substantial dowry. In order to impress her, he mounts a horse that does not belong to him; the horse throws him headfirst into a puddle beneath the windows of the woman he is wooing. This incident leads to his being recognized, and the result is another severe beating, followed by his having his face nearly slashed in half. The nightmare world of his childhood follows him into his adult existence.

In *The Swindler* there is only one egress from the hell of childhood: death. It is thus that one of the inmates of Dr. Goat's establishment escapes. The child lies moribund, having literally been starved to death, and the priest gives him the last sacrament. When the victim lays eyes on the Host, he speaks for the first time in weeks—and also for the last time: "Sweet Jesus Christ. Seeing you in this house is the only thing that has convinced me I'm not in Hell" (p. 99). Like Pablos's seven-year-old brother, who had been trained to strip the pockets of the clients his father was shaving and who had died from the lashing he was given in prison after having been caught in the act, this is one child who maintains his innocence in hell and must die for it.

The depiction of childhood hell is far more sophisticated

in Grimmelshausen's *Abenteuerlicher Simplicius Simplicissimus* (1668). From the outset, a paradisiacal existence is equated with ignorance, menaced by the instruction which the adult wants to impose on the child. When the story opens, the ten-year-old Simplicius is living in a state of bliss, but this is a condition that his father does not sanction:

> I had heard of neither God nor man, heaven nor hell, angel nor devil, and I did not even know the difference between good and evil. You can easily imagine that with such theology I lived in paradise, like our first parents who also knew nothing of sickness, death, or dying. . . . I was so perfect and excellent in ignorance that I could not possibly have known that I knew nothing at all. Once more I say, Oh, happy life.
>
> But my old man did not want me to enjoy such bliss any longer. . . . So he started to draw me toward higher things and to assign me more difficult lessons.[12]

Despite the father's efforts, Simplicius remains impervious to his lessons, and his absolute ignorance protects him from perceiving that he is actually living in the nightmare of the Thirty Years' War. When a troop of soldiers ransacks his home, the scene is one of incalculable horror: the hired girl is raped until she can no longer move, the servingman's mouth is held open by a wooden wedge and a milkpailful of liquid manure poured down his gullet, and the peasants are tortured and put to death in the most horrible fashion imaginable. Finally his parents and sister, who had tried to flee, are dragged in and brutalized in similar manner. The screams of the tormented shake the house and blood flows everywhere, but, in the midst of these monstrosities, Simplicius, a calm and untroubled witness, quietly turns the roasting spit. "I didn't know the meaning of it all," (p. 11) is his candid explanation for his lack of concern. His simplicity protects him from the realities of war at the same time that it permits him to record its absurdity.

When his home goes up in flames and when he is shot at by one of the marauding soldiers, Simplicius takes flight and loses himself in a forest as dark as his mind. A hermit who has built his refuge in the woods saves him from death by starvation or by exposure to the elements. This holy man does more than to restore him physically. He teaches him how to read and write and gives him religious instruction of a primitive nature. The faith he inculcates in the child is a fundamental one, and this education consists in the substitution of one type of simplicity for another. So after his passage through the inferno of warfare, Simplicius leads an existence that is dominated by the goodness of his new patron. This two-year respite is characterized by his isolation from mankind and consequently from the carnage being wreaked by his fellow creatures. It is as if the hell which he barely managed to survive had never existed. For a short while after his protector passes peacefully away Simplicius tries to emulate him. Soon, however, his lonely sojourn in the forest begins to weigh on him; bored with his prayers, he decides to see the world. He sets out for the nearest village to seek the advice of the pastor. He finds the town in flames and its inhabitants being brutalized by marauding troops. Soon a group of avenging peasants falls upon the soldiers and treats them with similar cruelty. Disillusioned with life in the outside world, Simplicius returns to his home in the forest, determined to pass the rest of his days in the tranquility of his retreat. But there is no longer any refuge from the horrors of warfare. On his way through the woods, Simplicius is witness to another dreadful scene in which a group of peasants is physically maltreated. When he finds his shelter, he discovers that it has been vandalized by soldiers. Deprived of his provisions and the feeling of security, Simplicius sets forth to discover the world that destroyed his first two homes. He makes his way to Hanau, where he is imprisoned and then, thanks to the intervention of the pastor (who had also sought refuge in the fortress), received by the governor. In listening to Simplicius's account of himself, the governor realizes that the hermit-mentor was his long-lost brother. In gratitude, he decides to protect the boy. The first part of Simplicius's sojourn in Hanau represents an encounter between simplicity and sophistication that reveals the brutality and coarseness of court life. Jealous of Simplicius's favored position, the other servingboys conspire to exploit his ignorance in order to bring about his disgrace. Simplicius is banished to the goose pen, and the governor subsequently decides to make of him his jester. Before Simplicius assumes this new role, he is subjected to a concerted effort to destroy his mind. The purpose of this cruel procedure is to make of the simpleton a fool. All the techniques of brainwashing are employed: he is made to drink wine for days on end, he is totally deprived of sleep, he is exposed to outlandish apparitions. Terrifying rituals are employed to convince him that through magic he is being transformed into a calf. Warned beforehand of the dangers to which he was going to be exposed, Simplicius survives with his mind intact by pretending to succumb to the efforts of his tormentors. When the treatment is over, it is he who makes a fool of them by simulating all the manners of the calf into which he had presumably been transformed. By feigning madness he survives the hell through which he has passed, but in doing so he loses not his sanity but his simplicity. From now on he will be able to get along in the world because he can surpass his fellow man in the art of duplicity.

Simplicius survives but does not immediately emerge from hell. As he himself admits, "Anyone can plunge into hell, but to get out again takes sweat and toil" (p. 111). Despite his eventual success in adapting himself to society, he remains fundamentally innocent. He is still troubled by a guilty conscience and feels uneasy about the deception he practices. So once more he goes to consult the pastor. His mentor, who himself had never shown any qualms about howling with the wolves, urges Simplicius to follow his example and to divest himself of any moral scruples. This advice has the same effect on Simplicius that the blind man's words had on Lázaro and Don Pedro's counsel on Pablos. After this consultation, Simplicius is completely disenfranchised and cultivates hypocrisy. In fact, he is such an enthusiastic adept that he is successful in deceiving the pastor himself even before the interveiw is over. He has shed his innocence and simplicity. His ascent from hell is indeed a slow one, and while he is a denizen of the nether regions he enjoys to the full the domain in which he now knows how to live. He becomes in turn an adventurer, a ruffian, a debauchee, a show-off, and a gigolo before he finally returns to the forest to resume the life of a hermit. It is only after having passed through all the stages of corruption that he can find again the lost innocence of his childhood.

The rise of the classical novel in the seventeenth century signals the demise of the picaresque novel, and after Le Sage's *Gil Blas* the genre virtually disappears. The twentieth century has witnessed an extraordinary renaissance of this archaic form, and the examples are legion: Céline's *Voyage to the End of Night*, Thomas Mann's *The Adventures of Felix Krull*, Günter Grass's *The Tin Drum*, and Thomas Pynchon's *Gravity's Rainbow*, to name just a few. The contemporary picaresque novel that is perhaps closest in spirit to earlier ones is Jerzy Kosinski's *The Painted Bird* (1965). Because of its episodic structure, the black humor that pervades the narration, the wartime horrors through which its protagonist passes, and the naiveté of the child-narrator, this work is more akin to *Abenteuerlicher Simplicius Simplicissimus* than to contemporary picaresque novels. It is a simple tale of a six-year-old boy from a city in eastern Europe whose parents have sent him to a distant village in the hope of saving him from the tribulations of war and of guaranteeing his safety in the holocaust the Nazi regime is preparing. But the boy's foster mother perishes shortly after his arrival, and the abandoned child roams from one village to another, while his parents, who have lost all trace of him, are themselves in hiding in order to avoid the concentration camp. During the course of his aimless wandering through the most primitive areas of eastern Europe, the child is subjected to a series of horrors that surpass anything that Lázaro, Pablos, or Simplicius endured. He is on more than one occasion flogged within an inch of his life, his ribs are kicked in, he is buried up to his neck in a field and attacked by ravenous crows, he is almost drowned in a manure pit; these are a few typical episodes in the first stages of his career. His innocent past fades from his memory rapidly. Only during the first months does he recall his teddy bear, his nanny, his parents: ". . . this past of mine was rapidly turning into an illusion like one of my old nanny's incredible fables."[13] The nightmare of the present obscures the remembrance of a childhood paradise. The brutalized child himself adopts brutality in order to survive. Thus he lures a carpenter intent on murdering him to a pillbox with the promise of loot to be found. When the unsuspecting adult leans over the edge, the child pitches him into the rodent-infested fortification knowing that his tormentor will be devoured alive by the famished rats. During the six years of his odyssey the child lives in constant terror, submitting to torture and witnessing even worse horrors. Mutilation, rape, and murder are the everyday scenes through which he lives. The unrelieved fear takes its toll, and the child, who has already experienced difficulties in communicating with the peasants, loses his voice. The war-torn world becomes ever more incomprehensible as White partisans fight against Red partisans, as some fight against the German occupiers and others against the Russian invaders. But somehow the child endures, and when the victorious Red Army arrives his physical tribulations are at an end. The twelve-year-old boy, well cared for in the hospital which the Russians set up, is restored to health. A political officer befriends him and teaches him to read and to write. At the same time, in a subtle form of brainwashing, he instructs him politically, replacing the boy's primitive superstitions and beliefs with equally simplistic Communist dogma. After his body had nearly been destroyed, his mind is poisoned. Consequently, when his parents do at last find him, they recover nothing but an empty shell. He is now a being more readily influenced by evil than by normalcy. After the family reunion the child frequently abandons the safety of his room, preferring to roam the dangerous city streets at night in order to seek out the worst company. Finally, a symbolic resurrection occurs. The boy is sent to the mountains to recuperate. After a skiing accident, he recovers his voice:

> The voice lost in a faraway village had found me again and filled the whole room. I spoke loudly and incessantly like the peasants and then like the city folk, as fast as I could, enraptured by the sounds that were heavy with meaning, . . . confirming to myself again and again and again that speech was now mine and that it did not intend to escape through the door which opened onto the balcony. (p. 213)

Fear has been banished and meaning restored to existence. The child can once more communicate. Although he may never recover the lost paradise of childhood, he has survived hell.

The picaro is not the only type of child figure who is a victim of warfare. In the romantic novel there are numerous examples of the hell created for children by adults locked in senseless combat. Although such depictions may not equal in physical horror the brutalities portrayed in the picaresque novel, in some cases they surpass them in the vividness of presentation and in the immediacy of individual scenes. In *The Man who Laughs* (1869), for example, Victor Hugo describes the vicious dealing in children that was prevalent in seventeenth-century England. A family that wanted to be rid of a child would sell him to the "comprachicos," who practiced an early form of plastic surgery. They would disfigure the little victim to such an extent that he became forever unrecognizable. The shock of the brutal operation also usually resulted in a total loss of memory. Such mutilation had a goal beyond that of making it impossible for the child ever to return to its past. The disfigurement was carried out with such art that the child was transformed into a freak, in great demand by carnival operators for their side-shows and sought after by royalty for their court fools. The protagonist of *The Man who Laughs* had been subjected to this torture, and his face cut up in such a way that on his countenance he wears a perpetual grin from ear to ear. As a ten-year-old this maimed orphan is abandoned by the "comprachicos" on a desolate peninsula in a raging blizzard. The half-starved, half-frozen child's search for shelter in a wasteland of snow and ice represents a frightful journey through hell during which, on two occasions, he encounters death in its most frightful form (a half-devoured body swinging from a gibbet and a mother frozen in a bank of snow). Blinded by the elements, burdened by the infant he has saved from its mother's stiff embrace, he staggers on until in the middle of the night he comes upon a village. There he discovers the ultimate horror: all the doors of the human community are closed to him. When he is on the point of collapse, the door of the caravan of a wandering entertainer miraculously opens. In the makeshift home of Ursus the boy and his charge find asylum, and the rolling hovel turns out to be a paradise of humanity. Like Oliver Twist and David Copperfield, Gwynplaine has traversed hell spiritually unscathed and finds heaven on earth. The mutilated child becomes the man who laughs.

A very different type of inferno is described in Hugo's last novel, *Seventeen Hundred and Ninety-Three* (1873), which opens with the dramatic encounter in a forest of the war-torn Vendée between a troop of soldiers loyal to the revolutionary government and a mother fleeing through the thicket with her three children, of whom the youngest is an infant and the oldest not even five. The protectress of the children does not know where she is leading them nor what she is taking flight from. All Simone Fléchard knows is that her husband has been shot and that war is raging all around. The children, equally unaware of what is going on, are terrified and hungry. However, thanks to the intervention of a kindhearted camp follower, an accommodation is reached between the troops and the small family. The soldiers adopt the children, and the mother accompanies them. Thus, ironically, the military provides a temporary refuge from the horrors of warfare. This introductory encounter prepares the way for the climactic episode in which the same children, taken as hostages by Lantenac, the implacable leader of the royalist insurrection, find themselves unwittingly at the center of the decisive battle between royalists and revolutionaries. The latter are preparing to storm La Tourgue, a previously impregnable medieval fortress that has been made vulnerable by the addition of a wing constructed over a moat. This renaissance structure houses the library, in which the children are kept prisoner. The symbolism is striking; the barbaric medieval tower is exposed to destruction through the civilizing force of culture. The library as the repository of the family archives is the sanctuary of history. It is history and the heritage that is represented by history that are now under attack.

The defenders of the besieged La Tourgue are hopelessly outnumbered, and, when the children awaken, an attack is imminent. But the young ones, in their innocence, are blissfully unaware of the impending danger. The author depicts their awakening consciousness in a manner that evokes the still-unformed nature of their thought processes:

It is the stammering of a human soul on the lips of childhood. This confused whispering of a thought that is yet nothing but instinct. . . . How are ideas decomposed and recomposed in these little heads? What is the nature of the mysterious movement of these memories that are still so unclear and so brief?[14]

As the day lengthens the children become bored, and one of them is intrigued by the volumes that surround them. The library houses more than the records of the past. It contains invaluable tomes, including the unique copy of a precious edition of Saint Bartholomew. As described in loving detail by Hugo, it represents the summit of the bookmaker's art. The oldest of the three children reaches for it, tears out one of the engravings, and gives it to his sister. His brother wants one too, and he detaches a second image. With an increasing momentum, page after page is ripped from the volume to the ever-increasing delight of the children. All the detached sheets are then carefully shredded, what is left of the book is stamped on and mutilated, and finally the three innocents throw all the scraps out the window. The mutilated pages of the past, transformed into confetti, drift down upon the besieging forces like butterflies. The symbolic massacre of knowledge terminated, the children return to bed and fall fast asleep. It is during their slumber that the bloody assault on the fortress begins. The sounds of the battle hardly disturb them, and only when the tower becomes a raging inferno do they regain consciousness, but even then without any awareness of danger. They are in the center of the holocaust, and there seems absolutely no hope for escape. Lantenac's vicious lieutenant has decided to take his revenge on the revolutionaries by immolating the children whom they had adopted. He sets fire to the library the moment before he himself expires. The screams of the mother, suddenly aware of the fate of the little victims, alert Lantenac. Although he knows that he will probably be guillotined and that the principles he has upheld with such brutality will be compromised, he returns to save them from the conflagration.

The children of Simone Fléchard have lived through a hell that in its horror equals the hells depicted in the picaresque novels. They, however, survive unscathed because their innocence protects them from any contact with the evil that surrounds them. And, unlike their picaresque counterparts, they become the agents responsible for the destruction of the very hell that had threatened to engulf them. Their presence has been the cause of a miracle, the transformation of the inhuman Lantenac. Even his revolutionary counterpart, Gauvain, is jubilant although he knows he must now perish for having, in a moment of compassion, liberated Lantenac:

. . . Gauvain had just seen a miracle. The victory of humanity over man. Humanity had vanquished the inhuman. And by what means? In what fashion? How had it overthrown a colossus of anger and hatred? What weapons had it employed, what kind of artillery? The cradle. (p. 208)

The children have triumphed over the hell created by the inhuman forces of war.

The horrors of a childhood disrupted by the internecine conflict of adults have been vividly depicted in literature, and such historical documents as the diary of Anne Frank bear eloquent witness to the fact that in this respect art translates a reality. But it is not only through warfare or through oppressive social institutions that adults have deprived children of what is often assumed to be their natural right to a carefree existence. While the conflicts of nations and the brutalizing calamities produced by evolving economic systems have resulted in forms of violence so spectacular that the voices of the youthful victims cry to the heavens for justice, there is another type of misery that, though less dramatic, is equally profound. This is the wretchedness that festers within the smallest unit of our society, the family. "We are not happy; our happiness is the silence of misery." With these words Jules Renard sums up the nagging dissatisfaction of the child alienated from the very milieu that is supposed to provide succor and protection from the menaces of the outside world. Such constant and unvarying misery is portrayed in Baudelaire's "Bénédiction" ("The Blessing") as that of the disinherited child whose mother curses him and vows "to twist this wretched tree, / So that its infected buds will never grow." Such is also the lot of Rimbaud's autobiographical "seven-year-old poet," whose mother is the incarnation of authority untempered by any vestige of maternal affection and in whose blue eyes the child perceives nothing but mendacity.

The theme of the child as the victim of intrafamily conflicts and whose home life is transformed into a domestic hell by the cruelty of parents is a recurrent one. Its prevalence in fairy tales (*Cinderella*, for example) indicates that it is deeply embedded in the human psyche, that it is an obsession which evokes feelings of guilt in the adult. For many grown-ups an unhappy childhood leaves an indelible imprint in the memory. Even for those whom one would hardly suspect of having spent a miserable period early in life, a relatively minor incident can have a profound impact. In his *Confessions*, Saint Augustine recalls the beatings inflicted on him by his schoolmasters and, worse yet, the indifference of his parents to his suffering:

. . . for as a child I began to implore Thee, my refuge and my help, and to ask Thee, small as I was yet with no small emotion, that I might not be beaten at school, and when Thou didst not hear me, my elders and even my mother and father, who would not have wished me any ill, laughed at the beating I received, great and heavy and ill as it was to me. (1.14)

The child is hurt more by the lack of comprehension of the adults who cannot fathom the pain inflicted upon him than by any corporal chastisement. Even if physical mistreatment is only episodic, a normal and minor component in his otherwise good relationship with his mentors and parents, it colors his whole vision of childhood. The import of this lashing becomes paradigmatic and explains the abhorrence Saint Augustine expresses in *The City of God* for the earliest stage in life:

In fact is there anyone who, faced with the choice between death and a second childhood, would not shrink in dread from the latter prospect and elect to die? Infancy, indeed, starts this life, not with smiles but with tears; and this is, in a way, an unconscious prophecy of the troubles on which it is entering. (21.14)

Saint Augustine draws a general conclusion from his concrete experience and manifests an almost physical horror of the first period of existence, a horror that was shared centuries later by a number of romantic and even preromantic writers.

The imprecations of Rousseau and Chateaubriand against their early years are powerful. However, it is a lesser-known author who, in more sober terms, gave expression to the misery caused by the rancor of hostile parents. Karl Philipp Moritz, in *Anton Reiser* (1785), the work he subtitled "A Psychological Novel," draws a dismal picture of a childhood perverted by adults who engage in mutual recriminations. Anton's mother had expected from her marriage more love and respect than she had previously enjoyed in her own family. She is bitterly deceived because her husband is a devout follower of Mme. Guyon and a fanatical quietist devoted to a life of renunciation and to the stifling of all human sentiments. Her ineffectual revolt against his cold and loveless character succeeds merely in creating an atmosphere of conjugal dissension. So Anton is born in discord.

> Anton was born under these conditions and it can truly be said that from his cradle he was repressed.
> The first sounds that pierced his ears and penetrated his dawning consciousness were reciprocal curses and imprecations against the indissoluble wedding band.
> Although he possessed both a father and a mother, yet he was in his earliest childhood abandoned by his father and mother, because he did not know whose side he should take or on which one of them he could rely, for they both hated each other.[15]

The boy knows the anguish of having to declare himself in a battle whose participants are equally at fault. So the child is totally deprived of affection, a condition the author dramatizes in his concise description of Anton's home: "When he stepped into the house of his parents, he stepped into a house of discontent, of anger, of tears and of plaints" (p. 9).

The situation is exacerbated when a second son is born. The remnants of parental affection are lavished on his brother while Anton is totally neglected. When his father and mother do design to take notice of him, it is with a scornful contempt that wounds him deeply. Such a life cannot fail to leave scars: "These first impressions were never in his life erased from his soul and often made it into a reservoir of black thoughts that no philosophy could disperse" (p. 9).

The bourgeois hell in which Anton Reiser spends his first years and which transforms him into a hypochondriac is, in its colorlessness, less dramatic than the infernos through which the picaresque heroes pass. But it has a dreadful permanence that the battlefields of Spain, Germany, and Poland lack. Nor is it constructed of momentary unpleasantness like the chastisements inflicted upon Saint Augustine. It is a hell that will remain with the protagonist forever.

Viciousness is by no means limited to the bourgeoisie; the perversely ingenious designers of childhood hells can be found in all strata of society. Jeremias Gotthelf is best known for his earthy but spiritualized portraits of God-fearing, upright Swiss farmers in novels like *Wealth and Welfare*, which are the pious incarnations of a patriarchal unity of peasant and Christian traditions. The deeply religious spirit that characterizes the works of his maturity is absent from his first work, *The Peasant Mirror* (1836), a pitiless exposé of the brutality of the corrupt, ignorant, and superstitious farmers which, in its violent naturalism and its portrayal of universal bestiality, anticipates Zola's *The Earth* by half a century. Gotthelf's semiautobiographical novel is the jeremiad of its suffering child-narrator crying out in a wilderness abandoned by God. Although no detail concerning his physical mistreatment is spared, it is the spiritual abuse inflicted upon the child that is appalling. After her husband's death, the debt-burdened mother can no longer support her seven-year-old son and takes the orphan to the weekly "beggar's community," a market where children are auctioned; each is *verdinget*, or handled as an object. So the pauper is put on the block, where prospective bidders look him over and feel his muscles. He is indentured to a man who treats his cheap acquisition harshly but without excessive cruelty; however, what hurts the child deeply is

that no one ever used my Christian name, but that I was called only "boy." Only later did I notice that every child auctioned off to an estate loses his name in order to be called "boy," that is to say to become a person who no longer belongs to anyone in the whole world but to the estate on which he is cared for.[16]

Like the ploughshare or the hoe, disposable and easily replaceable instruments of agriculture, the boy becomes an object to be used, misused, and abused, only to be exchanged at another "beggar's community" when his cost outweighs his usefulness. This is the ultimate degradation: the reification of the child.

The dismal hell in which Anton Reiser spends his youth can be considered the prototype not only of the one depicted in *The Peasant Mirror* but of those subsequently portrayed with variations in numerous fictional works of the nineteenth century. The bleak existence of suppressed and repressed children is one of the hallmarks of the Victorian novel, and the obsessive recurrence of this topos is ample evidence of a grim underlying reality.[17] The ostentatious concern with children, with their education, their upbringing, and especially their dress, during the nineteenth century seems intended to conceal the real hatred of adults for their progeniture. By a calculated and systematic denigration of spontaneity, they seem intent on destroying as ruthlessly as possible all vestiges of childhood and on making their offspring little adults as quickly as possible. The animosity implicit in such ruthless suppression is evoked in the second part of the dream sequence of Emily Brontë's *Wuthering Heights* (1847). In his sleep Lockwood hears the boughs of a fir tree whipped by gusts of wind rattling against the panes. Irritated by this sound, he tries to unhasp the casement but finds it soldered shut. He puts his fist through the window and reaches out to seize the branch, but instead his fingers close on a little ice-cold hand. Lockwood tries to disengage himself, but the sobbing figure clings to him. There ensues one of the cruelest scenes of the Gothic novel:

I discerned, obscurely, a child's face looking through the window—Terror made me cruel; and finding it useless to attempt shaking the creature off, I pulled its wrist on to the broken pane, and rubbed it to and fro till the blood ran down and soaked the bed-clothes: still it wailed, "Let me in!" and maintained its tenacious gripe, almost maddening me with fear.[18]

Finally the child's hold relaxes, and Lockwood pulls back his arm and blocks the jagged hole with a pyramid of books to prevent the intrusion of the menacing child. Implicit in this nightmare is the rejection of the neglected child by the disturbed and obdurate adult, who tries to isolate himself from its cries through printed material that represents pedantry at its worst. More sinister is the overall vision of the terrorized grown-up who takes a sadistic pleasure in torturing his tormentor.

In their depictions of the confining and inimical environment in which the helpless child is imprisoned, British novelists were not content merely to reproduce the pattern established by Moritz but gave it a significant and depressing extension. Often in their works the victimized child escapes from the terrors of the home only to be entrapped in a new ambience that is equally or more hostile. This passage from an intimate inferno to an institutional one is traced in Charlotte Brontë's *Jane Eyre* (1847). There is nothing spectacular about the torments inflicted on Jane at home. Her aunt treats the orphan harshly and as an inferior and displays a marked preference for her own son, who himself victimizes the unwanted waif. Jane is exposed to a stultifying lack of affection and to constant humiliation. She is ceaselessly reminded of her status as a ward of Mrs. Reed, the benefactress to whom she should be ever grateful. Though not fully aware of all its implications, she is acutely sensitive to this psychological degradation: "This reproach of my dependence had become a vague sing-song in my ear; very painful and crushing, but only half intelligible."[19] However, corporal punishment is never inflicted on her. The worst chastisement she receives is to be locked up in the "red room." Yet this unjust imprisonment in a chamber which contains all the terrors of death is such a traumatic experience that it drives the girl to the brink of a nervous breakdown. Haunted by the memory of her uncle, who died in this room of crimson drapes and scarlet rugs and counterpanes, she stares into the mirror and enters a nightmare world of reflections in which she is divorced from herself:

My fascinated glance involuntarily explored the depth it [the mirror] revealed. All looked colder and darker in that visionary hollow than in reality: and the strange little figure there gazing at me, with a white face and arms specking the gloom, and glittering eyes of fear moving where all else was still, had the effect of a real spirit (pp. 11–12)

This depersonalization is followed by a mindless panic:

My heart beat thick, my head grew hot; a sound filled my ears, which I deemed the rushing of wings: something seemed near me; I was oppressed, suffocated: endurance broke down; I rushed to the door and shook the lock in a desperate effort. (p. 17)

All her defenses destroyed, Jane succumbs to hysteria and screams wildly. The adults intrude momentarily, reproach her for her lack of submission, and lock the door upon her again. She has a fit and lapses into unconsciousness. This episode, whose memory will haunt her for years to come, precipitates her revolt against her guardian, who decides to pack her off. Jane's initial reaction to the prospect of being sent away to a boarding school is one of liberation, but her first impressions of her new milieu are ones of utter confusion. The author depicts the inability of a young mind to absorb and cope with a new and overwhelming reality. But soon enough her feelings crystallize as she tries to reconcile herself to an institution in which she is starving not merely for want of affection but for lack of sufficient food. Early on she takes stock of her precarious situation:

And then my mind made its first earnest effort to comprehend what had been infused into it concerning heaven and hell: and for the first time it recoiled, baffled; and for the first time glancing behind, on each side, and before it, it saw all around an unfathomed gulf: it felt the one point where it stood—the present; all the rest was formless cloud and vacant depth; and it shuddered at the thought of tottering, and plunging amid that chaos. (pp. 90–91)

Jane clings precariously to the dismal and uncertain present of the school, while she is on the verge of being engulfed at any moment by the terrors of the unknown.

Education as a method of destroying childhood systematically: this is the message repeated with insistence in novel after novel, from Dickens's *Nicholas Nickleby* to Musil's *Young Törless*. The narrator of Gotthelf's *The Peasant Mirror* gives poignant expression to the depressing effects of such instruction; after a brief session in school he cries out: "For two hours we were spiritually dead and physically immobilized, an eternity for a child!"[20] Not all children survive their schooling. Julian Boufflers, the pathetic hero of Conrad Ferdinand Meyer's "Das Leiden eines Knabens" ("A Boy Suffers") (1883), emerges from his school "his head sunk, his back broken, his body crushed, his eyes extinguished and with unsure step."[21] Shortly thereafter he succumbs as a result of a merciless lashing inflicted by the vindictive master of studies and of a brain fever brought on by the excessive intellectual effort imposed on him.

The revulsion voiced by so many writers against the currently prevalent pedagogy is given its ultimate expression in the bitterest of the many diatribes against Victorian society, Samuel Butler's *The Way of All Flesh* (1872–84). The fundamental Victorian view of children is presented in starkly simple terms: ". . . their wickedness at birth was but very imperfectly wiped out at baptism, and . . . the mere fact of being young at all has something with it that savours more or less distinctly of the nature of sin" (p. 31).

With maddening monotony the author proceeds to demonstrate the pattern that inevitably emerges from such a principle. In generation after generation, the members of the Pontifex family destroy with implacable patience any creative or generous impulses in the young, until the young themselves are old enough to assume the role of oppressors. And the results are always the same. The description of Ernest Pontifex is typical: ". . . he had not much of the buoyancy of childhood, and was more like a puny, sallow little old man than I liked" (p. 93). At one time these words would have fit his father or grandfather. Although the Victorian novelists and Butler, as well as their French and German counterparts, had exhausted the subject, later writers could not resist imitating them. The child as victim of pedagogical principles which negate those of Rousseau, Jean Paul, and Schlegel is found as protagonist of such popular twentieth-century works as Hermann Hesse's *Beneath the Wheel* and Somerset Maugham's *Of Human Bondage*. The efforts of liberal reformers like Pestalozzi and Gotthelf were overshadowed by the architects of hell.

According to Butler, the planners of Ernest's private hell are not motivated by wickedness; they are merely stupid. There are, however, parents whose actions are at least partially determined by sadism. The couple portrayed by Jules Vallès in his autobiographical account of the childhood of Jacques Vingtras in *The Child* (1876) is typical. The young narrator is so abused by them both physically and psychologically that it is a miracle that he loses neither his life nor his sanity. But amidst all his torments this child, like so many of his counterparts, does know moments of profound happiness and ultimately is able to escape from parents whose sadism is not devoid of affection and whose cruelties may be well intentioned.

The essence of a childhood perverted by the indifferent malice of authoritarian and capricious parents has been distilled in the work of Jules Renard, whose own early years scarred him for life, and especially in his *Carrot Top* (1894). His protagonist's parents are unambiguously portrayed as monsters and his hell is an exitless one. The youngest child of the Lepic family has been reduced to the function "of a hyphen between his father and his mother."[22] Symbolic of his status is the fact that, though his brother and sister and even the maids have proper names that are constantly used, his baptismal name is never mentioned. Like the "boy" of Gotthelf and the "petit Chose" of Daudet, he has been deprived of his identity and there is no need to refer to him by anything but the derogatory sobriquet that serves to describe not just the color of his hair but, as Mme. Lepic informs a neighbor, "the yellowness of his soul" (p. 327).

Carrot Top's existence is dominated by fear. In the very first episode of the book, when the child is sent out into the dark to close the door of the chicken coop, the tone of unmitigated terror is set once and for all:

His buttocks pulled tight, his heels firmly planted, Carrot Top begins to tremble in the shadows. They are so thick that he thinks himself blind. Sometimes a gust of wind envelops him like an icy sheet, as if to carry him off. Aren't there foxes, and even wolves, panting against his hands, against his cheeks? (pp. 11–12)

In a movement of panic he does succeed in reaching his destination and in slamming shut the chicken coop. The child returns to the living room triumphant, but his short-lived joy at having survived the nightmare is replaced by despair. For his mother informs him coldly that, because he was so brave, he would be charged with the same task every night. The nightmare will be a recurrent one from now on.

The fear to which the terrorized child is exposed is inspired not only by imaginary demons of the night. The real monsters of every day—his parents—are more menacing by far than the shadowy nocturnal beasts that stand between him and the chicken coop. It is his mother who maltreats him physically, beats him on a regular basis, and deprives him of food and drink. It is she who, in a scene reminiscent of *The Swindler*, forces the child, who has soiled his bed, to consume his own excrement. And as she spoons his droppings into his mouth, she smiles sweetly. Nonetheless, the atmosphere of *Carrot Top* is not, like that of the picaresque novel, primarily one of physical repugnance. More frightening than cruelty is the awful vacuity in which the young protagonist carries on his fight for survival. There is in his home a lack of any form of affection. The abode in which Carrot Top passes his time is a loveless and joyless one in which calculation replaces spontaneity, in which personal relationships have been emptied of fondness and reduced to bickering competitions. The impossibility of communication is dramatized in a scene in which Carrot Top unsuccessfully attempts to kiss his father:

On his tiptoes he tries to kiss his father. The first time his lips barely come into contact with his beard. But M. Lepic, with an automatic movement, raises his head as if he were trying to avoid him. Then he bends over only to withdraw again, and Carrot Top, trying to reach his cheek, misses it. He makes only superficial contact with his nose. He kisses emptiness. (pp. 138–39)

The absence of a spiritual or human dimension within this family unit and the lack of communication are rendered explicit by the almost palpable silence that characterizes this particular hell. Agathe, the new maid, is herself struck dumb by the stillness that hangs over the dinner table:

Nobody speaks.
   M. Lepic eats slowly, as if he were chewing crushed glass.
   However, Mme. Lepic, more talkative, gives her orders at the table with gestures and movements of the head.
   Sister Ernestine looks up at the ceiling.
   Big brother Felix sculpts a slice of bread, and Carrot Top is entirely preoccupied with cleaning his plate. . . .
   Suddenly M. Lepic gets up to fill the water pitcher.
   "I would have been glad to go," says Agathe.
   Or, to be precise, she does not say so, she only thinks so. Already afflicted with the communal malady, her tongue thick, she does not dare to speak. (pp. 111–12)

When words are exchanged, it is usually to deny the value of words. So, when Carrot Top tries to justify one of his unusually loquacious outbreaks by explaining that "One has to chat in order to make the time pass," M. Lepic responds by asserting, "It is even better to keep silent" (p. 294).
   Lack of love, the interdiction of communication, and physical

cruelty are the elements that make up the inferno to which Carrot Top is condemned. But his mother is not content to let him languish in his prison. As if afraid that her youngest son, with his irrepressible spontaneity, might bring some love into the vacuum of the house, she actively engages in injecting an element of gratuitous evil into his already doleful existence. It is only fear of affection that could justify her actions, which are willfully designed to render impossible the slightest manifestation of fondness. There is something more than malice in her cruelty to her young child. Thus, Carrot Top is not only ordered to execute the wounded game his father brings home from the hunt, but he is constantly told that this is his natural function because he is the one who enjoys inflicting pain. In one of her many carefully planned experiments, his mother tempts him into stealing from her and, when she entraps him, triumphantly declares that he is a natural thief. Thus she assiduously cultivates the child's inherited vices while extirpating his natural instincts for love. By insisting on the supposed pleasure he derives from his misdeeds, by repeated assertions of his lack of warmth, the bitter mother practices a highly successful form of brainwashing. So much so, that Carrot Top does indeed turn into the vicious, perverse child that she has always accused him of being.

Jules Renard's disillusioned vision of childhood is made explicit in a typically acerbic notation in his *Journal*:

Victor Hugo and many others have seen the chid as an angel. One must see him as ferocious and infernal. The candy children the reading public has been given to suck on until now must be smashed. The child is a small animal. Even a cat is more human. The child strikes his claws into anything that is tender, and the constant task of parents must be to make him retract them.[23]

In *Carrot Top*, Jules Renard depicts a child who is not naturally evil but who is meticulously deformed. The agent of this deformation is the mother who has assumed the responsibility of raising him as a ferocious and infernal child. Medea had been content to slaughter her children. Her modern incarnation, Mme. Lepic, destroys hers spiritually. The surgery that the "comprachicos" performed on infants to turn them into freaks finds its psychological counterpart in the operation to which Mme. Lepic subjects her youngest son.

The Revenge of the Maltreated Child

The race of children is monstrous.
Alain

The suffering child is not always a passive victim; sometimes, in his very agony, he contemplates a terrible vengeance. In his fifth epode (c. 30 B.C.) Horace tells of a boy who, having been tortured by the sorceress Canidia, is put to a slow death by her and her cronies. They bury him up to the neck and, while he is starving to death, pass fresh viands in front of his glazed eyes. In his death throes the youth sums up sufficient strength to curse Canidia and to threaten her with punishment:

> Nay, from the hour when bid by you I die,
>   O' nights I'll dog you hauntingly;
> And ghoul-like with bent claws your eyes I'll tear,—
>   For such the power blest spirits share,—
> Or seat myself upon each quaking breast,
>   And by sheer terror slay your rest.
> Mobs will from street to street pelt you with stones,
>   Or trample down, foul hags, your bones;
> Rent your unburied limbs will be, where gaunt
>   Wolves and night birds the Esquiline haunt.[24]

As a child he is incapable of protecting himself against the vicious hags. In the afterlife, however, he will inflict on Canidia torments that will repay him for his own suffering.

Despite his physical fragility and intellectual limitations, the child, in his confrontation with the adult, does not always prove to be an impotent adversary, and his capacity for vengeance can be limitless. This is the symbolic import of the relationship between the prostitute and her illegitimate son in Zola's *Nana* (1880). Like so many of the author's fictional children, Nana's Louiset, who never reaches his fourth birthday, is old beyond his years. However, unlike the wild urchins who roam the corridors and courtyard of the tenement of the Rue de la Goutte-d'Or in *L'Assommoir*, or the juveniles who suffocate in the bowels of the earth in *Germinal*, he is aged not by his physical environment but by his psychological one. Presumably he is well cared for by Nana's aunt, and, whenever Nana herself sees him, she assumes all the trappings of an indulgent mother whose major concern is to spoil her son. He is certainly not one of the deprived proletarian children who infest Zola's Second-Empire society and whose lives consist in a struggle against starvation and want. Nor is he one of the youngsters abused by adults who consider them either as competitors for sustenance or as breadwinners to be exploited. But the suffering that the courtesan inflicts on the child she professes to adore is more acute than the pain resulting from physical mistreatment: she reduces him to the status of an object, a toy with which to amuse herself when she feels like it and to toss aside when it begins to bore her. She treats him as carelessly as the gifts which she demands from her lovers and which she then breaks or loses. The profound humiliation to which she unwittingly subjects Louiset causes him to withdraw into an impenetrable inner world. Even in the midst of a crowd of merrymakers, Louiset remains a creature apart and maintains his gravity: "The child, without a smile, was looking at everybody. He seemed very old, as if engrossed in sorrowful reflections on what he was seeing." [25] In his debasement, the child becomes the lonely and aloof observer, estranged from the society in which he moves.

All children are at the mercy of adults, and Louiset is no exception. However, the tyranny he knows is the worst kind, for he is subject to the gratuitousness represented by his mother's whims. So, when Nana wants to assume the role of mother and to play at being a normal, kindhearted parent, she smothers him with the affection she believes fitting for the occasion. Because her abilities as an actress, whether in life or on the stage, are limited to miming cultural stereotypes, her histrionic efforts are unconvincing:

Nana's greatest pastime was to go to Batignolles, to her aunt's house, in order to see her little Louis. For two weeks she would forget him; then, overwhelmed with enthusiasm, she would run on foot, all modesty and tenderness, like a good mother, bringing the sort of presents considered appropriate for patients in a hospital, some tobacco for her aunt, oranges and cookies for the little one. (pp. 1338–9)

The child's subsidiary position in his mother's universe is exemplified by Nana's inability to distinguish between her lapdog and her son. One day she takes them to the races and, distracted, keeps forgetting about the two creatures who no longer amuse her. In a pathetic scene, the child and Bijou huddle together, are almost

stepped on several times, and are both finally picked up by the theatre director whose fortuitous intervention saves them from being
crushed by the press of people.

Despite his reticence, Louiset does succeed in imposing himself upon his mother's consciousness, and thus, though unaware of
the effect he produces, he takes his revenge on her. His constant
presence serves as both a continual reproach and a warning. His
debility, his scrofula, the plaques in his ears, and his eczema are in
striking contrast to Nana's radiant beauty and remarkable physical condition. Nana's reaction to her son's disabilities and ill health
is a troubled one:

When she saw him so pale, with his weak blood, his soft and yellow-
blotched flesh, she became serious; above all, she felt a sort of astonishment. What could be wrong with the dear that would explain his degen-
eration? She, his mother, was so very healthy! (p. 1359)

Nana has a horror of physical decrepitude, and her son's appearance, as a reminder of its inevitability, strikes her as ominous. She
has reason to be concerned, for the child's revenge will consist in
doing to her what nature had done to him. Louiset dies of small-
pox, but, before his death, he passes the fatal malady on to Nana.
So the courtesan who reveled in the beauty of her body dies maimed
and grotesquely disfigured, the victim of a child she has neglected.
This grim retribution is a fitting and, at the same time, ironic conclusion to the career of Nana, who, as a young girl in *L'Assommoir*, had by her presence caused the accident that led to the destruction of her father.

Embittered by the torments inflicted on him, the child occasionally takes revenge upon the adult world with a violence that
contains the potential for universal destruction. It is such a revolution that is at the center of Yukio Mishima's *The Sailor Who Fell
from Grace with the Sea* (1965). The story is a contemporary variation on an old theme, that of the child who has lost his father and
who resents the surrogate chosen by his mother. But in this modern version the classical situation undergoes a disquieting transformation. The thirteen-year-old Noboru does not seem a likely can-
didate for the role assigned him. The future agent of destruction is
always well treated, and corporal punishment is never inflicted on
him. He enjoys the advantages of an upper-class milieu and all of
the maternal comforts that his well-to-do mother can provide. Nor

does the young widow deprive him of maternal affection. Nonetheless, secretiveness and hypocrisy characterize all his relations with his elders. Thus he can smile ingenuously and look with the candid eyes of innocence at the old watchman who patronizes him and at the same time profoundly despise him. And in the dramatic finale of the novel, he can convincingly play the role of the trusting and admiring child, while plotting the destruction of the man for whose benefit he puts on this act. For Noboru harbors a deep resentment against the world of grown-ups, who have made a prisoner of him on the pretext of the very educational principles which he rejects. Every night, to prevent him from sneaking out to roam with a gang of like-minded friends, his mother locks him in the bedroom. His home is a gilded cage from which he can never escape because, even when he is given his freedom, he is expected not to use it. So the night that his mother conspicuously leaves the door unlocked, Noboru does not feel the exaltation of one who has been set free, but the depression of one who has been brought face to face with his own impotence:

It was a trap—a rabbit trap. The grownups expected the captive animal's rage and the familiar odors of his lair to transform themselves into the resignation and tolerance of a creature who has confined himself. . . . They were beginning his education, a terrific, destructive education. Trying to force *maturity* on a thirteen-year-old boy. *Maturity* or . . . *perversion.*[26]

The influence of adults is a civilizing one, and consequently debilitating. Noboru and the members of his gang struggle against it because they are convinced that only in childhood is there the potential for significant action. As the chief of their group explains, "There's a huge seal called 'impossibility' pasted all over this world. And don't ever forget that we're the only ones who can tear it off once and for all" (pp. 43–44). Because the goal the adults have set is to transform children into their mirror images and consequently to deprive them of the impossible, all adults are considered as mortal enemies. Noboru's companions envy him for not having a father.

Initially, Ryuji, the second mate of a tramp steamer, who becomes the mother's lover, seems to fall into the category of the exceptional hero. He represents for the child the romance of the sea, the lore of the deep, the violence of hurricanes, the exoticism of far-off countries. Even though disillusionment sets in quickly, Noboru tries to maintain the fiction, for he must protect the "hallowed figure" whom, in a moment of ecstasy, he had seen coupling with his mother. Because the sailor must return to his vessel in two days and to the sea whence he came, this task is relatively easy. After the mariner's departure, the letters, covered with colorful stamps from faraway places and recounting fabulous adventures and tropical storms, reinforce the child's initial vision.

Six months later the sailor returns, having shed his pea jacket for a western-style business suit and renounced the sea in order to marry Noboru's mother and take over the management of her shop. Unaware of the banality of the fictitious vision that he has created of Ryuji, the betrayed child seeks violent vengeance. Previously, he and his companions have butchered a cat, so they already know how to take a life. They lure the unsuspecting sailor to their hideaway, where they have prepared the opiate they will administer in his tea before proceeding to his vivisection. This murder is a symbolic one. It is the murder of the tawdry fictions created by adults and accepted by the unsuspecting child. By this assassination the child thinks to displace the adult and thus himself become master of the world. "Woe to thee, O land, when thy king is a child." (Eccles. 10:16) This biblical admonition could serve as a warning to those who would accept the reign of Noboru.

The Heaven of Childhood

> Where children are, there is a golden age.
> Novalis

As counterparts to the depictions of the infernal horrors of childhood, there are the countless descriptions of its more joyful aspects. As can be expected, the latter only rarely measure up to the former. Bliss is harder to communicate than suffering, and the many attempts to recreate a childhood paradise all too often result in uncomfortably sentimental effusions that are made even more intolerable by an equally mawkish enthusiasm for nature. The tears evoked by scenes of children frolicking in an alpine landscape or dreaming by a peaceful brook are not those of joy but of excessive yawning provoked by an insipid lyricism. Hugo can become dreary when he practices the art of being a grandfather, and even Mörike can go beyond the bounds of good taste when he tries to identify with children. In *Histoire du véritable Gribouille* (*The*

Story of the Real Gribouille) (1850) George Sand captures the attention of the reader when she describes the child's sufferings under the tutelage of his cruel parents and then of the monstrous M. Bourdon, but loses it as soon as Gribouille escapes to the lovely but insipid realm of the fairies. Not that the children of paradise are less attractive than the children of hell. The difficulty is that few writers or artists have both the requisite genius and the humility to portray a state that is the essence of simplicity and that is, at the same time, extraordinarily complex, a state that is always the same and yet of an infinite variety. Like Plato's eternal harmony, it is a condition that by definition must be monotonous but that cannot provoke boredom. In general, painters and musicians have been the most successful in resolving this paradox. Composers as diverse as Schumann and Debussy have made audible the tonalities of the blissful child, while Franz Marc and Paul Klee have transcribed its vision. Among artists it is perhaps Henri Rousseau who has come the closest to capturing the eternal awe and wonderment of the childhood Eden in those detemporalized and motionless jungle paintings which are as sophisticated as they are naive. Among poets it is Baudelaire who in one brief formulation communicates the essence of childhood bliss in the famous verse concerning "les verts paradis des amours enfantines." Among modern novelists, it is Proust who has achieved the same feat in more extended form. Not the Proust who recreated the intolerable waiting for the goodnight kiss, or who rediscovered the infernal anguish of jealousy, or who reinvented the disturbances of a neurasthenic child, but the Proust who revealed for the first time the spires of Martinville and the lilacs of Combray.

For many writers the only gateway to the childhood paradise is through death, and the child must pass through hell on earth in order to gain admittance to heaven. It is this pessimism concerning the human condition that informs the moving anecdote "A Little Boy at Christ's Christmas Tree" (1876), which Dostoevski recounts in his *Diary of a Writer*. The tale itself is constructed of an alternance between the stark realism of the impoverished child wandering through the cold city streets and the unreality of the dreamworld he eventually finds. The author's ambivalent attitude toward the material he exploits precludes the superficial emotionalism inherent in the structure and the material. Dostoevski's remarks casting doubt on the veracity of his recital create an ironic mode that lends credibility to a banal story portraying the misery of the human condition. The six-year-old beggar boy does find his blissful realm, but only after passing through the culminating nightmare of his life that begins when he is unable to awaken his mother and is horrified by the coldness of her flesh. He leaves the cellar where they had sought refuge and roams the unfamiliar streets of the strange city to which they had come in search of food. It is Christmas Eve, and everything is festively illuminated. Despite his hunger and the bitter cold, the waif is entranced by the bright lights, the Christmas trees, the banquets and games that he sees through the windows. But the enchantment is broken by an older boy who hits him on the head, kicks him, and steals his cap. Terrified, the little child runs through the labyrinth of streets and finally collapses behind a woodpile in a courtyard. Comforted by the sense of security accompanying his realization that nobody can find him, he is about to doze off when he hears what he presumes to be the voice of his mother. Then an idealized female figure leads him to the real feast with real children and real mothers, an eternal celebration with the Christ child. Earlier he had been separated from the spectacles he had witnessed by panes of glass; now he becomes an active participant in the most magnificent feast of them all. This is the jubilant climax of a story that ends on a sober note: on the following day, the authorities find the frozen corpse of the child in the courtyard and the body of the mother in the cellar. The introductory and concluding speculations of the author concerning the reality of the episode add a particularly somber tone to what is a fairy tale within a realistic setting. In these comments Dostoevski admits that the entire story might be nothing more than a poetic fiction. But of one thing he is certain: what took place in the cellar and in the courtyard could have happened. In other words, the hell of childhood is a certainty, whereas heaven may be a figment of the imagination.

A similar though temporary paradise amid desolation can be found in dreams. In one of Rimbaud's first poems, "Les Etrennes des orphelins" (1871), the antiphonal effect of the title sounds throughout. The misery of the bereaved children is contrasted with recollections of a familial past as reassuring as the most comforting of Hugo's scenes. The warmth of these memories provides intermittent relief. However, in the children's room the somber funeral clothes scattered about predominate, and the sleep to which they finally succumb is such a disconsolate one that even with their eyes closed they seem to weep. But the "angel of cradles" arrives with a dream for them and they are transported to a "pink paradise" that is a sublimation of their anterior existence. The wondrous quality of the past can even influence the state of wakening. When the children are aroused from their dreams, their eyes immediately fall on the sinister paraphernalia of death, but which have been marvelously transformed:

> Là, sur le grand tapis, resplendit quelque chose . . .
> Ce sont des médaillons argentés aux reflets scintillants;
> Des petits cadres noirs, des couronnes de verre . . .
>
> > (lines 101–3)

> There, on the large carpet, something is glittering . . .
> It is the silver medals with sparkling reflections;
> Little black frames, wreaths of glass . . .

The end of the poem is ambivalent, and the reader is left to wonder how long this splendiferous paradise can survive the absence which dominates the house.

A strikingly similiar imaginative pattern, but in extended form and without any of the ambiguity of Dostoevski's text, is found in Gerhart Hauptmann's dream play, *Hanneles Himmelfahrt* (*The Ascension of Hannele*) (1893). It, too, is a romantic fabulation within a crassly realistic framework, but the irony present in Dostoevski is totally lacking. After her mother's death the child-heroine becomes the victim of an alcoholic stepfather who brutalizes her ceaselessly. Hannele seeks to rejoin her mother in heaven by drowning herself. She walks out on the frozen pond until she reaches a spot where the ice is so thin that she falls through. The well-meaning schoolteacher pulls her from the water in extremis and carries the semiconscious, fever-racked girl through a nocturnal blizzard to the poorhouse. Like Dostoevski's boy, Hannele is cold, hungry, and almost mad with dread. The doctor's examination reveals the cause of her panic fear of her guardian: her entire body is covered with the weals of the lashings he has inflicted on her. The girl's terror is such that she has no desire to be cured, and, in a desperate attempt at communication, she utters three times to the uncomprehending adults the simple phrase, "I don't want to get well." Physical convalescence would mean a return to what she calls her home, which is the equivalent of the childhood hell. All she desires now is to be admitted to the realm inhabited by her mother, which is the equivalent of the childhood heaven. Sister Martha watches over her in agony, during the course of which the child has several visions. After an initial nightmare in which her stepfather threatens her, she sees the figure of her mother, who describes heaven to her and gives her a bunch of marigolds. The symbolism is clear in the original text, for in German marigolds are *Himmelsschlüssel*, literally "keys to heaven." Hannele's final dream is of an encounter with a stranger, who is quite clearly a Christ figure. It is he who leads her into a paradise which he describes in a poem whose opening lines are: "Ecstasy is a marvelously beautiful town, / Where peace and joy have no end." This promised land is an extraordinary mélange in which elements of mythology are blended with Christian symbolism, fragments of fairy tales are interspersed with verses from children's lullabies, and exotic and even erotic imagery coexist with the legends of saints. A naive ludic strain gives coherence to this beatific dream; the culminating metaphor is that of celestial children playing with their golden balls. It is a paradise that is in striking contrast to the sordid reality of the poorhouse in which Hannele expires and in which the only games are adult ones of debauchery.

The celestial domains depicted by Dostoevski and Hauptmann are modern variations on a theme that can be traced to the Bible. The association between childhood and paradise after death is a well-established one, deeply rooted in Christianity. So in the *Paradiso* Dante accords a special place to children. It is Beatrice who propounds the doctrine of the purity of children, at the same time that she acknowledges that both their trust and their innocence are eroded by the passing years:

> Only in little children are found
> Faith and innocence; then each one
> Takes flight before the cheeks are covered.
>
> (27. 127–29)

Saint Bernard, who explains to Dante the sacred order of paradise in which nothing is left to chance, locates "this swift-sped people" precisely within the eternal kingdom (32. 39–84). He envisages the redeemed as the petal of a divine rose, which a line cleaves in half. On one side are those who anticipated the coming of Christ and on the other those who had looked back upon it. Midway along the line, and thus in an atemporal zone, is the circle of the children, endowed with grace and living in the eternal realm from which the sorrow, thirst, and hunger that have plagued both Hannele and Dostoevski's child are forever excluded.

Unlike the childhood heaven that is preceded by an earthly hell, the concept of a terrestrial childhood paradise which anticipates the eternal one is usually considered a modern one, a product of the preromantic imagination, invented by Rousseau and popularized by Bernardin de Saint-Pierre. Although it is true that the worldly Eden of childhood was not a prevalent theme in literature before the inception of the "cult of the child" in the eighteenth century, there are a few earlier, significant examples that cannot be dismissed. The emphasis placed on a benevolent form of pedagogy during the Renaissance assumes that, at least among a certain class, adults made a serious attempt at creating for the child a propitious framework in which it could thrive. Chaucer shows a deep concern for the intellectual well-being of his son Lowys in the educational *Treatise on the Astrolabe*,[27] and its very composition is a demonstration of his friendship for the ten-year-old boy. An even more striking case is that of Montaigne. Despite his professed indifference toward infants ("I lost two or three sucklings, not without regret, but without vexation"), he depicts in the essay "Concerning the Education of Children" an idyllic period of development during the course of which the youngster is first nurtured in the country and given as much freedom as possible. The child's later, intellectual education is to be undertaken by his father and is also characterized by a lack of rigor and constraints. The symbol of this luxurious upbringing is the music of the flute with which the child is to be awakened every morning. Montaigne's contemporary, Rabelais, described an equally joyful if far more boisterous childhood for Gargantua and later on for his son Pantagruel. These attempts by fathers to create a paradise for their offspring are given their rationale at the end of Gargantua's letter of advice to Pantagruel: "My old age will reblossom in your youth." These children, who never know the miseries that the picaresque children from Lázaro to the narrator of *The Painted Bird* had to endure, are privileged because they represent the hope of the adults who see in the child the possibility for the fulfillment of their own dreams.

The nostalgia characteristic of Gargantua's attitude toward his son is the hallmark of some of the most moving childhood poetry from Henry Vaughan to Wordsworth. Like them, Jean-Jacques Rousseau is a poet of retrospection, and much of his life and work can be seen as an unconscious effort to create a childhood paradise that he himself had never known. Whether at Les Charmettes cradled by his "maman" or on the Lac de Bienne rocked by his boat, he is obsessed by the desire to revert to a preadolescent state. The yearning which informs such major poetical works as the *Confessions* and the *Reveries* is the essential component of his pedagogic treatise, *Emile* (1762). Although it is dangerous to reduce such an ambitious project to modest proportions, it is no simplification to claim that it represents an attempt to establish for a fictitious child the paradise that its author had never known. With the application of what Rousseau calls a "negative education," he creates the perfect denizen of the perfect Eden. Before sketching the portrait of Emile at the age of ten or twelve, Rousseau depicts his equally fictitious counterpart who had been trained in the classical method. We see the young victim of a repressive education at the very moment when his mentor calls him to his books:

The poor child let himself be taken away, he turned to look backward with regret, fell silent, and departed, his eyes swollen with the tears he dared not shed and his heart heavy with the sighs he dared not exhale.[28]

In contrast, Emile's tutor addresses the child he is charged with raising in rapturous terms:

Oh you, who have nothing similar to fear, you, for whom no time of life is a time of constraint or boredom, you who look forward to the day without disquiet and to the night without impatience, and who do not count the hours but by your pleasures, come, my happy and good-natured pupil, come and console us. (p. 419)

This effusion is couched entirely in terms of negatives. The idyllic state consists not of any positive presence, but of the absence of pain, ennui, and displeasure. Continuing in this vein, the preceptor remarks that he and his charge get along so well because Emile knows that "he will never be a long time without distraction" in his company and because "we never depend on each other." The atmosphere of emptiness produced through this stylistic device is reinforced by the structural one of contrast. By describing Emile as the opposite of the unhappy child, Rousseau is able to define him more in terms of what he is not than in terms of what he is.

The insubstantiality of the state of nature in which Emile spends "the age of joyfulness" is entirely consonant with the behavioral scheme on which it depends. In order to profit from this paradise, the child must be taught to dispense with all habits, or, as the author adds, to commit himself completely to one habit, namely that of not contracting any others. The pupil thus finds a purely negative freedom in his domain, freedom from the attachments that habit creates, freedom from fear, freedom from pain, and freedom from responsibility. The question Rousseau avoids (and for good reason) is: freedom for what?

The defining feature of the negative paradise is liberty, but this liberty is only an apparent one. For Rousseau hastens to add that the freedom he accords Emile is a "well-regulated one." Paradoxically, the preceptor must take great pains to maintain his charge in a state of absolute ignorance as to the laws that regulate—and hence limit—his freedom. So, a basic hypocrisy underlies this entire pedagogic system. Inculcated with a false sense of freedom, the pupil is caught up unwittingly in the intricate web of lies that is his education, an education that is nothing more or less than a sham. Emile is as much a victim of a plot as his creator. Even though the pedagogical machinations do not lead to the paranoia which eventually clouded Rousseau's mind, their results are appalling. Thus Emile is happy because he believes that there is no interdependence between himself and his guide, when in fact the tutor has made Emile entirely dependent upon him. The child is conditioned without realizing it, and instruction becomes the ultimate form of mind control. Rousseau's paradise is not Walden, but "Walden Two," whose end product is the well-adapted citizen of the modern world. Through his method, Rousseau complacently predicts, it will be possible to make the pupil "patient, level-headed, resigned, and peaceful" (p. 320). In other words, the tutor's role is to tame the "wild child" by manipulating him.

Rousseau's originality lies in his recognition of the fact that the childhood world is an autonomous one, different not only in degree but in kind from the adult one: "Nature requires that children be children before being men" (p. 340). Furthermore, his pedagogic working hypothesis is that the instructor must never

violate the childhood state: "Treat your pupil according to his age.
. . . Respect childhood" (pp. 342–43). These well-meaning exhortations are empty ones. Rousseau does create a paradise for the youngster, but it is based on a fraud. In a moment of unguarded cynicism, B. F. Skinner claims that "we can achieve a sort of control under which the controlled, though they are following a code much more scrupulously than was ever the case under the old system, nevertheless *feel free*."[29] Rousseau is less frank than the unabashed advocate of cultural engineering, but he is equally committed to an experimental method that treats the pupils to be formed as guinea pigs, manipulated without their knowledge or consent. So it is not the child's paradise, but his own artificially constructed one which Rousseau uses as a prison-laboratory.

Despite the influence Rousseau had on Bernardin de Saint-Pierre, the childhood paradise depicted in *Paul and Virginia* (1787) is a more healthy one than that found in *Emile*, more akin in its naive simplicity to the paintings of Henri Rousseau than to the sophisticated artificiality of the milieu in which Emile seems to prosper. The island in the Indian Ocean which provides the exotic setting for the novel constitutes a refuge from civilization in which the illegitimate child, Paul, and the orphan, Virginia, grow up side by side in an uncorrupted state of nature. Their minimal but not negative education is an honest one, and their joyful existence is based on a full awareness and acceptance of their interdependence. With their mothers and with their old friend (the narrator of their history) they form a harmonious community whose motto could well be the biblical "ora et labora." In the simplest terms Bernardin de Saint-Pierre describes their childhood in the tropical garden of Eden:

Their entire education consisted of learning to please each other and to help each other. They were ignorant of anything else . . . wherever they were, in the house, in the fields, in the woods, they raised their innocent hands toward heaven, and their hearts were full of the love of their parents.

Thus passed their early years, like a beautiful dawn which announces an even more beautiful day.[30]

The advent of the radiant future promised in this passage is intermittently threatened by the intrusion of the outside world. The children first become aware of the existence of evil in a somber encounter with the brutal master of a fugitive slave whom they have helped. But an even more destabilizing menace is the hope of inheriting the fortune of Virginia's capricious aunt in Paris. And it is the intervention of this eccentric relative that precipitates the disaster. She sends a letter in which she promises her wealth to Virginia if the latter stays with her in France. Despite Paul's vehement protestations and despite Virginia's own reluctance, the grown-ups accede. Her two-year European sojourn turns out to be a wretched experience which Virginia finally gives up when her aunt tries to force a suitor upon her. The incorrigible ward is disinherited and sent back to Mauritius. When Virginia is within sight of the coast, a hurricane strikes, the ship founders, and Paul watches helplessly as Virginia is drowned. It is not the whim of the aunt nor the chance encounter with a tropical tempest that destroys the childhood paradise. Its disintegration was necessary from the beginning, and the dramatic events that brought it about merely precluded its more gradual but inevitable disintegration. Trying to console Paul in his bereavement, the old mentor tells him that the harshness of the life of labor to which he and Virginia had been condemned would have taken its toll eventually. Had Virginia lived, the narrator explains to Paul, ". . . you would have seen her succumb every day, while she was trying to share your fatigue" (p. 221). But Paul's psychological constitution is too feeble to bear this affliction, and, after a few months of near madness, the distraught child passes away. This fatal debility can be attributed directly to his sheltered upbringing. The mentor's comments on this flaw in his natural education are unambiguous: "Sorrow had submerged him. Alas! The misfortunes of childhood prepare man for entry into life, and Paul had never experienced any" (p. 230). Unlike Rousseau, Bernardin de Saint-Pierre recognizes the dangers of the idyllic existence he created for the two children. Paul had lived too long in the childhood paradise to survive reality.

From Bernardin de Saint-Pierre to Proust, the childhood paradise regained through the memory and eternalized in the work of art is presented as a sublime one, as a rich lode from which the most precious metals can be extracted. But just as during this period there are examples of a bourgeois hell less spectacular than the monstrous infernos depicted in the picaresque novels, so there are bourgeois paradises that are more modest than the splendid visions of the lake poets. Typical of the latter is the swarm of idealized children who surround Lotte in Goethe's *Werther*. The nuclear family, within the idyllic setting of Wetzlar, constitutes the framework of an undisturbed and undisturbing paradise. Similarly engaging are Hugo's grandchildren, who scatter the poet's books and distract him from his work. The most convincing example of such conventional but nonetheless enchanting paradises is represented by the childhood of George Sand. Even in her old age she dreamed of the tranquil happiness and the peaceful joy of her girlhood. In her autobiography, she evokes her former existence as Aurore Dupin in terms which refute Saint Augustine:

> One cannot help but believe that life is in itself an awfully good business, since its beginnings are so sweet, and childhood such a happy age. There is not one of us who does not remember this golden age as a vanished dream which cannot be compared to anything in the future. I say a dream, as I think of these early years during which our remembrances float uncertainly and seize only a few isolated impressions within a vague totality. It is impossible to say why a powerful charm is attached for each of us to these revelations of the memory which for others remain insignificant.[31]

It is this peaceful paradise that she reinvents in her later, pastoral novels, *François le Champi* and *The Devil's Pool*. The ecstasy of the great romantic poets may be lacking in these undramatic portrayals, but in spirit they are not that far removed from *The Prelude*. And, after all, in *Remembrance of Things Past*, the young narrator's favorite novels were the ones in which George Sand depicted the childhood of François le Champi and of Petit Pierre.

Rousseau, Bernardin de Saint-Pierre, Wordsworth, and Proust —these are the authors one most frequently associates with the concept of the childhood paradise. But it is Emile Zola who, in *The Sin of Abbé Mouret* (1875), gives what is perhaps the most detailed description of two very different types of Edenic existence. This is not as surprising as it might seem at first, because in the entire *Rougon-Macquart* series children occupy a central role, so much so that the then still-childless author might have been suspected of being obsessed with them. The diversity of the race of children which dominates the family chronicle is striking, comprising as it does the entire range from the demonic to the angelic. In *Germinal*, Jeanlin, Bébert, and Lydie play their monstrous adult games of fornication, theft, and murder in the infernal region dominated by the coal mine Le Voreux, and in *Restless House* the over-protected Angèle, daughter of the bourgeois Compardon couple, belies her name and finds bliss in the arms of the maid. She is the incarnation of precocious perversity. Most sinister of all is the hirsute bastard in *Money*, who by the age of twelve has been initiated into necrophilia and shortly thereafter commits rape. At the end of the novel he is set loose to prey upon a defenseless society. At the other end of the spectrum are the children who represent salvation and who are symbolized in *The Dream* by the protagonist, Angélique, an embroideress of chasubles, and at the conclusion of the last volume, *Le Docteur Pascal*, by the infant who is described as "a flag to life." Aside from the bevy of parish brats who by their antics desecrate the sanctity of the church, there are no preadolescents in *The Sin of Abbé Mouret*. And yet the central theme of the book is childhood and its eternal presence. The novel opens and closes with the appearance of the twenty-two-year-old sister of Father Mouret, Désirée, whose intellectual and psychological development was arrested before she had attained the age of ten and who remains forever a prepubescent girl, simple in spirit. She is a constant point of reference, for not only does Zola use her to begin and end his story of the fallen priest, but he comes back to her at regular intervals throughout the novel. It is she who represents the primitive force of life from which her brother shrinks. In the concluding scene, while Serge Mouret is lowering the body of Albine into the grave, Désirée, standing on a dungheap, triumphantly announces the birth of a calf. Isolated in her Eden, she is oblivious of the drama being consummated in the cemetery, just as she has always been oblivious of her brother's spiritual travails. She lives in her own terrestrial paradise, the fertile farmyard in which animals constantly copulate, give birth, and die. Désirée, the eternal child in her natural beauty, presides over the forces of nature that encroach upon and threaten to engulf the white, sterile church in which Serge officiates. Désirée's earthly paradise provides the framework of the novel and at the same time is a recurrent presence which is reflected in the paradise of the senses that her brother later discovers.

The permanence of Désirée's paradise is dependent on her retardation. Her brother lives side by side with her in his own paradise, whose continuance is assured by his emasculation. Eden seems to exist only because its inhabitants are not fully developed or subsequently mutilated; its stability, therefore, is a direct function of their incompleteness. Thus most earthly paradises are of a fleeting nature, and the attempt to eternalize them is a dangerous and in some cases illicit enterprise. Despite the seductive charm with which he entrances his companion, the protagonist of Alain-Fournier's *Le Grand Meaulnes (The Lost Domain)* (1913) is irresponsible to the point of criminality and ready to sacrifice everyone to his self-centered quest. He is determined to find again the mysterious domain into which he inadvertently stumbled and to relive the splendor of the three enchanted days he spent there. This period was devoted to the celebration of an engagement that had never taken place. The festive occasion centered on children, who dominated it by their innocent games. Upon his arrival, the adolescent Augustin Meaulnes was seized by a wonderment that provoked him to exclaim, "This must be a wedding party. . . . But it is the children who run everything here? . . . Strange domain!"[32] It was children, too, who led him by the hand to his quarters. During his sojourn he had met Frantz de Galais, the abandoned fiancé, as well as his sister, Yvonne, with whom he fell in love. Of course, the feast never reached its culmination; the party disintegrated, the guests scattered, and Meaulnes returned to school, obsessed with the urgent need to recover the lost realm.

The brief passage through the magic paradise of childhood has completely transformed Augustin. His discovery of never-never land has made him incapable of playing his natural part in the real world of youthful pleasures. This earthy young peasant with his crew-cut hair cannot resume his former role as popular leader of his schoolmates. He becomes a pariah, and his only friend and confidant remains François Seurel, the young son of the schoolmaster. Augustin's efforts to find the road to the domain remain fruitless and his attempts to recreate it in his relations with others are destructive. He does find Valentine, the fiancée for whom the celebration had been prepared and who had deserted Frantz, but his intervention in her life undermines it. The simple-spirited country girl is driven, because of his clumsy persistence, to abandon her home and seek her livelihood on the streets of Paris. He does come close to a reconstitution of the event which had transformed his life, when, through the efforts of François, he finds Yvonne at an idyllic picnic. The reunion is a mournful one, and the general degradation is symbolized by the activities of a group of the same children who had once gently taken him by the hand to lead him to the castle. This time their function is a different one: they are showering blows on a stubborn donkey. Yvonne herself disillusions her admirer by telling him that the castle has been sold to people who razed it for a hunting ground. In a desperate attempt to recreate his lost happiness, Meaulnes does marry Yvonne, but deserts her the morning after the wedding in order to search for her childlike brother. The forlorn bride dies shortly after giving birth to a child, which the narrator takes under his protection. Eventually Meaulnes returns, his mission apparently fulfilled. He brings back Frantz and Valentine, whom he has reunited. Even this success is a questionable one; it has made of the fantastic Frantz and the equally strange Valentine a domesticated couple. As for Meaulnes, he sees his young daughter for the first time, and the narrator recognizes at once that he will take her away and make of her his companion in the continuation of his hopeless quest.

At the beginning of the novel young Seurel recalls the arrival of Meaulnes and notes, "Someone came who robbed me of all the pleasures of a peaceful childhood" (p. 21). Despite this disillusioned tone, the advent of his companion is an auspicious one. It signals the convalescence of François, who had been suffering from coxalgia and who, as their friendship develops, learns to walk again without limping. But when Meaulnes at the end of the novel returns for his child, François sadly writes, "I now knew that big Meaulnes had come back to take from me the only joy which he had bequeathed me" (p. 315). In his attempt to find the lost domain of childhood, the romantic adventurer has become what Supervielle called "un voleur d'enfants," a thief of children.

The pessimistic implications of *The Lost Domain* have been consistently ignored, while the paradise represented by the lost domain for which the protagonist searches in vain has been exalted.[33] Undaunted by the failure of Meaulnes, a number of recent authors have attempted to find the paradise which eluded him. This renaissance is located in the Provence, and its most notable representatives, Jean Giono and Henri Bosco, have their roots in southern France. In the former's *Jean le bleu* (1933) the garden is the symbol of a paradise which is always present in the soul of the child; in the latter's *Culotte the Donkey* (1937) the young protagonist draws all his strength from a garden, as mythic as it is real, from which he never loses contact. The seigneurial estate of Frantz has become overgrown, and the Eden of Bosco is not a park surrounding a castle, but a lush tropical jungle reminiscent of Albine's Le Paradou. But the undeniable beauty of these childhood paradises has been previously compromised. After *The Lost Domain* we know the cost of a paradise which is but the imaginary fulfillment of an adult's dream of childhood. As Yvonne de Galais said, "The world is empty, vacations are finished, . . . and finished too is the mysterious feast." The attempts of Giono and Bosco to create the illusion of a paradise within the real world are as touching and futile as the attempts of children to prolong vacations which are definitely over.

The search for the childhood paradise leads to its ruins, ruins which had already been prefigured by the disintegrating shells of the huts of Paul and Virginia. The sorrowful query of Paul Eluard becomes a natural one which we must all ask ourselves:

> Ai-je jamais été enfant
> Moi qui peux parler de l'enfance
> Comme je parle de la mort[34]

> Have I ever been a child
> I who know how to speak of childhood
> As I speak of death

The poet can talk of the childhood paradise only as of a period which he has never experienced. Indeed, the fragility of the childhood paradise appears all too vulnerable to adult cynicism. Aldous Huxley, in his virulent conclusion to *Point Counter Point* (1928), attempts the final assault and employs derision as his weapon. Burlap, the aging and hypocritical editor of a pious journal, has finally succeeded in seducing Beatrice, a repressed spinster, by playing the role of a helpless child and appealing to her maternal instincts. A few days later his secretary and former inamorata, whom he had sacked as a sacrifice to his new love, commits suicide:

But that was something which Burlap could not foresee. His mood as he walked whistling homewards was one of unmixed contentment. That night he and Beatrice pretended to be two little children and had their bath together. Two little children sitting at opposite ends of the big old-fashioned bath. And what a romp they had! The bathroom was drenched with their splashings. Of such is the Kingdom of Heaven.[35]

It is easier to mock paradise than to sing of it. Nonetheless; Huxley succeeds merely in destroying the sentimental facade of a realm whose erstwhile inhabitants, like St.-John Perse, will continue to celebrate its essence.

The Revenge of the Well-Treated Child

> The unique concern of children is
> to find the weak spot in their masters.
> La Bruyère

Like his infernal counterpart, the child for whom adults attempt to create a paradise occasionally takes his revenge on his well-meaning elders. It is such a revolt, a demonstration of pure ingratitude, that Zola depicts in *A Love Affair* (1878). The novel opens with a scene of high drama. In the middle of the night, the eleven-and-a-half-year-old Jeanne, daughter of the young widow Hélène Grandjean, has a near fatal seizure and is saved thanks to the devotion of her mother and the intervention of Doctor Deberle. Because of the high-strung nature of the child, the physician advises that she "lead an untroubled, happy life without any disturbances."[36] Hélène follows his counsel, creating for her only child the protective, well-regulated paradise in which her chances for survival are enhanced. The well-intentioned suggestion of the doctor and the mother's assiduity in implementing it create a situation which the child exploits shamelessly. Indeed, despite her deep affection for her mother, there is something disquieting about Jeanne. She seems to be the spiritual sister of some of the more disturbing of the enigmatic children. Like them, she is a *puella senex*: "She looked like a little old woman, with the pale eyes of very aged spinsters whom no one will ever love any more" (p. 1040). Among the reassuring fixtures in her peaceful universe is an elderly gentleman, Rambaud, who comes to dinner once a week. Jeanne adores him, and, when he once asks her if she would like him to live with her and her mother forever, the child replies, "Oh, I'd be happy; we would play together, wouldn't we? It would be such fun" (p. 876). However, when Rambaud proposes to her mother, the child turns on both of them and demolishes their dream of a happy family existence. "You know perfectly well that it would kill me" are the simple words with which she destroys their plans. And this is the phrase that she uses over and over to counter any of her mother's natural desires.

Jeanne is not merely a spoiled child; she is a monster of egotism and jealousy. The episode with Rambaud establishes a pattern that is repeated. Thus she idolizes the doctor who had saved her life. When she has her second attack and while her mother and Doctor Deberle are watching over her bedside, she murmurs to them, "I only want you two, real close, oh, close, together" (p. 931). And for a time the two adults live in the illusion that the child sanctions and even sanctifies their love: ". . . the child did not separate them; on the contrary, she brought them closer together, added her innocence to their first night of love" (p. 937). As soon as Jeanne suspects that her mother is genuinely fond of the doctor, her attitude is transformed into a menacing one:

Both were laughing at the child. But Jeanne seemed gradually to be overcome by a malaise; she looked at them furtively, then lowered her head, no longer eating, while a shadow of distrust and anger drained the blood from her face. (p. 939)

From that moment on she turns against Deberle with ferocity and begins unabashedly to tyrannize her mother. The formerly gentle and kind child "now spoke to her mother curtly and imperiously, as if to a maid, bothering her with trifles, becoming impatient, always complaining" (p. 945). And so she undermines the happiness of her mother, who even in her moments of joy thinks to hear the threatening coughing of the child all around her. When one evening her mother does yield to her lover, the child senses it and realizes that she has been vanquished. But in her very defeat she succeeds in destroying this love, even though at the cost of her own life. While her mother lies in the arms of Deberle, Jeanne does what she has always been forbidden to do: she sits by an open window and lets herself be soaked by the storm raging outside. The result is an incurable pneumonia. During the course of her three-week-long agony, she makes it clear to her mother and to Deberle that it is their one night of bliss that is the cause of her impending death. Willfully the child demolishes the relationship between the two architects of her Eden, and in doing so dismantles the paradise they had created for her.

Proust's "Confession of a Girl" (1896) is a variation on this theme of a sadomasochistic daughter who turns upon an adoring and adored mother. In this early story, as in *Remembrance of Things Past*, the childhood paradise is symbolized by "the matinal perfume of lilacs"[37] and is corrupted by the fetid odor of a perverse sensualism. The fourteen-year-old girl lets herself be debauched by a vicious cousin, and this first, passively accepted experience leads her to welcome indiscriminately the advances of other men. Her licentiousness is determined by a terrible inertia against which she offers no resistance. Her will seems to be as lamed as that of Baudelaire. Although her mother is totally unaware of her daughter's conduct, it seems to have a pernicious influence on her and she becomes dangerously ill. This cardiac malady, subconsciously linked with the daughter's behavior, has a profound effect on the girl. With an immense effort she reverts to the role of a dutiful daughter. She pulls herself together, gives up her profligate way of life and accepts as fiancé a suitor acceptable to her mother. The daughter senses that her conduct is closely linked to the health of her mother, and so is hardly surprised that "as if there were a mysterious solidarity between her and my soul, . . . my mother was almost entirely cured" (p. 155). It is during this period, when she "savors the harmony of this profound and pure joy with the fresh serenity of the sky" (p. 155), that she betrays her mother again. The occasion is provided by a party given during the absence of her fiancé. Like the narrator of *Remembrance of Things Past*, who torments his beloved grandmother by drinking cognac, she downs glass upon glass of champagne despite the gentle admonition of her mother. As the dinner is breaking up, she withdraws with one of her former lovers to another room. At the very moment when her face is distorted by the ecstasy she finds in his embrace, she catches sight of herself in a mirror in which she also sees reflected the astonished countenance of her mother, whom the shock of this discovery kills. Like Jeanne, Proust's girl destroys the very person whom she loves most, the author of her happiness.

Conclusion

> The race of children has its sacred laws and keeps
> them for itself.
>
>   Alain

The high drama enacted within the confines of childhood is one entirely internal to the time-bound state of childhood itself, and it assumes heroic proportions only within this strictly limited context. From the adult point of view, the heartrending sobs of a child or its ecstatic transports of pure joy are but immature reactions to trivial episodes which, although their imprint may be indelible, leave no visible scars. Their manifest consequences fade during the course of a long existence. The vicious treatment to which Oliver Twist is subject does not result in any long-lived traumas, and Hugo's mutilated Gwynplaine becomes an adult without psychotic tendencies. The childhood paradise and hell are only temporary realms which at best can be resuscitated through the memory. Constantly at work within the dynamics of a work of art depicting these states there is a dialectical relationship between the present of adulthood and the past of childhood. It is this contrast, perfected in Proust, between different stages in life that gives the drama of childhood a significance which transcends the state itself and which retrospectively can transform it. This double perspective serves as the basis of "Rose Lourdin" (1911), the opening story of Valéry Larbaud's collection of childhood scenes, *Enfantines*. The bulk of this fictional portrait is devoted to the first year the twelve-year-old protagonist spends in a boarding school. Rose Lourdin's dismal existence as a "sad and taciturn girl"[38] with clearly delineated masochistic tendencies is transformed by her adoration for Rosa, a somewhat older fellow pupil. This passionate but not explicitly sexual relationship is interrupted when Rosa, whose overt affair with one of the teachers comes to light, is expelled. Many years later and long after the memory of this childhood tragedy has faded, Rose Lourdin, as a mature and successful woman, finds an old school photograph. From her adult vantage point, there is a disillusioning reduction in proportions. She had earlier depicted a group of pubescent girls, lesbian Lolitas torturing and loving each other in a hothouse atmosphere of female voluptuousness. Now she sees the images of these same pupils and asks herself: "All these girls in their dress uniforms with hair combed straight, was that really us? What miserable figures of orphans, what sad little faces! Faces as ignorant and rough as those of boys" (p. 406). But as she continues to stare at the faded group picture, the face of her beloved Rosa takes on clearer contours, and in the process Rose Lourdin's love reemerges. Her adult indifference gives way to a passion which transforms the former hell of the boarding school into a lost paradise. The proportions of the childhood realm are so indeterminate that shifts in perspective can transform an insignificant event into a critical moment and vice versa; its contours are so vague that heaven and hell become interchangeable.

As mutable as the child's world is when perceived from the exterior, it has an extraordinary internal coherence when experienced from within or when invoked by the involuntary memory. Then the temporary universe through which the child passes on his way to adulthood or extinction takes on many forms, but whatever its shape, its essence is still characterized by intensity. The suffering that the child in hell knows is, unlike the suffering of adults, an all-consuming one. By the same token, the child in paradise experiences a pure bliss that is not vouchsafed to grown-ups. The reason for this heightened experiential existence is that the child, like the animal, has an underdeveloped sense of time. Because the past and future are for him at best abstractions, he lives in an absolute present. Thus the inferno of warfare in which the picaresque child, from Lázaro to the narrator of *The Painted Bird*, exists is an eternal condition. For the child war has no remembered beginning or foreseeable end. Equally permanent is the familial hell. While the reader thinks to know that the child will eventually grow up and escape, Anton Reiser and Carrot Top know only the immediacy of a timeless present of anguish. The children who live in an earthly paradise are equally oblivious of time. Paul and Virginia do not realize the fragility of their island paradise, and childhood in *The Prelude* and in *Remembrance of Things Past* are rendered eternal through memory. Serge Mouret escapes from the timelessness of Le Paradou but finds the unending essence of innocence in the priesthood, while his sister, Désirée, remains a nine-year-old forever.

The childhood world is a separate and yet dependent reality; therefore, contact, even though usually intermittent, is maintained with the adult world. Although such communication is by its very nature imperfect and determined more by necessity than by sympathy, it can assume the most intense forms. This forced interrelationship is most often expressed through hostility. It seems to matter little whether benign parents, such as Jeanne's mother in Zola's *A Love Affair* or the equally devoted one in Proust's "Confessions of a Girl" try to create a paradise for their children, or whether malignant parents, like those portrayed in Vallès's *L'Enfant* (*The Child*), imprison their offspring in a hell which they have constructed. In either case, the child seems resentful of the very effort by adults to shape his world and thus attempts, often successfully, to take revenge on the presumptuous architects of his universe.

In extreme cases this resentment is replaced by indifference, and the child breaks off all communication in order to withdraw into an autonomous universe shaped uniquely by his own imagination. This ultimate isolation is sensitively portrayed by Conrad Aiken in "Silent Snow, Secret Snow" (1932). Young Paul's initial excursion into an imaginary world of eternal snow seems to be a natural extension of a very normal dream and is subconsciously prompted by his equally natural need to maintain his identity as a child. His secret domain provides him with a solitude which occasionally every child needs, "a fortress, a wall behind which he could retreat into heavenly seclusion."[39] Little by little his flights assume neurotic proportions, and his continued explorations inevitably force him to lead a double life which can be only precariously maintained. On the one hand he feels obliged to keep up the appearances of a bright school child and a dutiful son; on the other, he feels seduced by the magic realm from which all others are excluded. To strike a balance becomes more and more difficult as he discovers the marvels of his new universe: ". . . the new world was the profounder and more wonderful of the two. It was irresistible. It was miraculous. Its beauty was simply beyond anything— beyond speech as beyond thought—utterly incommunicable" (p. 221). As he becomes more and more infatuated with the imaginary snow which muffles the external world and separates him from it, he begins gradually to lose touch with reality and simultaneously to become aware of the menace of this absolute beauty:

He loved it—he stood still and loved it. Its beauty was paralyzing— beyond all words, all experience, all dream. No fairy story he had ever read could be compared with it—none had ever given him this extraordinary combination of ethereal loveliness with a something else, unnameable, which was just faintly and deliciously terrifying. (p. 226)

It becomes increasingly difficult for Paul to function in the world of school and family. His automatic responses to adult demands begin to fail, and he finally rejects his mother, who is the incarnation of the others, in order to sink in total isolation into the silent, secret snow of his inner world. The split personality characteristic of so many children results in Paul's case in an extreme form of schizophrenia. This terrifying flight into another world is far from typical. More frequently, some contact remains between children and adults that makes it possible for the latter to describe, even if only through gross approximations, the former's contiguous but foreign habitation.

Although heaven and hell are separate domains, there are children who are destined to pass from one to the other, and who do so with apparent impunity. The evil world of Fagin and Monks is the antithesis of the virtuous world of Mr. Brownlow and Mrs. Maylie. Oliver Twist knows both of them, but as entities forever separated by the buffer of the unconscious. This coexistence of two opposed realities is symbolized in *Remembrance of Things Past* by Combray, the scene of tranquil bliss and morbid jealousy, the locale in which the young Marcel sees Mlle. Vinteuil, in the company of her lesbian lover, desecrate her father's image and in which he also sees his room transformed by the enchantment of a magic lantern. But whether confined in the dungeons of hell or rejoicing in the freedom of heaven or moving from one to the other, the child lives in his universe with intensity. And so the "voci puerili," the childish voices that greet Dante in his ascent toward paradise, are always audible, singing of extreme suffering or extreme bliss.

CHAPTER THREE

Corruption in Paradise

How can I live as a stranger in a house
whose child I was?

Rousseau

Thanatos and Eros

> Je ne sais en quel temps c'était
> Je confonds toujours l'enfance et l'Eden
> Comme je mêle la Mort et la Vie—un pont de douceur les
> relie.

> I know not in what time it was
> I always confuse childhood and Eden
> As I conjoin Death and Life—a bridge of gentleness links
> them.

Léopold Senghor

The various literary depictions of the childhood world have yielded some clues as to its nature. As the examples have demonstrated, it is one of extremes, and, in most cases, it is a dynamic one. As best illustrated by Dickens and Proust, there is a recurrent movement between heaven and hell, between an existence of transcendent ecstasy and one of utter despondency. In a few cases, however, motion is lacking in this universe. The retarded Désirée of Zola's *The Sin of Abbé Mouret* is suspended forever in the atemporal Eden of her physicality, and in *Carrot Top* Jules Renard's protagonist will never emerge from the hell which his parents had constructed around him. But whether it is one of motion or immobility, there seems little formal structure to the childhood universe. If it is a dynamic one, its motion seems characterized by a random vacillation without any discernible progression. If it is one of stasis, there obviously cannot be any development within its continuum of intransmutability. Even the oscillation of the mobile world is sustained by a static fundament, demonstrated in all its monotonous regularity in Alphonse Daudet's *Le Petit Chose* (1868). Like Oliver Twist, Daniel Eyssette passes through a series of alternating heavens and hells in a regular rhythm which does not abate when he attains an age normally associated with adulthood. Even in enterprises which presuppose a certain degree of maturity, like his marriage, with which the volume ends, he acts exactly like the callow, dependent child he was at the beginning. Neither death nor sex has sufficient impact to transform in any significant fashion the course of his life. Throughout his dramatic existence he remains as essentially unchanged as does Désirée in her placid life.

There are some striking exceptions to this general principle of stability. The random and indecisive motion between lethargy and creativity which is typical of the life of the narrator of *Remembrance of Things Past* culminates in his heroic decision to reconstruct Combray. The self-centered Pip of *Great Expectations* does develop into a generous person, and Estella regains the heart which Miss Havisham had ravished from her. A careful study of some important though atypical works shows that the transformations depicted in them are not always fortuitous but a necessary consequence of a preordained pattern.

In general, these metamorphoses assume one of two forms. The aptly named *Bildungsroman* sketches the process of maturation that results in the formation of an adult. It usually traces the gradual passage of its protagonist from childhood to adulthood in a normal development which, no matter how many peripeties, is progressional. In a classic of the genre like Gottfried Keller's *Green Henry* (1854–55), the hero moves through undelineated but incremental stages which merge into each other, and the displacement of the child by the adult is an almost imperceptible process. The boundaries between a naive paradise of transparency and an opaque world of responsibility are indistinct, and it is impossible to tell at what precise point the gates of the former close forever behind the protagonist.

This gradual evolution stands in direct contrast to the violent transformation posited by Jean-Jacques Rousseau and on which all his major works, whether autobiographical, fictional, political, or philosophical, are based. It underlies even such writings as the "Essay on the Origin of Languages," which ostensibly do not deal with childhood. This mythological foundation,[1] which is a formal system of signification, finds its most unambiguous and sumptuous expression in the first part of the *Confessions* (1781–88). The two years (1722 and 1723) that, in the company of his cousin Bernard, the ten- and eleven-year-old Jean-Jacques spent as a boarder in the Lambercier home in Bossey represent the culmination of his childhood. It is a paradise whose inhabitants possess a "reciprocal transparence of consciousnesses"[2] that in retrospect makes possible the impossible state of total communication based on absolute trust. The only menacing note is represented by the voluptuous pleasure Rousseau derives from the corporal chastisement occasionally inflicted on him by Mlle. Lambercier. The inevitable fall, however, is not precipitated by this intrusion of sex. It is an apparently trivial episode that destroys this ideal condition: Jean-Jacques, incriminated by sufficient circumstantial evidence, is unjustly accused of having broken a comb and punished not so much for the crime he had not committed as for his adamant refusal to confess. This is the flimsy but eloquent material which the author uses to create the myth of Bossey and of its destruction, a myth which assumes the significance of its biblical prototype, the expulsion from the garden of Eden. The premises are of universal import: the magnification of the insignificant is, after all, the very basis of most of those serious conflicts between generations which lead to the abolition of childhood. Rousseau presents the drama as a definitive resolution of a condition whose only defect had been its vulnerability:

There was the terminal point of my childhood. From that moment on I ceased to enjoy a pure happiness, and even today I feel that the remembrance of the charms of my childhood stops there. We stayed on for a few more months. Like the representation of the first man, we were still in the terrestrial paradise, but we had ceased enjoying it.[3]

A sudden awareness of injustice precipitated the catastrophe which resulted in the disenchantment of paradise. No longer are the children immune to shame and guilt; instead, they are exposed to all the human vices that lurk within "the obscure and muddy labyrinth" (p. 18) into which they stumble upon their dispossession. Unlike Adam and Eve, who were expelled from a paradise which continued to exist without them and which therefore might be regained, Rousseau and his cousin remain in Bossey but have lost forever the capacity to take delight in it. Their estrangement has made their idyllic abode uninhabitable. Moreover, their exile is not the result of a committed sin but seems rather to be the inevitable result of a preordained and ineluctable process. This, indeed, is what is astonishing and original about the text of the *Confessions*: a translation into universal terms of Rousseau's individual paranoia. The terrible loss of paradise is not due to a fault of the children, who are innocent, nor of the adults, who have every reason to believe in their culpability. In fact, no one is at fault, and the disaster is precipitated by forces beyond the control of those who are their victims.

The Bossey episode represents a radical reinterpretation of the ancient myth of the expulsion from paradise and in its comprehensiveness assumes the status of an original and autonomous myth. The significance of this particular variation on a story which has been retold endless times lies in its structure. Most modern versions of the Fall scrupulously reproduce the linear account of Genesis in which exile, as a punishment for a sin, is a unique experience never to be repeated. In this respect the conclusion of George Eliot's *The Mill on the Floss* (1860) is typical. When, as a consequence of the sale of the mill, Tom and Maggie Tulliver are dispossessed, they enter the adult world of responsibility from which there is no turning back:

They had gone forth together into their new life of sorrow, and they would never more see the sunshine undimmed by remembered cares. They had entered the thorny wilderness, and the golden gates of their childhood had for ever closed behind them.[4]

The closure with which childhood existence at Bossey is terminated is equally conclusive. However, the destruction of Rousseau's paradise is an archetypal event, divorced as it is from any specific fault and emerging from an inherent culpability. Consequently its incessant repetition will dominate the child-adult's existence. After Bossey, the unique event is replayed at Les Charmettes, where, upon his replacement by the rival Wintzenried, Rousseau loses both his regained paradise and his refound mother. Then there is L'Hermitage, where Mme. d'Epinay installs him in the personalized paradise which she has constructed for him and from which he is driven by the calumnies of his "friends." After this he takes up residence in Monlouis, the "enchanted habitation," a small pleasure castle which M. de Luxembourg had restored for him.

Threatened with arrest, he flees to Switzerland and finds an idyllic haven at Môtiers. Eventually stoned by the outraged citizenry, he seeks another refuge, the Ile de Saint-Pierre, from which he is exiled by the officials of Berne. Each of these localities becomes the site of the original paradise, which forces that Rousseau could never understand ultimately rendered uninhabitable. These formalistic repetitions assume the stature of an ineluctable malediction whose victim, like so many heroes of ancient mythology, is doomed to eternal punishment.

So the intrusion of evil into the seemingly innocent universe of children at play is more than a metaphor; it is a ritual that structures a rather important body of the literature that deals with childhood. Initially these works conform to a Rousseauistic vision. They posit the existence of the child within a state of benign nature whose vitality is gradually but inexorably sapped by the forces of civilization. Thus weakened, paradise becomes vulnerable to all the forces inimical to childhood. The actual corruption of what Baudelaire called "le vert paradis des amours enfantines" is subsequently brought about by an incursion of such brutality that the fragile structure of paradise collapses. Whereas in the case of Rousseau this evil originally took the form of a manifest injustice, in most works the childhood world is destroyed by a not unrelated disclosure, namely by the sudden, and often simultaneous, revelation of the mysteries of sex and death. Because Thanatos and Eros have no place in the cosmogony of children and because these two gods cannot be expelled, Eden must be destroyed. The child's sudden awareness of the profound reality of death and sex—so different from an intellectual comprehension of them as concepts— takes the form of a shattering encounter which forever annihilates the prelapsarian world for which, in some cases, the child retains a wistful yearning. This dramatic collapse and the subsequent nostalgia can produce a variety of effects. It can, as in some of Vaughan's and Wordsworth's poems, stimulate and nourish a mystical desire to return to a previous existence. It can also lead to self-abnegation through an absolute faith in a divinity, as in Flaubert's *A Simple Heart*. It can compel its victim, as illustrated by Proust, to a titanic effort at reconstruction, or it can bring about the decision to create a completely new and different world, as in Romain Rolland's *Jean-Christophe*. More frequently, it produces an equally powerful negative effect, in which case the disintegration of paradise can even entail the demise of its former inhabitants, who do not have the stamina to live in another, harsher world. This is certainly the case of the bereaved youth in *Paul and Virginia*, whose death is preceded by madness. Its most terrible consequence is, without a doubt, the total despair into which Chateaubriand's René plunges, for this is a spiritual death as opposed to the physical annihilation of Paul. The most common outcome is also the least dramatic: the eventual acceptance of adult reality on the emotional plane, as in Abel Hermant's *Eddy and Paddy*,[5] or on the political level, as in Sartre's *Childhood of a Leader*.

This obsessive pattern with all its variations will strike most modern psychologists as an aberration, as an artificial construct which represents a negation of reality. Ever since Freud's famous "Essay on Infant Sexuality" (1905), the tendency has been to deny the very possibility of the concept of childhood innocence and hence that of its subsequent corruption. The observed physiological phenomenon of sexual arousal prior to puberty on which Freud based his theory seems an insufficient reason for denying innocence as a viable category. After all, the natural sexual curiosity of an infant must be regarded as being guiltless. In any case, the Freudian argument is irrelevant, for the fact remains that the equation between childhood and innocence is firmly fixed in that popular imagination to which the writers we shall examine appeal. And it is perfectly possible that it is the Freudian hypothesis which is an artificial construct, and that the deep structure underlying certain fictional and poetic works translates a profound reality.

Certainly not all the writers who treat the destruction of innocence conform to a pattern derived from Rousseau. Some, like Jerzy Kosinski, simply ignore it. Others, like Stendhal, seem bent on wilfully denying it. In the latter's *The Charterhouse of Parma* (1839) Fabrizio del Dongo's first encounter with the reality of death appears indeed to be a shattering one. On the battlefield of Waterloo a corpse blocks the path along which the young enthusiast is riding and Fabrice stops short, paralyzed with horror:

Fabrice's face, naturally very pale, took on a most pronounced greenish tinge. . . . Fabrice remained frozen. What struck him most vividly was the filthiness of the feet of this corpse which had already been stripped of its shoes and on whom nothing was left but a ragged pair of pants completely soiled with blood. . . . A bullet had entered next to the nose and passed through the opposite temple and disfigured the corpse in a hideous fashion; one eye had remained open.[6]

The canteen-keeper accompanying Fabrice is not satisfied with the potential warrior's reaction. So that he might become inured to the horrors of death she invites him to descend from his horse and shake hands with the mutilated cadaver. Afraid to appear a coward, Fabrice does her bidding:

Without hesitation, though on the point of vomiting with disgust, Fabrice dismounted, took the hand of the corpse, and shook it firmly; then he stayed there as if demolished; he felt that he no longer had the strength to remount. What had induced his horror more than anything else was that open eye. (p. 59)

The nausea provoked by the physical details of death (the dirty feet and the open eye) prefigures that of Sartre's Roquentin; however, Fabrice's revulsion has no lasting effect. When the kindhearted canteen-keeper sees that her impressionable protégé is on the verge of fainting, she restores him with a glass of aquavit. A few moments afterward, Fabrice is back in his childhood paradise unscathed and, like a little boy playing at war, goes charging off with four other soldiers. When the first bullets whistle by his head, his reaction is one of delighted wonderment, and Stendhal comments sardonically, "Fabrice remained in the enchantment of this curious spectacle" (p. 61). Just as Fabrice is invulnerable while his companions fall all about him, so his childhood paradise remains for the time being intact and, like an impregnable fortress, protects him.

Even Fabrice's paradise of wonderment is not an eternal one. The romantic illusions that give a semblance of substance to the opéra-bouffe world in which he functions are destroyed by the ugly reality so imperfectly hidden by the tarnished façade of courtly life in Parma. Fabrice seeks consolation in the arms of Clélia Conti, but his blissful existence is forever destroyed by the expiatory death of his illegitimate child, Sandrino. Fabrice must retire to the charterhouse of Parma because he has killed his own child and simultaneously his own childhood. So, while denying the power of Thanatos and Eros, Stendhal ultimately renders them homage and affirms the fatalistic vision which makes the corruption of paradise inevitable.

Paradise Lost

The ignominy of childhood; the distress
of boyhood changing into man.
W. B. Yeats

Although the structure of annihilation through death and sex
was first given fictional legitimacy by Rousseau's disciple Bernardin de Saint-Pierre in his *Paul and Virginia,* he did have some pre-
cursors. Most of them, however, had only hinted at the pattern
that he was to impose on his novel, and treated death and sex as
separate elements. Eros as a segregated agent of destruction is a
common topos exploited as early as Horace. In his "Ode on Lalage"
(2.5), he describes the young girl frolicking in carefree fashion
with the bullocks. The calf, however, is destined to become a
charging, passionate bull, and Lalage will bear his full weight, a
weight which will crush her innocent ludic world. By this isolation
of sex Horace anticipates Rousseau, whose first childhood paradise is weakened by his predilection for flagellation and whose second one is undermined through the unease provoked when Mme.
de Warens gives him his sexual initiation. Furthermore, his eventual expulsion from Les Charmettes is immediately preceded by
his brief affair with Mme. de Larnage.

Death as an even more sinister force of corruption is also a
frequent theme in literature. So Grimmelshausen, in the first part
of *Simplicissimus,* clearly distinguishes between death as an abstract concept and death as a reality. When the picaresque child
protagonist first encounters mortality, it has no effect on him. He
is witness to the brutal slaughter of his entire household but remains unmoved because he cannot fathom what is taking place.
Even when confronted with the distinct possibility of his own annihilation, he envisions the soldiers taking aim at him as playing
some abstract game drained of all reality. It is only when he stands
at the deathbed of his first patron that he becomes aware of death
as a reality. Simultaneously, his naive vision of the world begins to
disintegrate. The forest in which he has found a refuge and which
symbolizes the childhood paradise is now filled with marauding
troops who menace his very existence, and he must part from this
innocent world forever.

While some early writers had analyzed the impact of either

death or sex upon the childhood realm, others had hinted at the destructive impact of their dual onslaught. Shakespeare's Ophelia is undone by them, as is Racine's Hippolytus. But it was Bernardin de Saint-Pierre who first systematically analyzed the effects of this unholy alliance and thus posited, in its most elemental terms, the pattern we are studying, and earlier works like *Hamlet* and *Phèdre* serve to give his treatment of the theme a mythic resonance. As we have seen in the analysis of *Paul and Virginia*, a number of elements threaten the Edenic existence of the two children: the social repression of the master-slave relationship that revealed to them the existence of evil, the temptation of wealth, and the civilizing force of the education to which Virginia is subjected. However, these three potentially dangerous influences are ones the children are capable of withstanding. Their innate charity alleviates the pressures of a repressive society, their joy in the pleasures of a simple existence makes them immune to the desire for money, and Virginia's essential goodness protects her against the sophisticated education which her aunt attempts to impose upon her. But these children are powerless when faced with sex and death, for they are two realities which cannot be avoided. The crisis of puberty forces upon them the separation for which the aunt's pressing invitation serves as a convenient excuse. Even without this ostensibly compelling reason for Virginia's departure, their profound sentiment of friendship could not have survived the incestuous implications of a sexual relationship. And so, when Virginia returns, years after their initial separation, it is not for a reunion but for the ultimate divorce which only death can provide. Virginia thought that she was fleeing France in order to regain an innocent childhood paradise, but, because she was actually returning not to the brotherly embrace of a companion but to the arms of a potential lover, the storm which drowns her within Paul's sight must arise just as surely as the monster must emerge from the ocean in order to destroy Hippolytus. And Paul must go mad and die because he does not have the strength to adapt himself to a world in which Thanatos and Eros reign supreme.

This fearful but simple design is what makes of the Gretchen tragedy, embedded at the very center of Goethe's *Faust I* (1808), a drama which surpasses in grandeur the pathetic and potentially sentimental situation on which it is based. It may seem contradictory to consider Gretchen, who is after all over fourteen years old, a child, but that is how both Mephistopheles and Faust see her. They constantly refer to her as such, and the former claims that she is so innocent that she has no reason to go to confession. As for Faust, when he first intrudes into her chamber, he is overwhelmed by the innocent atmosphere of tranquility, order, and contentment that transfuses it. And, as he sits alone dreaming in her bedroom, he imagines her as a child standing by her grandfather's armchair, waiting to receive her Christmas presents. This vision, whose simplicity anticipates the naive childhood images of Victor Hugo's "L'Art d'être grand-père" ("The Art of Being Grandfather"), is followed by one in which he sees her as a little girl lying in her bed:

> Hier lag das Kind, mit warmem Leben
> Den zarten Busen angefüllt,
> Und hier mit heilig reinem Weben
> Entwirkte sich das Götterbild.
> (lines 2713–16)

> Here lay the child, its delicate bosom
> Filled with warm life,
> And here with sacred pure weaving
> Came into being the divine image.

Despite the latent eroticism of these verses, with their barely veiled hints of a sexual awakening, it is the image of the sacred, untouchable child that emerges. The resultant atmosphere of purity is so overwhelming that Faust is ready to renounce his project of seduction: he is afraid to sully an innocence that is holy. But it is too late. Mephistopheles has already brought for Gretchen the box of finery that will tempt her and bring about her downfall. Although she does give in to her mother's insistence that the treasure be turned over to the priest, she agrees to the imposed sacrifice only with resentment. In a natural consequence of external submission accompanied by inner revolt, she conceals from her mother the next gift she receives from Faust. And so deceit enters her world and weakens its foundations. Her childhood paradise is definitively destroyed when, in order to be able to receive her tempter in her bedroom, she agrees to administer an opiate to her mother. The sleep produced by this potion proves eternal. So death and sex enter the sanctum of Gretchen's formerly clean chamber simultaneously. And death continues to be intimately linked with sex: Gretchen's brother, outraged by the seduction of the girl whom he considered the ideal of purity, is slain by Faust, and Gretchen herself drowns the child resulting from her illicit union. As her dying brother tells her brutally, Gretchen the child has become Gretchen the whore. Her virginal chamber represented her childhood paradise. It is replaced by the prison cell in which Faust last sees her prior to her execution.

During the course of the "Walpurgis Night," a central question is raised concerning the reality of the paradise destroyed by sex and death. In the midst of the surrealistic hallucinations of the Blocksberg, Faust, drunk with the unholy evil of the witch's sabbath, suddenly has a sobering vision. He thinks he sees a figure reminiscent of Gretchen: "A pale, beautiful child standing alone and far off" (4184). Mephistopheles vehemently denies the reality of this apparition and admonishes Faust, "Let it be . . . it is a magic image, lifeless, an idol" (4189–90). But Gretchen in her innocence has existed and, despite the negations of the evil spirit, will continue to exist. Her naive, bourgeois Eden has been destroyed, but by her refusal to let Mephistopheles and Faust save her from prison and inevitable execution she gains entrance to an eternal paradise.

The simple design which structures *Paul and Virginia* and the first part of *Faust* recurs constantly and can be seen in such diverse works as Kleist's *Kätchen von Heilbronn*, Musset's *Il faut qu'une porte soit ouverte ou fermée* (*One Door Has to Be Open or Closed*), and Balzac's *Le Lis dans la vallée* (*The Lily in the Valley*). Whereas in them it plays a secondary role, it forms the very substructure of Tolstoy's first published work of fiction, the semiautobiographical novella *Childhood* (1852), which Dostoevski characterized as "a most serious psychological essay dealing with a child's soul."[7] The opening words of the youthful narrator's recital portray in symbolic terms the shattering of his childhood world, an event that will be realized at the end of his story:

On the 12th of August 18——, exactly three days after my tenth birthday, for which I had received such wonderful presents, Karl Ivanych woke me at seven in the morning by hitting at a fly just over my head with a flap made of sugar-bag paper fastened to a stick. His action was so clumsy that he caught the little ikon of my patron-saint, which hung on the headboard of my oak bedstead, and the dead fly fell right on my head.[8]

The sticky flyswatter is an instrument of death, but at the same time it has a phallic form and its coating of syrup is certainly suggestive of sex. So the slumbering child is awakened by an aggressively sexual gesture and by the corpse of the fly, which strikes him in the very center of his intelligence. Sleep, from which he was so rudely wrenched, is the privileged domain of the child in which his "light, serene and reassured soul" drifts. It is an oneiric realm of indistinct but blissful visions: "Dreams would follow one another in quick succession—but what were they about? Elusive and intangible they were but full of pure love and hope of radiant joy" (p. 54).

It is from such an ecstatic state of somnolence that the clumsy actions of the preceptor arouse the child. And as the boy is expelled from this realm, the image of his patron saint (Nicholas) receives a glancing blow that sets it swinging. The assault of sex and death threatens a simple faith. With this portentous episode, the birthday party, with all its festive connotations, recedes far into the distant past (represented by the three days), and even its memory is sullied by the filth of the crushed fly. And so, upon awakening, the boy weeps and, when asked why, instinctively lies by making up the story of a nightmare in which his mother dies. The truth is too awful to reveal, for the tears he sheds are for an innocence he will soon lose, and so he must create a self-fulfilling fiction as a temporary screen from a reality with which he cannot yet cope. This symbolic expulsion from paradise is followed immediately by an all-too-real one. At breakfast the narrator and his older brother are informed that the following morning they are to leave the country estate that is their home for Moscow, where they will receive a "serious" education.

Despite this displacement and despite the arousal of sexual instincts, which brings about two violent accesses of voluptuousness, the soul of the child remains intact during his initiation into civilization. It is only when his fictitious dream is actualized, when he returns to the country estate to be present at the death of his mother, that his childhood comes to a brutal end. However, the impact of death is not immediate. When he sees his comatose mother, his self-consciousness impels him to act as the others expect him to. Such mechanical playacting makes true sorrow impossible, and authentic emotions are replaced by lucid observations. Later on, alone with the open coffin that contains his mother's body, Nicholas is still incapable of anything but feigned feelings. He sees the reality of the cadaver in all its physical details but cannot equate the inert object with the woman he loved. While he gazes fixedly at her remains, his imagination begins to work almost automatically, reconstructing his mother as she had been. There ensues an extraordinary movement between present and past:

Then again visions replaced the reality, to be shattered by the consciousness of the reality. At last my imagination grew weary, it ceased to deceive me. The consciousness of the reality vanished too and I became oblivious of everything. I do not know how long I remained in this state, nor what it was: I only know that for a time I ceased to be aware of my existence and experienced a kind of exalted, ineffably sweet, sad happiness. (p. 93)

This shuttling back and forth, which leads to complete oblivion, also serves to protect the child from the powerful reality of death. It is only at the conclusion of the actual funeral service, during which he has performed the ritual of weeping, and when the mourners pay their last respects, that the young boy encounters death. The originality of Tolstoy's presentation lies in the fact that it is only through another who functions as a temporary surrogate that this meeting takes place. A peasant woman with her five-year-old daughter approaches the casket to depose a final kiss on the brow of her former mistress. The little girl becomes terrified, and her hysteria is imparted to Nicholas:

. . . the peasant woman was standing on a stool by the coffin and struggling to hold the little girl in her arms. The child was pushing with her little fists, throwing back her frightened little face and staring with dilated eyes at the dead woman as she uttered a succession of dreadful frenzied shrieks. I too uttered a cry that, I think, must have been more terrible than the one which had startled me, and ran from the room. (p. 96)

For the first time the child realizes what the insidious and heavy odor was that blended with the smell of incense. The corruption of death, with all its sexual overtones and the revelation of its bitter truth, puts a definitive end to the childhood of Nicholas.

Not all the exploitations of the formulaic pattern are as powerfully simple as that of Tolstoy. It is in Zola's *The Sin of Abbé Mouret* that one of its most complicated expressions is to be found. As we have already seen, the framework of the novel is provided by the immutable physical paradise of Désirée, a universe which is protected by the timelessness implicit in her mental retardation. The substance of the novel consists of the two childhoods of her brother, Serge Mouret, each of which he relives through memory. The first of these is the one he constantly yearns for: the condition of priesthood as a natural extension of his infancy. Despite his apparently detached attitude, he is deeply committed to this state:

> Sometimes he said smilingly that he was continuing his childhood, imagining himself never having grown up, with the same feelings, the same judgments; then at the age of ten he knew God just as well as now at the age of twenty-five. In order to pray to him he had similar inflections of the voice, the childish pleasure of joining his hands with exactness. The world seemed to him the same as the world he used to see when his mother held his hand while walking.[9]

As village curate, he thinks to have found this paradise of eternal infancy, and he has no further desires. And so to his complaining housekeeper he explains, "We have everything we need, we are living in the peace of paradise" (p. 1228). This beatitude is disturbed by a troubling sense of dissatisfaction that has its origins in his first, brief encounter with the pagan world of Le Paradou, an estate which has been abandoned and is now inhabited only by an atheistic caretaker and his daughter, Albine. This troubling incursion provokes a feverish meditation during which the priest recalls his tranquil childhood and the equally peaceful days at the seminary, a period in which his childhood innocence had never been menaced. Now, at this moment of spiritual crisis, he addresses a fervent prayer to the Virgin Mary, whose constant refrain is provided by his desire to remain a child forever: "I would still like to be a child. I would like to be nothing but a child, forever, walking in the shadow of your gown. . . . Make it possible for me to become a child again, . . . make it possible for me to be five years old" (pp. 1313–14). This prayer is vouchsafed him, though not in the form he had expected. A violent brain fever, the consequence of his religious ecstasy, almost costs him his life, and his brother, Doctor Pascal, has him transported in secret to Le Paradou. It is Pascal's hope that the invigorating atmosphere of this wilderness and the ministrations of Albine will restore him.

The second part of *The Sin of Abbé Mouret*, which recounts the convalescence of the young man, is an allegorical recital, a secular version of Genesis. Le Paradou, which is isolated from the rest of the world by a high wall, has fallen into disrepair, and nature has reasserted itself. Only traces of the formal gardens and fragments of statuary remain; the artifice of man is engulfed in a lush, tropical garden. When Serge finally regains consciousness in this Eden, he is quite literally reborn: "He did not remember anything, he was really in a condition of happy infancy. He had the impression that he had just been born the night before" (p. 1319).[10]

Albine treats her patient as the child he is and, when his strength begins to return, teaches him first to walk, and then to speak again: ". . . she enjoyed naming the objects for him which he touched. He was capable only of babbling, stumbling over the syllables, not pronouncing any one word clearly" (p. 1331).

In this first stage of his education, Serge knows the wonderment of a child incapable of comprehending reality and enchanted by the discovery of a new world at which he can only marvel:

It was constantly the astonishment of eyes wide open which did not understand, a hesitation of gestures not knowing how to go where they wanted to go, a beginning of existence, purely instinctive, outside of the knowledge of its surroundings. The man had not yet been born. (p. 1332)

Gradually Serge does become aware of his surroundings, and, in the subsequent months of his recuperation, in the constant company of Albine, he explores the immense garden of delights into which he has miraculously been born. Each day brings a new discovery greeted with the unalloyed joy of a child who has not yet learned that there are limits to his world. Only when he attains adolescence for the second time does Serge see a part of the wall that circumscribes his domain. Unfortunately, this second childhood, unlike his first, must come to an end. In his previous incarnation Serge had never known temptation, but this time, together with his Eve, he becomes gradually aware of the attractions of the flesh. As soon as he succumbs, as soon as he knows Albine carnally in the shadow of the tree of knowledge, he becomes aware of the outside world and is expelled from paradise in order to resume his life as the village priest of Les Artaud. So the brilliant childhood paradise of Le Paradou is but a hiatus within the colorless infantile paradise of his sacerdotage.

Just as Serge relived his original childhood through memory, so, in the same fashion, he reexperiences his second one. In an extraordinary evocation, provoked when Albine confronts him in the church in a desperate attempt to persuade him to return to her, the entire experience of the many months at Le Paradou are compressed into a moment which contains their essence:

> Then he awoke one morning as if new. He was born a second time, disencumbered of all that twenty-five years had successively accumulated within him. In Le Paradou, when he opened his eyes again, without memory of the past, without a vestige of his priesthood, . . . he had saluted the sun, he had marveled at the first tree. (p. 1481)

Automatically and without desire, the priest attempts to give a new ending to the story evoked by memory. He will return to Le Paradou and to Albine. Instead of regaining his paradise lost, an earlier prayer is fulfilled: he is deprived of all the attributes of manhood that he acquired during his stay in Le Paradou. Imprisoned in his sacerdotal childhood, he is as impotent as a newborn infant. Despite Albine's efforts to arouse his virility, he remains completely unresponsive. While she attempts to resuscitate for him memories of their happy past, he hears only the chiming of the church bell announcing the elevation. While she tries to show him the beauties of their garden, he sees only monstrances tracing fiery crosses in the sky. When finally she presses her lips against his, the emasculated priest can only weep. And so Albine, feeling herself rejected, drives him from Le Paradou. This is his second and definitive expulsion, and now, when he returns to the church, it is forever: "The world no longer existed. Temptation had been extinguished, like a fire that was no longer necessary for the purification of this flesh. He was entering a super-human peace" (p. 1510).

The Christian God has vanquished Pan. Without a twinge of regret Serge buries Albine and in doing so consecrates the dominion of death and the abjuration of sex. The eternal childhood paradise of pure innocence has triumphed over the childhood paradise of the senses. But the real paradise of childhood has been destroyed, because the aspirations which give it its dynamism have been extinguished. Désirée lives on in the eternal childhood of a joyful physical existence, while Serge succumbs to the sleep of nothingness.

The utilization of the pattern that becomes so complex in Zola's novel is by no means limited to authors of fiction but can be found in poets from Novalis to Eluard. In "Le Bateau ivre" ("The Drunken Boat") (1871) Rimbaud gives it its richest lyrical expression. The poem opens with the jubilant liberation of the child from all the restraints of civilization, represented by the ropes with which the haulers had been guiding the ship down the river. The imagery, violent as it is, is characterized by the primeval innocence of the children's picture books that did, in fact, inspire it.[11] "More unheeding than the minds of children" ("Plus sourds que les cerveaux d'enfants") (line 10), the boat plunges into the ocean. The tempest blesses this joyful departure, which is as lighthearted as only a child's carefree excursion can be: "Lighter than a cork, I danced on the waves" ("Plus léger qu'un bouchon j'ai dansé sur les flots") (line 14). At the outset of this fabulous navigation the child is blissfully unaware of the menace of death and is heedless of the fact that he is dancing on the surface of an element "which is called the eternal roller of victims" ("Qu'on appelle rouleurs éternels de victimes") (line 15). But this oblivion is shattered by repeated encounters with the reality of death in the form of corpses descending silently into the depths of the ocean: "Drowned men sank down to sleep, backwards" ("Des noyés descendaient dormir, à reculons") (line 68). Simultaneously, the reality of sex, more powerful than the intoxication of the child and greater than his inspiration, sullies the waters through which he moves:

> Plus fortes que l'alcool, plus vastes que nos lyres,
> Fermentent les rousseurs amères de l'amour!

> Stronger than alcohol, vaster than our lyres
> The bitter russets of love ferment!
>
> (lines 27–28)

So it is death and sex that bring about the shipwreck of the intoxicated vessel and destroy the childhood paradise so irrevocably that the poet is incapable of depicting it even to his peers. "I would have liked to show children these dolphins / Of the deep blue . . ." ("J'aurais voulu montrer aux enfants ces dorades / Du flot bleu . . .") (lines 57–58) the poet cries out, but the past conditional tense he employs proves his inability to communicate the marvels he had discovered. The delirious voyage has been reduced to the limited drifting of a fragile toy boat set afloat on a puddle by a disconsolate child.

The vulnerability of the childhood paradise is obvious. Because the consequences of its destruction can be as dreadful as the madness and death of Paul and Gretchen or can lead to the emptiness and sterility of Serge or of the narrator of "The Drunken Boat," extraordinary measures are often taken to maintain it. The vanity of such efforts is a recurrent topos in literature. In Chrétien de Troyes' *Story of the Holy Grail* Perceval's mother raises her son in absolute isolation and in total ignorance of the world, but his eventual escape from his childhood paradise causes the death of his protectress. Holden Caulfield, in Salinger's *Catcher in the Rye*, wants to protect his little sister's innocence at all costs, but he is incapable of effacing from the walls of her school the obscenities that threaten her virginal existence. The enterprise of defending what is doomed by fate is ineffectual and can be as disastrous as simple submission to an ineluctable destiny. This is the bitter lesson which the governess of Miles and Flora in Henry James's *The Turn of the Screw* (1898) seems incapable of learning.[12] When she arrives at Bly, the estate is to her eyes the perfect childhood paradise as envisioned by adults, a haven all the more lovely to her because she had been deprived of a similar retreat when young:

I remember as a thoroughly pleasant impression the broad clear front, its open windows and fresh curtains and the pair of maids looking out; I remember the lawn and the bright flowers and the crunch of my wheels on the gravel and the clustered treetops over which the rooks circled and cawed in the golden sky. The scene had a greatness that made it a different affair from my own scant home, and there immediately appeared at the door, with a little girl in her hand, a civil person who dropped me as decent a curtsey as if I had been the mistress or a distinguished visitor.[13]

The denizens of Bly appear to the governess as perfect as the paradise which they inhabit. Of Flora she notes that she "affected me on the spot as a creature too charming not to make it a great fortune to have to do with her. She was the most beautiful child I had ever seen" (p. 7). Furthermore, ". . . it was a comfort that there could be no uneasiness in a connection with anything as beatific as the radiant image of my little girl" (p. 8). The governess goes on to describe her first sight of her little charge as a vision of angelic beauty. The initial impression made by Flora's brother, though he had been expelled from school, is equally positive. As soon as the governess perceives him, she thinks to have encountered the essence of perfection, that same translucence to which Rousseau had aspired at Bossey: "I had seen him on the instant, without and within, in the great glow of freshness, the same positive fragrance of purity. . . . He was incredibly beautiful" (p. 13). The enthusiasm of the governess knows no bounds, and she is certain that there is something divine about him because of "his indescribable little air of knowing nothing in the world but love" (p. 13). Even the housekeeper is depicted in idyllic terms. Mrs. Grose is a "stout simple plain clean wholesome woman" (p. 7) with whom the governess can establish a good relationship. So, out of the fragments of life at Bly, the governess constructs the Victorian fairy-tale paradise for which she has always longed and from which the sullying realities of death and sex are banished. The transparence of this world and its inhabitants is illusory; only the shimmering surface that bedazzles the governess blinds her to the possibility that it is a brilliant creation woven of self-deceit and the lies of the others. As in so many paradises, there are suppressed and sinister forces at work which cannot forever be denied and which menace its stability, forces in this case represented by the "ghosts" of Miss Jessel and Peter Quint. As former lovers who had met a violent and mysterious end, the apparitions of this disreputable couple clearly represent death and sex in an unholy alliance. The governess interprets their goal as the seduction of the two innocent children, and, in order to preserve the childhood paradise of Flora and Miles, she is prepared to risk everything by precipitating a direct encounter with evil. Flora must leave Bly forever in the company of Mrs. Grose, and Miles is left alone with the self-appointed guardian of his paradise, a guardian who is prepared to sacrifice him for the maintenance of the ideal dreamworld. Ultimately the governess grasps Miles in her arms to save him from the blandishments of Peter Quint, but the boy dies in her embrace. Thus she plunges him into the very realm from which she sought to save him; and in doing so she loses everything. The governess has refused to recognize the inexorability of the forces with which the children consorted. Her obduracy does not preserve the childhood paradise intact; one of its inhabitants escapes it through death and the other through expulsion.

The desperate defense of a childhood paradise which transforms the governess in *The Turn of the Screw* into a murderess is also the motivating force behind Elizabeth's equally portentous measures in Jean Cocteau's *The Holy Terrors* (1929). However, the paradise which the latter seeks to maintain intact has little superficial resemblance to the rustic domain of Bly. Its locale is not a country estate but a squalid Parisian apartment, and its inhabitants are not a couple of beautifully dressed, handsome children who might have stepped straight out of a Gainsborough portrait, but a pair of perverse urban teenagers who would have felt at home in the underworld of Toulouse-Lautrec. The magic realm of childhood as depicted by Cocteau is not as simple as that of Bernardin de Saint-Pierre, and it contains as many terrors as it does charms. Its cult requires of its participants "ruses, victims, summary judgments, horrors, tortures, human sacrifices."[14] Not that Cocteau is blind to the delights of childhood. All its wonders are apparent in the snowstorm with which the novel opens and which casts an enchantment over the "cité Monthiers." The enclosed square is transformed into a medieval courtyard, and the ruddy-faced boys, released from school, make of it a battleground for a splendid snowball fight. However, what has all the makings of a childhood idyll turns into a nightmare.[15] As young Paul runs ecstatically toward his idol, the older Dargelos, he is struck in the chest by a tightly packed snowball containing a stone. The missile has been hurled by Dargelos himself, still standing proudly on the imaginary ramparts, and the impact is so powerful that Paul reels and falls to the ground, bleeding from his mouth. This blow, struck by death in the guise of a schoolboy, is not sufficient immediately to shatter Paul's imaginary universe, and he remains suspended in an unreal atmosphere conducive to hallucinations. So it is only natural that, as his friend Gérard takes him home in a cab, the regular movement of the vehicle rocks him into a dreamworld: "This entire dream lifted him up into a zone of ecstasy" (p. 23).

Neither the snow-covered battlefield of the "cité Monthiers" nor the magical interior of the swaying cab contains the "real" paradise of childhood into which Paul must find his way back:

Above all, it was necessary, at whatever price, to return to this reality of childhood, a serious, heroic, and mysterious reality, whose magicality is nourished by humble details and which the questioning of adults interrupts brutally. (pp. 24–25)

The realm of this separate reality is the room which Paul shares with his sister Elizabeth, a warehouse of trash accumulated—and transfigured—by the children. It is in this magic chamber that they play their "game," which begins in "the semiconsciousness into which children plunge" (p. 26) and which, through a hypnotic trance, leads them into a kingdom apart, a dream within the dream of the room: ". . . he had learned to remain awake while sleeping a sleep which makes you invulnerable and which gives back to objects their real meaning" (p. 27). It is a visionary world, similar to one induced by drugs and far removed from the sordid one of reality that is dominated by their mother, the widow of an adulterous dypsomaniac who had been paralyzed by a stroke. It is also a world to which they can devote themselves exclusively, for Paul, in the aftermath of his chest wound, is indefinitely excused from school.

The ideal realm of the children is a protected one, and even their brutally shocking discovery of their mother's death (they collide with her corpse while chasing each other) seems only to enhance its sinister beauty. One adult, the maid Mariette, understands their world and acts as the beneficent spirit who provides the material means for its continued maintenance. In her total simplicity ". . . this uneducated Breton deciphered the hieroglyphs of childhood" (pp. 69–70) and ". . . her simplicity communicated to her the comprehensive genius which made it possible for her to respect the creative genius of the room" (pp. 70–71). The strange existence which Paul and Elizabeth, in their total isolation from practical exigencies and societal demands, lead is disturbing enough as it is; what makes it even more troubling is its continuance over the years: "Elizabeth and Paul, made for childhood, continued to live as if they inhabited two twin cribs" (p. 111). What seemed dubious enough when the children were fourteen and sixteen years old becomes monstrously perverse when they attain the ages of seventeen and nineteen. But just as during adolescence they had remained "incapable of discerning good from evil" (p. 89), so it is as young adults that they achieve "the plenitude of innocence" (p. 95). Without a trace of self-consciousness they take baths together in the presence of Gérard, but their universe is so sexless that there are no incestuous overtones to their communal nudity. Similarly, when Paul begins to frequent streetwalkers, he describes the physical details of his casual encounters to his sister with a disarming frankness that is a proof of his essential innocence. As for Elizabeth, her virginity is impregnable. When she does marry the wealthy American Michaël, he is killed between the wedding ceremony and its consummation in a bizarre automobile accident that is both a macabre reenactment of the death of Isadora Duncan[16] and that of the biblical Absalom. The impact of this death is minimal: Elizabeth and Paul reconstruct their magic room within the mansion that her husband has left her, and the "game," from which Michaël is no longer excluded now that he has shed his corporeality, goes on as before.

Eventually, however, this artificial childhood paradise is undone through the dual onslaught of sex and death. The agent of destruction is Agathe, a simple girl whom Elizabeth has introduced into the room and whom she has initiated into its mysteries. Cocteau chose the name of this nemesis carefully and must have had in mind the Agathe of Baudelaire's "Moestae et Errabunda" (from *The Flowers of Evil*), who had enabled the poet to discover "the innocent paradise replete with furtive pleasures" as well as "the green paradise of childhood loves." Paul immediately recognizes Agathe for what she is: a reincarnation of Dargelos, the harbinger of death who had so fascinated him. She exerts a powerful sexual attraction on him, and, for the first time, he falls in love. Simultaneously, there is a disintegration of the "game," and Cocteau notes that the "children's feasts were completely disorganized by her presence" (p. 131). When Elizabeth (who has been dreaming of *Paul and Virginia*) learns of their love, she sets everything in motion to render it impossible. Like James's governess, she is determined to protect the childhood paradise no matter what the consequences may be. She plays the role of an intriguer in a Racinian tragedy and, by marrying Gérard off to Agathe, is at first successful. But high drama rapidly disintegrates into cheap melodrama, and, while Elizabeth temporarily maintains the semblance of their former paradise, which is now based on lies and thus fragile, her plotting "made of the secret room a theater open to spectators" (p. 227). The double suicide of brother and sister is the inevitable outcome of the revelation of Elizabeth's scheming, but it is precipitated by a powerful drug sent by Dargelos. Paul's existence in his artificial paradise has been only a hiatus between the initial blow of the snowball and the deadly consequences of its impact. Over the years, the fatal snowball has been transformed into the sphere of poison which destroys paradise and reduces the magic games of childhood to the dimensions of a series of tawdry incidents that at best could provide matter for a sensational newspaper item.

The Holy Terrors is but one of numerous twentieth-century

works based on the undermining of a paradise by sex and death, and the popularity which many of them have achieved indicates that this pattern is one that corresponds to a deep human reality to which the reader responds with an unconscious shock of recognition.[17] These various manifestations of an immutable formula range from Graham Greene's *The Fallen Idol* (1935), which represents a classical model,[18] to Jean Varoujean's *Viendra-t-il un autre été?* (*Will There Be Another Summer?*) (1973), one of the best of the more revolutionary variations. Few novels, through the originality of their presentation of the theme, occupy a place apart, and among them is Richard Hughes's *A High Wind in Jamaica* (1928). Superficially there may seem little to distinguish this fiction from many other thematically related ones. The lush tropical jungle of the West Indies in which the Bas-Thorntons, unencumbered by the burdens of civilization, thrive is not that different from the equally exotic Ile-de-France in which Paul and Virginia grow up without the benefits of a formal education. Of the former, Hughes notes that "it was a kind of paradise for English children to come to,"[19] and with merely a change in nationality Bernardin de Saint-Pierre might have said the same about the island he depicts. Moreover, Hughes's world is as devoid of sex as that depicted by his predecessor: "The difference between boys and girls . . . had to be left to look after itself" (p. 16), and the children have no compunctions about swimming together in the nude. But there is a profound difference, which is typified by the omnipresence of death in *A High Wind in Jamaica* and by its ambiguous impact on the lives of the children.

Initially, death seems to have no reality for the children, but actually there is only a postponement of recognition far more extensive than the one in Tolstoy's *Childhood*. The true impact of death, like the impact of the snowball in *The Holy Terrors*, is felt only long after the initial encounter with it, but in the interval it accrues an immense force. The self-centered nature of the children's universe seems to protect them against an immediate realization of the implications of mortality. A Negro, gorged with green mangoes, has drowned in their bathing-hole, but this accident, grim as it is, does not interrupt the pleasure they take in swimming. In fact, they are rather pleased because the superstitious natives, for fear of the dead man's "duppy," avoid what now becomes their private domain. Another, far more dramatic death, which they witness firsthand, leaves them equally unmoved. During the hurricane that lays waste the island, Old Sam is struck by lightning. The father drags the limp corpse into the house and, to protect the sensibilities of the children, leaves him in the corridor. But the two older children discover the body and are fascinated, not traumatized, by the sight: "Emily and John slipped unbeknownst into the passage, and were thrilled beyond measure at the way he [Sam] dangled: they could hardly tear themselves away" (p. 35). But there is another victim of the violent storm whose brutal death has a much more powerful effect on the children. During dinner, their Tabby flashes into the house, pursued by a whole gang of murderous wildcats. The ensuing scene is one of high drama:

. . . they were, in the passage, caterwauling in concert: and as if at their incantation the thunder awoke anew, and the lightning nullified the meagre table lamp. Tabby, his fur on end, pranced up and down the room, his eyes blazing, talking . . . in a tone of voice . . . which made their blood run cold. He seemed like one inspired in the presence of Death, he had gone utterly Delphic: and without in the passage Hell's pandemonium reigned terrifically. (p. 33)

The horror is hardly mitigated by the incongruous slapstick humor of the scene, as Tabby and a dozen of the jungle beasts come crashing through the fanlight, onto the dinner table, upsetting the lamp and supper. The animals disappear into the jungle, where Tabby is torn to pieces by his tormentors. The fate of their pet does indeed upset the children, and especially Emily.[20] It "seemed a horror beyond all bearing. It was her first intimate contact with death" (p. 39). And yet even such an unmediated encounter with the reality of death shakes her only intermittently. Her remedy for this, as for all other unpleasantnesses, is the evocation of the memory of the earthquake she has once witnessed, a memory which serves as a miraculous refuge and which thus protects, at least temporarily, the innocence of her childhood paradise.

There is another, even more effective defense mechanism than memory against a reality that is too overwhelming to face, and that is the absolute refusal of recognition. It is to such a negation that the children have recourse when the eldest, John, is killed. The incident occurs after their parents have shipped them off on the *Clorinda* with England as their ultimate destination and after they have been inadvertently captured by a disreputable band of totally incompetent buccaneers. Hughes used the beginning of what turns out to be their not-so-innocent voyage as a demonstration of the irrelevance for children of the actual geographic locale of their paradise. So the memory of their parents and their life in Jamaica recedes as rapidly and as irrevocably as the shoreline, and the little ones reconstruct their own world on board the passenger ship without even thinking about it. When they are transferred to the pirateer, the transition is equally smooth. The youngest, Laura, hardly four years old, at once sets out to transform the heterogeneous objects she finds into the inhabitants of her imaginary menagerie, and she does so in the midst of the unruly pirates as easily as she had in the sanctity of her home. This adaptability is made possible by the atemporal nature of their fundamentally malleable universe: "They lived in the present, adapted themselves to it, and might have been born in a hammock and christened at a binnacle before they had been there [on board the schooner] many weeks" (p. 109). The tragedy that fails to disrupt their existence occurs when the schooner lands at Santa Lucia, where Captain Jansen and Otto, his first mate, vainly attempt to dispose of their loot and the troublesome children. On the evening after the disastrous auction one of the sailors takes some of his charges to see a premature nativity play with live animals, which is to be staged by the local priest. The burlesque humor which undermines the drama gives this event the same surrealistic, mad quality of the wildcat battle. A recalcitrant cow, supported by a broad bellyband, is being hoisted to the top floor of the building. John watches in fascination the "slowly revolving cow treading the air a yard from the sill, while at each revolution a Negro reached out . . . trying to catch her by the tail" (p. 82). In his excitement, the boy leans out too far, loses his balance, and plunges out of the window to the ground forty feet below. In a wild sequence (probably inspired by the zany burlesque of the silent movies) the sailor jumps onto the back of the suspended cow and is hastily lowered to the ground, but to no avail; John's neck is broken. The reaction of the children is quite simply to deny this reality and even the reality that was represented by their living brother. When they return on board they do not mention John's disappearance and talk only about the cow-catching trick. Nor do the others, in silent complicity, ever broach the subject of the forever absent brother. So effective is this total negation that they, like their confidante at the end of the novel, might have exclaimed: "*John*? Why who is John?" (p. 173).

Emily's childhood world seems as impervious to the reality of sex as to that of death, but this, too, is the effect of delayed reaction. One night there is a brutal encounter between her and Jansen (whom all the children idolized). Totally inebriated, he staggers toward Emily with the obvious intention of raping her. Instinctively she bites the captain's thumb hard, and he retires sobered. All the children, including the intended victim, are deeply shocked, not by the captain's attempt, which they had not even understood, but by Emily's violent and rude reaction. That sexual innocence cannot be perpetually maintained, however, is exemplified by Margaret Hernandez, the daughter of a Creole family, who had also been sent on the *Clorinda*. Only a few years older than Emily, she is taken advantage of. Before her voyage is over, the sexually abused child lapses into autistic imbecility.

Sex and death cannot be denied forever and in a crucial scene assert their power. While her younger brothers and sisters continue to live on in their make-believe world, playing at being pirates in emulation of their captors, Emily's universe is corrupted. Severely wounded in the leg by a marlin spike which Rachel inadvertently dropped, Emily is bedded down in the captain's cabin. During her convalescence, the pirates undertake the capture of another ship, tie its recalcitrant captain up in the cabin, and leave him in Emily's care while they inspect their booty. Thus the stage is set for the third of the macabre scenes in which outrageous comedy is juxtaposed with a stark depiction of death. The only loot the luckless sailors find is liquor, to which they help themselves freely, and two cages containing a lion and a tiger. Inspired by drink, they decide to set up a circus for the children by releasing the two seasick beasts; by prodding them, they hope to encourage the unwilling animals to do battle with each other. In a brilliant exploitation of the technique of simultaneism, Hughes depicts Emily in the isolation of the cabin, all this while watching over the trussed-up Captain Vandervoort with terror. While Otto twists the lethargic tiger's tail in a vain effort to get him to attack the lion, Emily sees the Dutchman trying to roll himself near a knife that the ever-careless pirates have left on the floor. Feverish because of her wound and feeling menaced by the hapless captive, who merely wants to cut the cord that imprisons him, Emily manages to roll out of the bunk and seize the knife. While Otto is cuffed and severely mauled by the suddenly aroused tiger, Emily hysterically stabs her victim a dozen times. The only witness to the slaying of the captain, and a silent one at that, is Margaret, whom the intoxicated pirates, upon their return, take to be the murderess.

This dramatic encounter with death, and a death which she herself has inflicted, does not bring about the immediate collapse of Emily's paradise. It becomes the focal point of a gradual process of disintegration that has begun earlier. It is around it that the previous encounters with death, which had seemed so insignificant at the time, assume all the reality that previously unnoticed they had always possessed. After the murder Emily reminisces, as before, about her life in Jamaica. But now her memories center on the sinister corpse floating in the swimming pool, on Old Sam struck by lightning, and on Tabby torn to pieces by the wildcats. Under the burden of these accumulated deaths with their delayed impact, she becomes a "poor little outcast" (p. 130), and, as in the case of Margaret, her illness and misery "had been in direct proportion to the childhood she had belied" (p. 126). An equation is made between sex and death: in one of Emily's terrible nightmares the look of her terrorized cat when faced with annihilation and that of the captain when she had bitten his thumb merge and become indistinguishable. Her dread is not limited to her dreams. At first her intermittent moments of awareness while awake are not so threatening because they are interrupted by periods when she can still play in the world of little children. But gradually lucidity becomes more frequent and more persistent:

. . . those times of consciousness . . . were become sinister. Life threatened to be no longer an incessant, automatic discharge of energy: more and more often, and when least expected, all that would suddenly drop from her, and she would remember that she was *Emily*, who had killed . . . and who was *here*. . . . (p. 130)

It is only weeks after the murder, just prior to the children's rescue, that permanent disillusionment sets in. As so often before "The awful, blood-covered face of the Dutch captain seemed to threaten her out of the air" (p. 154). Although as previously the hallucinatory countenance fades, this time she is left stranded forever in the sober world of adult reality:

... her eyes roamed round the sinister reality of the schooner. She suddenly felt sick to death of it all: tired, beyond words tired. Why must she be chained for ever to this awful life? Could she never escape, never get back to the ordinary life little girls lead, with their papas and mamas and ... birthday cakes? (p. 155)

It is at this very moment that the pirates succeed in making the arrangements to transfer her and her companions to the passenger vessel which will carry them to England for the long-delayed reunion with their parents. And it is high time for Emily to debark, for the pirate ship has lost its aura of magic for her. Emily's world has been permanently disenchanted and so she is expelled from it.

The depressing finality of this exile seems belied by the apparently optimistic concluding paragraph of the novel. After all she has gone through, her parents place Emily in an English school, and, while they are having tea with the headmistress, Emily joins her new playmates and seems to find her place in a newly reconstituted childhood paradise. It is on this note that the story ends:

Looking at that gentle, happy throng of clean innocent faces and soft graceful limbs, listening to the ceaseless, artless babble of chatter rising, perhaps God could have picked out from among them which was Emily: but I am sure that I could not. (p. 191)

This cheerful portrait becomes highly ambiguous if we consider that the author may be mocking the obtuseness of the narrator. It becomes even more dubious if we consider the events which take place between the family reunion and Emily's entry into an idyllic school life. The pirates have been brought to trial, but their conviction depends on evidence that they had murdered the Dutchman, whose body has never been found. Emily, the only articulate witness to this incident, has never mentioned it since her return, and the prosecutor's blandishments do not succeed in eliciting any information from her. It is only when she is put on the stand and questioned by the attorney for the defense that the self-contained girl seems to become hysterical and through her tears blurts out the very words that will put the noose around the necks of Jansen and his crew. Is she an overwrought child who does not know what she is doing and who gives way under the pressures of the interrogation, or is she a calculating adult, desperately defending herself and knowingly sending others to the gallows for the crime she has committed? Has she condemned her erstwhile heroes inadvertently or sacrificed them knowingly? After her damning evidence her father lifts the sobbing girl out of the box, and, as her eyes meet those of Jansen, she recognizes his look once more as the same one she saw when the captain's face, in a moment of sexual arousal, merged with that of Tabby on the point of being dismembered. After this fleeting reevocation of Eros and Thanatos, the gods who had dismantled her paradise, she finds herself back in the protective cab, regains her self-composure and artlessly asks her father, "What was it all about?" Mr. Bas-Thornton's reaction is significant:

Mr. Thornton made no attempt to answer her questions: he even shrank back, physically, from touching his child Emily. His mind reeled with many possibilities. Was it conceivable she was such an idiot as really not to know what it was all about? Could she possibly not know what she had done? He stole a look at her innocent little face, even the tear-stains now gone. What was he to think? (p. 189)

And what is the reader to think? That depends very much on whom he considers more perceptive, Mr. Bas-Thornton or the narrator.

William Golding's allegorical adventure tale, *Lord of the Flies* (1954), though equally dense, is far less ambiguous in its rigorous demolition of the Rousseauistic vision of children as noble savages, incorruptible within a state of nature, than *A High Wind in Jamaica*. Nor is the paradise presented at the outset as being as resistant as that of Emily. In fact, because the inherently evil nature of the human species can manifest itself in early childhood, it collapses almost before it is possessed. The group of boys (whose number remains indeterminate) ranging in age from six to twelve are the survivors of the crash of an airplane that had been chartered to evacuate them from the perils of World War II. Ralph and Piggy, the first of the children to find their way to the beach of the uninhabited tropical island where the others will soon gather, exult in the freedom which they discover in their paradise. And Ralph is perfectly aware of the nature of the newfound land: "Here at last was the imagined but never fully realized place leaping into real life."[21] The defining feature of their pristine world is a negative one that, because of the lack of a positive counterpart, will lead to its rapid dismantlement. This quality is the absence of grown-ups and consequently of the arbitrary rules which they impose. Optimistically, Ralph shouts to his new friends, "This is our island. It's a good island. Until the grown-ups come to fetch us we'll have fun" (p. 30). Little does he realize that before the adults arrive to save him he will become the panicky prey of boys turned into far-from-noble savages intent on skewering him on the sticks they have carefully sharpened at both ends for this purpose. Nor does he imagine that, when the navy does come to the rescue, he will "weep for the end of innocence" (p. 186). Blissfully unaware of the fate which awaits him, fresh with the joy of discovery and his spirits buoyed by the realization that there are no more adults, Ralph gives expression to his ecstasy by turning somersaults. Then, in another physical manifestation of unadulterated joy, he strips off his clothes and plunges naked into a tidal pool. This cavorting in the nude and the subsequent ablutions are an exuberant expression of absolute innocence. However, his eventual realization that salt water, like perspiration, is unsuitable for washing a body and clothes made filthy by the grime of the jungle signals a sullying of innocence as well. Even grimmer is the fact that the carefree prancing on the beach will degenerate into the ritualistic tribal dance that culminates in the slaughter of Simon.

Paradise, if it is to be meaningful, must be appropriated, and so it is only natural that one of the first acts of the boys is to take possession of their property. After exploring the island and climbing a peak which dominates it, Ralph turns to his companions and proudly proclaims, "This belongs to us" (p. 25). In their thoughtlessness and lack of experience, the boys waste no time in mistreating their newly claimed dominion. While trying to light their first signal fire, they set half the island ablaze, and in the conflagration one of the little children is lost. As in *A High Wind in Jamaica*, there is a steadfast refusal by all those concerned to acknowledge this disappearance. In any case, the murderous fire is only the first step in a process of despoliation, for the arrival of the children constitutes an ecological disaster. They besmirch everything, and their indiscriminate disposal of their own excrement threatens to befoul the fruit that is the surest source of their sustenance. By polluting their environment, the children poison the paradise they have found. In a striking parallel, "that glamour, that strange invisible light of friendship, adventure and content" (p. 35) with which their heady adventure began cannot endure.

Paradise is corroded first by fear, the nameless and unutterable terror of the smallest children, but which all of them share to a greater or lesser degree and which has been provoked by their nightmare of a "beastie," a monster which they imagine may have emerged from the ocean. It is a horror that will eventually dominate them all. Its source of inspiration is the "lord of the flies" and it is given concrete shape by a cadaver swaying to and fro in the treetops. Their thoughtless happiness is undermined as well by a sentiment not unrelated to their fear, namely the feeling of discomfiture that accompanies the awakening of an awareness of potential evil. During one of their walks Jack attempts unsuccessfully to slay a wild piglet. At the last minute he stays his hand because he realizes what an enormity the downward stroke of his knife would be. As the little animal scurries away, "He [Jack] noticed that he still held the knife aloft and brought his arm down replacing the blade in the sheath. Then they all laughed ashamedly . . ." (p. 27). This sense of embarrassment, which is the direct consequence of incipient self-consciousness, is akin to the dissatisfaction arising from the failure to consummate a sexual act which had been initiated out of bravado. It is the same shame that Adam and Eve experienced upon their expulsion from the garden of Eden, and, like their forebears, the children renounce nudity. But to hide their bodies from themselves, they do not use fig leaves but war paint, a grotesque form of makeup that prevents them from recognizing themselves and makes it possible for them to transform themselves into the killers whom their civilized education had suppressed.

The aborted slaughter of the piglet and the subsequent successful massacre of a pig are ominous but unheeded warnings which serve as the prelude to the actual slaying of a sow. The depiction of what is evidently a vengeful attack upon the mother is famous for its Oedipal overtones:

. . . she [the sow] squealed and bucked and the air was full of sweat and noise and blood and terror. Roger ran around the heap, prodding with his spear whenever pigflesh appeared. Jack was on top of the sow, stabbing downward with his knife. Roger found a lodgment for his point and began to push until he was leaning with his whole weight. The spear moved forward inch by inch and the terrified squealing became a high-pitched scream. Then Jack found the throat and the hot blood spouted over his hands. The sow collapsed under them and they were heavy and fulfilled upon her. (p. 125)

This communal attack, with its overt, heavy-handed sexual symbolism, and the ensuing feast, in which all the boys participate in the consumption of the victim, mark the simultaneous triumph of Eros and Thanatos. Prior to this horrifying act of group sex, murder, and cannibalism, Ralph, even when disenchanted, has managed occasionally to reinvoke paradise through memory, and even when retrospection fails, there is still hope for the future. He can be cynical: ". . . remembering that first enthusiastic exploration as though it were part of a brighter childhood, he [Ralph] smiled jeeringly" (p. 70). But the bitterness provoked by the juxtaposition of a radiant past and a desolate present is alleviated by intuitions of a brighter future. So Ralph calls the others together and exhorts them:

"We've got to talk about this fear and decide there's nothing in it. I'm frightened myself, sometimes; only that's nonsense! Like bogies. Then, when we've decided, we can start again and be careful about things like the fire." A picture of three boys walking along the bright beach flitted through his mind. "And be happy." (p. 76)

But after the killing of the sow, Ralph, whose memory becomes progressively more defective, is no longer able to find consolation in the past; nor is he able to envisage a future, a failing symbolized by his sudden inability even to remember why he wanted to keep the signal fire going. As cruel as the subsequent actions of the children are (the sacrificial murder of Simon, who had tried to bring enlightenment down to them from the mountain; the calculated assassination of the intellectual Piggy, whose spectacles had made possible the fire with which they roast pigs; and the attempt on the life of Ralph, who had tried to provide them with the shelter of moderate leadership), they are but ceremonial reenactments of the archetypal slaughter of the sow, the original act that substituted for a world of innocence one dominated by what Bernanos called "the sun of Satan."

It is not only in its radical pessimism concerning the durability of the childhood world that Golding's Jansenist novel differs from earlier models. The author also presents an equally somber analysis of the relation and correlation of the adult and child worlds. Initially, the vestigial restraints of civilization serve to maintain the rudiments of order. The children themselves create a primitive form of government sustained by laws and tradition. They even enter upon a rudimentary social contract with Ralph as their elected leader. But when the memory of adult rules and regulations fades, the children plunge into the chaos of self-indulgence in which nothing, least of all human life, remains sacred. This retrograde evolution is demonstrated in the gradual descent to savagery of Roger, one of the erstwhile choirboys who, under the leadership of their former chapter chorister, become hunters. Early on, Roger observes Henry, one of the little ones, playing in the sand. The potential killer begins to throw stones in his direction, always coming closer but without striking him. There is a protective zone around Henry which, for the time being, remains inviolate:

Here, invisible yet strong, was the taboo of the old life. Round the squatting child was the protection of parents and school and policemen and the law. Roger's arm was conditioned by a civilization that knew nothing of him and was in ruins. (p. 57)

There is something sinister about the fact that the adult world that has provided the protective regulations has disintegrated, and there is the clear signal that the same fate awaits the children's world. Later, when the overwhelming majority of the children have renounced Ralph as chief and turned into a tribe of savages under the leadership of Jack, Roger succeeds in divesting himself of the last restraints of civilization. When below him he sees the defenseless Piggy, blinded because Jack and his cohorts have stolen his spectacles, his murderous instincts overwhelm his repressions. He pushes an immense, precariously balanced boulder which crushes Piggy to death.

The adult world is being torn asunder by a murderous conflict, and yet it is to this world that the marooned children, in their distress, look for succor. When they are terrified by the imaginary self-created monster of their nightmares, they invoke the majesty of adult life and then pray for a salutary communication: "'If only they could get a message to us,' cried Ralph desperately. 'If only they could send us something grown-up, a sign or something'" (p. 87).

As if their prayer has been heard, it is answered that very night: "A sign came down from the world of grown-ups, though at the time there was no child to hear it" (p. 88). But as so often when the gods respond, the answer confounds the suppliants·and prepares their doom. The longed-for sign is the corpse of an aviator, entangled in the shroud of his parachute. The cadaver floats from the sky and becomes enmeshed in the branches of a tree, where it flaps in the breeze with an unearthly sound. The following day the children perceive the harbinger from on high but, afraid to approach the monstrous object, fail to recognize him for what he is. The "beast from water" of their imaginations is replaced by the infinitely more terrorizing "beast from air" created through their ignorance.

Yet ultimately the adults do save the children. In an effort to smoke out Ralph, who has become their prey, the "savages" for the second time incinerate the jungle. A British battleship sees the fire and comes to their rescue. Immediately the proportions of the drama are reduced, and the murderous pack of savages is transformed into a group of disheveled little boys with matted hair and filthy bodies. But as there is reduction, so also there is magnification. For in this ending is embedded a deep irony. The boys are rescued by uniformed officers themselves engaged in a violent struggle. The "trim cruiser" which is their vessel of rescue may well transport the no-longer-innocent victims into a world of which their devastated island is the prototype. Golding's parable brings the pattern of paradise destroyed to a conclusion whose import transcends earlier versions because in it the fate of the child is equated with the fate of humanity.

Paradise Regained

> "Ha!" said Doctor Blimber. "Shall we make a man of him?"
> "I had rather be a child," replied Paul.
> "Indeed!" said the Doctor. "Why?"
>
> Charles Dickens

The paradise corrupted by forces over which the child has no control is irrevocably lost. Nonetheless, in a few privileged instances, annihilation is followed by the discovery of a new paradise that is richer than the lost one. The unidimensional childhood sensibility no longer operates within the limitations of solipsistic games and unrealizable dreams. Rather, it informs a mature vision which operates within the reality of an adult world. The limited realm of practicality is infinitely enhanced by the unlimited force of innocence, a force which derives its strength from the childish refusal of compromise. Adult life transfused by the permanent presence of childhood becomes a realization of the art of the impossible. This is the triumphal message of "Das fremde Kind" ("The Strange Child") (1817), one of the most curious fairy tales in E. T. A. Hoffmann's *Die Serapions-Brüder* (*The Serapions' Brothers*). It is a message with archetypal resonances, not merely because of the mythic form of the fiction itself but because the lesson is repeated on two generational levels as well as on the levels of both dream and reality.

The two children around whom this allegory is constructed, Felix and Christlieb von Brakel, inhabit an idyllic but modest world. The means of the parents are severely restricted, but the simple home they have created for their children is characterized by hospitality and love. The brother and sister spend most of their time in the forest that surrounds the "castle," or their simple dwelling. The sylvan world that serves as their playground is for them both familiar and mysterious and seems to anticipate the nature which Baudelaire describes in the first stanza of "Correspondances":

> La Nature est un temple où de vivants piliers
> Laissent parfois sortir de confuses paroles;
> L'homme y passe à travers des forêts de symboles
> Qui l'observent avec des regards familiers.

> Nature is a temple where living pillars
> Occasionally allow confused words to emerge;
> Man passes there through forests of symbols
> Which observe him with familiar looks.

The relationship of the children with their environment is one of harmony, but a harmony that, through its mystical overtones, transcends the mundane.

The first disruption of the children's ideal existence comes with the visit of their father's wealthy cousin (a Baron von Brakel), his wife, and their two children. In preparation for this elegant company, Felix and Christlieb are carefully groomed and, for fear that they might soil their finery, forbidden to go into the forest. This is the first restriction of their liberty. The subsequent encounter between the two pairs of children represents in stark terms the opposition between a natural and a conservative education in which the artificiality of the civilized learning of the more sophisticated pair is satirized in the best romantic tradition. Although Felix and Christlieb violently reject their two counterparts and everything for which they stand, they are tempted by the amenities of civilization. The decoy takes the form of a sack of toys which their relatives give them, a dangerous treasure trove which plays a role similar to that of the box of jewels that Mephistopheles leaves for Gretchen. After the departure of the importunate visitors, the instinctive reaction of the relieved children is to revel in their regained freedom by running into their beloved forest. But before doing so, they cannot refrain from investigating the contents of the bag. They are so intrigued by the ingenious playthings that they completely forget their project of going out. On the following day they again cannot resist the pleasures afforded by their acquisitions, but in the midst of their new games they are seized by nostalgia for their anterior existence. Torn between the desire to play with their toys and the longing for a resumption of their life amidst nature, they reach the logical decision to take their presents into the forest. This is their first compromise, and it proves to be an unfortunate one. The delicate playthings are too fragile to compete with the forces of nature and, before the day is done, they are all broken. The brother and sister throw them away disdainfully and yet with a twinge of regret. The following day, unencumbered, they run into the forest to resume their former games. But, as if their compromise had represented a betrayal of childhood, the aura of magic has been dissipated. None of the amusements that had formerly enchanted them are of any avail, and, despite all their efforts, they are overcome by boredom and disgust. Furthermore, the erstwhile friendly forest has become hostile. They stumble on stones while running and catch their clothes on briars. Their disillusionment is depicted by their disconsolate joylessness: "They slunk peevishly through the forest, then sat down discontentedly and stared silently at the ground."[22] And so they weep, but their tears are shed not for their disintegrating paradise but for the lack of knowledge which has made them incapable of utilizing the amenities of civilization represented by the toys.

It is at this moment of despair that a miracle occurs: the apparition of "the strange child." This unreal personage of an indeterminate sex does more than restore their paradise in all its pristine beauty; he invests it with a new magic. By demonstrating to Felix and Christlieb the infinite superiority of nature over civilization, he reinculcates them with their former faith. His touch suffices to animate nature and to give a supernatural beauty to all its forms. This initial encounter is followed by daily meetings that enable the brother and sister to appreciate fully the incredible joys which the forest hides from the profane, that is, to rediscover the multiple splendors of the childhood paradise which has been menaced by the influence of their cousins. After the repeated entreaties of Felix and Christlieb, the strange child tells his story, a parable of paradise threatened and subsequently saved, but at a price. The strange child is a prince whose fairy mother reigns over a kingdom of innocent joy in which the most splendid feasts are those prepared for the children. Once the entire universe was her domain, and her child was secure everywhere. But ever since his mother banished an inimical minister, whom she originally appointed without knowing his true identity and evil intent, the strange child is always in danger whenever he leaves the realm of the elves, to which his mother's power is now restricted. This minister is a mighty spirit and a scholar, who, during his tenure in office, made a serious attempt to spoil the feasts of the children and to still the voices of the singers by throttling them. His culminating and most abominable act was to soil with a black fluid the brilliant stones of the palace, the flowers of the garden, and even the rainbow. It was this last act that made it clear to the queen that her defiant minister was none other than the monstrous fly, Pepser, the king of the gnomes who is bent on the destruction of her kingdom. With the help of her loyal allies, the queen succeeded in expelling him and in restoring the beauty of her domain. However, the fact remains that this domain is now circumscribed and that beyond its frontiers there lurks constant danger.

This Rousseauistic allegory is replayed in the lives of Felix and Christlieb immediately after its recital, and in its second version the anti-intellectual tendencies of the original are reinforced. As soon as brother and sister return home eager to tell their parents the miraculous story of the strange child, they are introduced to the tutor whom their uncle, Baron von Brakel, has sent them for their improvement. The name of this pedant is Master Ink,[23] and physically he resembles a large fly. The formal introduction turns into a practical joke with sinister undertones. When he shakes hands with his new pupils, he stabs them each with a hidden needle. This symbolic inoculation is the first step in a process of education designed to inculcate them with that very knowledge for which, ironically, they had wept, a knowledge that will sully their innocent world. The children are ostensibly saved when they lure the preceptor into the forest, where the allies of the strange child do battle with this reincarnation of Pepser. But only moments after the children have recounted the defeat of their schoolmaster to their parents, he returns and, as if drunk, plunges into the bowl of milk. The father, disgusted with his filthy habits and realizing his true identity, tries to smash him with a flyswatter and succeeds in maiming him and in chasing him from the house. Once again the children are apparently saved. However, the intrusion of death masked as pedantry has definitively destroyed their paradise. They can no longer find the strange child; in fact, in looking for him they become lost in their once familiar forest and, in a nightmare scene, are attacked by the resurrected toys that they have broken and thrown away. In the meantime, their father, as if contaminated by his contact with the tutor, is gradually wasting away. One day he takes his children, who are now afraid to go alone, into the forest and tells them of his own childhood paradise, which he had lost but has now regained in a different form thanks to his children's tales of the strange child. The discovery, in his maturity, of a new paradise which contains his former one enables him to bear his physical afflictions with tranquillity. A few days after this confession, he passes away in peace. His family are left destitute and are expelled (by Baron von Brakel) from their modest home. On the road to exile the mother, overcome with grief and despair, faints. At this moment the strange child appears once more to the despairing siblings and promises them that if they remain faithful to him they will find another life in which they will have nothing to fear from Pepser. And indeed the guardian spirit keeps his promise. The mother revives, and the trio finds a new home with hospitable relatives. The children prosper in the real world while in their dreams they continue to play with the strange child. Their original paradise has been destroyed, but it has been replaced by one in which dream occupies its rightful place within reality.

The perfect and paradigmatic expression of the destruction of the childhood paradise through death and sex and its ultimate replacement by another paradise is found in Thomas Mann's *Joseph and His Brothers* (1934). Joseph makes his first appearance in the pastoral setting of Hebron, which is a reconstitution of the garden of Eden. It is a magnificent scene of unearthly beauty illuminated by the pure light of myriad stars and the full moon. Joseph has just washed himself in the waters of the well and, in the splendor of his pristine beauty, sits naked on the edge of the cistern. Cleansed by his nocturnal ablutions and rocking himself, he addresses the heavenly bodies in a mysterious and almost inaudible chant. The enigmatic sounds which his lips form are not a prayer but a quiet singsong in which he loses all consciousness of himself and enters a state of ecstasy. This devotee of the moon is not "a child" but "the child," and that is how his father addresses him and how he refers to himself. And in this paradisaical setting, the lunar child is the incarnation of innocence. However, this prelapsarian state is menaced from the onset. The words with which Jacob awakens his favorite child from his reverie are, "A child sits by the depths?" and this query is followed by a command which is a reproach: "Cover your nakedness." While Joseph for the moment remains oblivious to the awareness of shame which his father seeks to awaken in him, he is conscious of the danger posed by his proximity to the well. This menace is not so much physical as spiritual. For the well is the very one which is the subject of the prelude of the novel and is described in its first sentences: "Deep is the well of the past. Should it not be called bottomless?" To fall into it is tantamount to the fall from grace and would signify the embarkation on the "voyage through hell" that is proposed in the overture. But it is also the same pit into which his brothers will throw Joseph and in which he will encounter death. So the innocent child in his pre-Adamic Eden sits on the edge of the timeless cistern that contains both past and future and in whose depths Joseph's paradise will disappear.

A child firmly ensconced in his paradise is a trusting creature whose confidence in others is so great that he does not attempt to comprehend them. This indifference, which characterizes the young Joseph, is such that he does not make the slightest effort to understand those who are the instruments of his destiny. At the same time, this insensitivity serves as the basis for his sublime egotism and results in the unquestioning conviction that "all people love him more than themselves."[24] Such self-centeredness, though natural and inherent in the very being of the child, is culpable, for it implies a blind self-confidence in which is implicit an attitude of condescension toward one's fellow creatures. Hence, it is an egotism which negates the egotism of others, a position so unrealistic that it must lead inevitably to a conflict that will annihilate Eden. So it is Joseph's very nature which not only leads to a conflict with his brothers, but actually creates the intolerable situation that impels them to eliminate his presence. Only the oldest and the youngest of his eleven siblings are so in awe of Joseph's childlike quality that they do obeisance to it. Reuben, despite himself and despite Joseph's betrayal, which has led to his disgrace, is dominated by "an unnameable compassion and a veneration of wonderment at the babbling innocence of the chosen one" (4. 514), and Benjamin worships him as the teller of dreams. But the latter is too young to become involved, and the former is helpless when confronted with the communal rage of the others.

When Joseph appears before the self-exiled sons of Leah and the concubines in his splendid regalia, in that colorful garment which signifies the child's supremacy, they fall upon him like a pack of wolves incited by his haughty words of greeting. With their teeth they rend his raiment and with their fists they mercilessly mutilate his body. Simultaneously, they tear to shreds his childhood, and their brutal blows shatter his faith in his egocentric universe. In his brothers' violence he comes face to face with a pure hatred which has transformed them from devoted elders to what they had in reality been all along, his murderers, who proceed to consummate their violence by throwing him into a dry cistern, where he is left to die. Before his entombment he is stripped naked. Whereas earlier his nudity had been an expression of innocence, now, in his spirit "Unveiling is tantamount to death" (4. 582).[25]

This encounter with Thanatos leaves the childhood paradise in rubble. Simultaneously, it brings about an extraordinary conversion as Joseph's selfishness is replaced by compassion. In his agony he no longer thinks of himself, but is deeply concerned with the effect that the news of his death will have on his adoring father. And even more impressive is the pity which he feels for his murderers and his pathetic concern with the ultimate effect of their criminal act on themselves. In his illumination within the darkness of the cistern he becomes conscious of the fact that it is his presence that forced them to a crime whose spiritual consequences for them could be disastrous. So in Joseph's death the fault that led to his downfall is eliminated.

Joseph's death, which he, his brothers, and his father consider a real death, has extraordinary historical and cosmogonic dimensions. The well that serves as his grave and as the passageway to the nether world and ultimately to the kingdom of the dead is not merely "a deep crevice, an abyss which separated the present from the past, a grave."[26] It is the eternal locus for the reenactment of an archetypal drama. Abraham's bride was wooed next to a well, Jacob encountered Rachel by a well and later imposed himself by digging a well for Laban. And it was by a well that Joseph danced in the moonlight. This same ancestral well, a natural symbol for the shepherds who depend on its waters for their very existence, has now engulfed Joseph. It is also the well into which the moon shines, and in which every month it drowns for three days, the exact span of time which Joseph spends in it. It is the same prison into which many years later Joseph, in his second downfall, will be thrown.

Young Joseph really does die, just as surely as Isaac died under the knife of Abraham, and his dress, soaked in the blood of a sacrificial animal, is the sign of that death. He dies, and his emergence from the well is a resurrection. He returns to the earth nameless and without a family. The merchants are midwives who have dragged him, naked and sullied, from the well as from a womb. When they give their speechless foundling milk to drink, it dribbles over his lips just as it would over those of a newborn babe. Death has destroyed a paradise which will now be recreated only to be destroyed again.

Joseph is dead, eternalized in the memory of his father as a seventeen-year-old youth immune to the ravages of time, and it is Osarsiph who is led by the merchants down into Egypt, the land of death and mud. And it is Osarsiph the child who is sold as a house slave to Potiphar in order to become the overseer of his estate. In the magnificent palace of the Egyptian lord he finds himself in a garden of forbidden delights very different from the one from which young Joseph had been expelled. It is a brilliant paradise of pure appearance whose fragile harmony, like that of Genet's bordello, is contingent upon absence, and whose master, as an infant, has been emasculated by his incestuous parents. The nature of this world is revealed through the description of Potiphar, who has realized the ideal of the transvestites in *The Balcony* by having become pure function, no longer encumbered by the realities of his symbolic position: "In his titular inactuality he stood outside of humanity; all reality was foreign to him in the exitless closure of his being and pure form was his essence" (5. 1323).[27]

This sterile domain of a voluptuous but fruitless beauty which is reminiscent of Baudelaire's artificial paradises is dominated by the child Osarsiph: "He stood there in the darkening structure of pillars of this garden of trees like an ecstatic child in the temple in whom God glorifies himself" (4. 894).[28] Unlike his predecessor Joseph, Osarsiph is not blinded by egotism but by an equally culpable self-confidence which will lead to his destruction by "the steer of fire" representative of sexuality and whom he provokes to battle.

Mann's interpretation of the biblical account is an astonishing but convincing one, in which the adulteress, like Racine's Phèdre, is as much of a victim as her prey and in which the exemplary Old Testament hero is far from blameless. So it is not just a question of the attempts of Potiphar's lustful wife to seduce an innocent boy whom in frustrated spite she then accuses of having tried to violate her. He is as responsible for her crime as he has been for that of his brothers. For Osarsiph, the ostentatious virgin, is not content merely to remain pure. He wants to prove his chastity and to flaunt it: "The second catastrophe of his life, the repetition of his downfall, was brought about by that very force to which, out of youthful pride, he had felt obliged to refuse to do tribute" (5. 1138).[29]

Just as it was Joseph's mere presence that excited his brother's hatred, so it is Osarsiph's existence that awakens the dormant sexual potential of Mut. It is he who arouses the emotionless idol and who transforms her from a "swan virgin" into a "witch." Osarsiph is at fault, for he has dared to play with fire, to take the bull by the horns, "whether out of confident bravery . . . or whether out of rashness and secretive lust" (5. 1156). In a culminating reenactment, Mut rends Osarsiph's garment and has him thrown into the pit which is the prison of the pharaoh. Eros has destroyed the second childhood paradise.

Joseph spent three days in the well, and it is three years before a messenger from Pharaoh frees Osarsiph from the pit. However, the latter emerges from prison not as a newborn infant but as a mature thirty-year-old man. In this newly created adult is realized the necessity expressed by Hölderlin: "The intimations of childhood must be resurrected as truth in the spirit of Man."[30] Joseph comes, as his prison keeper had foreseen, "in the form of the awaited one and the savior, who comes to put an end to the old and the boring and, accompanied by the rejoicing of humanity, to inaugurate a new epoch" (5. 1329).[31] It is Joseph the nourisher who arises from the depths and who will be able to greet his brothers by revealing himself with that simple but meaningful formula, "Children, it is I. It is I, Joseph your brother" (5. 1685).[32] The childhood paradise has been obliterated by the onslaught of Eros and Thanatos, but in its place arises the kingdom ruled over by God's chosen one.

Conclusion

> Children are like the years; you never see
> them again.
>
> Céline

The childhood paradise cannot withstand the dual impact of Eros and Thanatos. Although normally its Rousseauistic transparency is gradually tarnished by time, under dramatic circumstances the appearance of death and sex can becloud it with such violent suddenness that there occurs an immediate substitution of adult opacity for childhood limpidity. This instantaneous revelation produces utter desolation. At the conclusion of *Paul and Virginia*, the tropical garden so carefully cultivated in the heart of the Ile-de-France has been despoiled and has reverted to a wilderness dominated by the ruins of the huts in which the two protagonists spend their fleeting years. Hughes's Jamaican jungle, which has served as a playground for the Bas-Thornton children, is demolished by a hurricane, which also wrecks their house. In *Lord of the Flies*, the south-sea island on whose beach Ralph frolicked with the choirboys is ravaged by a conflagration and by a tempest which also sweeps away the flimsy shelters the children have erected. The structures established by or for children in paradise have no permanence. Ruins, graves, and rubble are all that is left in the wake of the destructive forces to which they are exposed. The erstwhile inhabitants of these Edens, now homeless, are, like Paul and Virginia, entombed, shut up in a school like Emily, or carried off, like Ralph and his companions, in a warship.

Innocence cannot be maintained when exposed to the Faustian drive. Gretchen's virginal chamber is doomed to be desecrated and its sullied inhabitant thrown into a prison cell whose only exit is death. Attempts to preserve childhood purity, even when well intentioned, lead only to disaster. Gretchen's mother fails dismally as the guardian of her daughter's virtue. And in *The Turn of the Screw* the governess's unremitting efforts to exorcise the ghosts which haunt Bly result in the death and exile of her two protégés. The far more ambiguous enterprise of Elizabeth in *The Holy Terrors* to preserve life intact in the room of childhood culminates in madness and suicide. There seems to be an infernal and implacable machine at work which assures the eventual destruction of the childhood paradise. To escape from the inextricable web of this plot directed by the unknowable forces that haunted Rousseau is possible only at the price of self-annihilation or spiritual suicide. Only by lapsing into imbecility, as in the case of Désirée, or by self-emasculation, as in the case of Father Mouret, can an unreal childhood be maintained.

Although in most cases paradise lost is replaced by the drab monotony of a mundane existence, occasionally its destruction can be transcended. By her refusal to follow Faust and by her acceptance of prison and death, Gretchen is saved. Such transcendence is not contingent upon an escape from the realm of terrestrial reality. Even in the world of the living it is possible to find a substitute for the lost domain, and one which can even be superior. This heroic re-creation is represented by the successful enterprise of Joseph, who integrates the two childhood paradises he has forfeited into his new life as Joseph the Nourisher.

There is an alternative to the divinely inspired undertaking of Joseph. It is the secular acceptance of the forces which simultaneously destroy childhood and define maturity. This demonic counterpart is evoked in an expressionistic fictional fragment of Hugo von Hofmannsthal entitled "Dämmerung und nächtliches Gewitter" ("Nightfall and Nightly Storm") (1912?), one of the most powerful depictions of the impact of the conjunction of Eros and Thanatos on the existence of a child. It opens at dusk when the boy Euseb and his companions crucify a sparrow hawk against the barn door. The agony of the bird of prey, with its universal import, is a terrible one: ". . . from his burning eyes madness shot forth, as he convulsively tore himself to death against the iron nails which had penetrated his wings."[33] The piercing screams of the hawk's mate, circling high above in ever-widening gyres, seem to free the lightning bolts from the threatening clouds and to release the storm that breaks over the boy's head and shatters his innocent world. There are other ominous signs of death: the lightning illuminates the grave of a premature infant and, when Euseb leaves the cemetery for the village, another bolt lights up a recently slaughtered calf hanging head down. It is the latter image which provides a natural conjunction of death and sex, for it is the butcher's daughter who excites the boys by flaunting her breasts. The climactic episode of this brief sketch comes when Euseb in front of the tavern sees a pregnant servinggirl brutally rejected by her former lover. The young boy violently lusts after her and follows her in the dark of the night. As he stalks her, he is simultaneously a man seeking a woman and a butcher tracking down a runaway animal in order to lead it to its death. During this mad pursuit, Euseb feels ecstatically at one with the nocturnal storm and he embraces the wild wind with which he finds himself in league. Now that he has accepted his new condition not only willingly but with joy, the lightning illuminates the entire forest down to the very roots of the trees so that his prey cannot escape into the dark.

Like E. T. A. Hoffman's "Das fremde Kind" ("The Strange Child"), the story of Euseb is a fairy tale, though a somber one.[34] As such it posits a violent alternative to the pious maintenance of childhood ideals with which Felix and Gottlieb make the adult world habitable. Euseb rejects the paradise he has lost and with intoxication revels in his marriage to the adult forces of sex and death. His reign, unlike that of Joseph, will mark the triumph of the savage god, for he glorifies the very divinities responsible for corruption in paradise.

CHAPTER FOUR

The Death of the Child

After the first death, there is no other.
Dylan Thomas

The Mortality of Children

Dance there upon the shore;
What need have you to care
For wind or water's roar?
. . . .
What need have you to dread
The monstrous crying of wind?
W. B. Yeats

The mortality rate among fictional children is exceedingly high. In ancient mythology, Cronos, the father of Zeus, having been warned that one of his children might usurp his power, devours them all, and Saturn, his Roman counterpart, does likewise. The Greeks emulate their god's act of political self-preservation by hurling Astyanax, the son of Hector and Andromache, from the walls of Troy in order to prevent the fulfillment of Calchas's prophecy that the kingdom of their enemies would be restored. For equally pragmatic reasons, King Herod orders the extermination of all male infants in Bethlehem. The massacre of the innocents is not always rationally motivated. Medea, driven mad by jealousy, slaughters her offspring by Jason in order to wreak vengeance on her unfaithful husband. Similar carnage can be prompted by sheer necessity. Saint Jerome, in his letter on the death of Marcella (412), depicts in lurid terms the extremes to which adults were driven by the famine that preceded Alaric's sack of Rome. Cannibalism was not uncommon, and famished parents, in order to survive, ate their own offspring: ". . . the mother did not spare the infant suckling at her breast, but devouring it, took back into her stomach flesh and blood which her womb had just brought forth."[1]

In one of the most grotesque variations on this theme, Dante, in *The Inferno*, tells of the imprisoned sons of Ugolino who slowly starve to death; according to one interpretation, their father consumed the wasted corpses in order to put off the inevitable moment of himself succumbing to the same fate. These are but a few of the many gruesome reenactments of the Saturnian repast. In fact, feasting upon the tender flesh of the young is a commonplace in literature, and there are innumerable folktales, of which *Little Tom Thumb* is the prototype, in which children are destined to become the victims of pedophilic anthropophagists. Child murder often has sexual connotations, as in the history of Gilles de Rais and its many variants, of which the most recent is Ionesco's *La Leçon*. Occasionally there are also racial overtones to the assassination of youthful creatures. So the prioress in *The Canterbury Tales* recounts the story of the seven-year-old whose throat was slit and whose body was thrown into a privy by the Jews who had been outraged by his chanting of the *Alma redemptoris*. The wanton killing of the babes of Queen Elizabeth in Shakespeare's *Richard III* is another example of the callous disregard for the life of the young by psychopathic grown-ups, who demonstrate no compunction about spending their fury on a child. Among these lurid recitals perhaps the most terrifying of all are those that deal with the abduction of the child from the realm of the living by a nameless incomprehensible deity or by the forces of evil. Thus there is a sense of sacred horror when in Goethe's "Der Erlkönig" the father discovers at the conclusion of his nocturnal ride that it is but the inanimate corpse of his son that he holds clasped in his arms and that, despite the paternally protective embrace, the Erlking had abducted his child. A similar sense of dread permeates the conclusion of Henry James's *The Turn of the Screw*, in which young Miles escapes from the murderously protective embrace of his governess to the realm of the dead who had seduced him.

Less spectacular but in its grim sobriety equally horrendous is the death of children due to historical circumstances beyond the control of the adults responsible for them. During years of famine brought about by crop failures, the three children of Amanda Woyke in Günter Grass's *The Flounder* starve to death:

> And when the girls
> pale, blue and deformed by hunger,
> grievously premature crones,

just born, barely stilled—Louise
was almost ready to run—were laid in a crate,
nailed shut and shoveled over,
Amanda lamented loudly.[2]

Not only vicious adults, bloodthirsty ogres, malignant deities, and ineluctable economic forces are responsible for such wholesale carnage. Children themselves can be their own worst enemies. In Thomas Hardy's *Jude the Obscure* Little Father Time hangs all his brothers and sisters before putting an end to himself. In André Gide's *The Counterfeiters* young Boris is driven to suicide by his merciless peers. And in William Golding's *Lord of the Flies* the children butcher one of their own in a barbaric expiatory sacrifice.

As prevalent as death may be among the young, its potential victims are for the most part fearless. According to Freud, this attitude is dictated by the child's inability to conceptualize mortality: "The child knows nothing of the horrors of decay, of shivering in the cold grave, of the terror of the infinite Nothing. . . . Fear of death is strange to the child."[3] So children, as a rule, do not need the adult reassurance proffered by Emerson in "Compensation I":

Fear not then, thou child infirm,
There's no god dare wrong a worm.

They emulate the son of Macduff, who is so blissfully unaware of the menace to his existence that he denies the very possibility that children can be caught up in the deadly machinations of their elders:

LADY MACDUFF: Poor bird! thould'st never fear the net nor lime,
The pitfall nor the gin.
SON: Why should I, mother? Poor birds they are not set for.
(*Macbeth*, act 4, scene 2, lines 33–35)

Thomas Gray, in his "Ode on a Distant Prospect of Eton College," expresses this lack of awareness even more succinctly:

Alas, regardless of their doom
The little victims play!
(lines 51–52)

Preadolescents for the most part are protected by a simplicity that causes them to negate the fact of their vulnerability even in the face of incontrovertible evidence. In "We Are Seven" Wordsworth tells of the little girl who knits at the graveside of two of her siblings and yet steadfastly refuses to acknowledge the reality of their absence. The rhetorical question of the opening stanza assumes the impossibility of comprehending mortality from within the context of pure being:

> —A simple Child,
> That lightly draws its breath,
> And feels its life in every limb,
> What should it know of death?

A far less gentle expression of the indifference that is a natural consequence of innocent ignorance is dramatized in a scene from Balzac's first major novel, *Les Chouans* (1827). The double agent Galope-chopine, after a summary trial, is decapitated by a pair of vengeful royalist executioners who tie their bloody trophy by its hair onto a hook in the hall. When the unsuspecting young child returns home and sees his father's bloody head, with its eyes still open, his reaction is not one of horror but of passionate interest: "He opened his eyes wide, stared for a long time at the head of his father with an uncomprehending look which betrayed no emotion. Then his face, stupefied by ignorance, succeeded in expressing a savage curiosity."[4] An attenuated version of this macabre episode is found in one of the sketches from George Eliot's *Scenes of Clerical Life* (1884). Young Dickey attends the funeral of his mother and sees in this event a pretext for a new game: "He [Dickey] stood close to his father, with great rosy cheeks and wide open blue eyes, looking first up at Mr. Cleeves and then down at the coffin, and thinking he and Chubby would play at that when they got home."[5]

The natural inability to believe in death is, as Thomas Mann said, "the negation of a negation."[6] It is a helpless faith whose very strength lies in its helplessness. Such ignorance can provide a psychological defense against constant terror. It can do nothing to prolong an existence that is constantly in the balance.

The corpse of the child as a persistent presence in literature demands an examination not limited to a mere determination of the cause of death. It should also attempt to isolate the components of what may seem to be a morbid subject that have exerted such a continuing fascination on authors and to discover what it is that writers are trying to express through their manipulation of

these elements. Even the most cursory investigation leads to a conclusion as evident as it is unsatisfactory. The destruction of innocence is an event that has a universal if somewhat perverse appeal
and that is sure to evoke sympathy, even if of a rather tainted kind,
in the soul of every sensitive reader. In *The Betrothed* Manzoni
used the death of children to create the emotional climax of his
depiction of the plague, and Fogazzaro constructed his entire *The
Little World of the Past* around the pathetic drowning of little Maria. But it is Dickens who most relentlessly exploited those heartrending aspects of premature death that were sure to attract a
large audience. In doing so he, and even more so his less gifted im-
itators, exemplified the dangers inherent in the theme itself. In utilizing such material, most writers find it difficult or impossible to
avoid succumbing to a mawkish sentimentalism. The consequences
of such self-indulgence are often lamentable and seem to confirm
Léon Bloy's contention that "in the presence of the death of a little
child, Art and Poetry are really wretchedly inadequate."[7] When
broaching this topic, even as fine an ironist as Tieck becomes
maudlin and as great a poet as Hugo becomes insufferable. The
worst and most famous excesses are found in novels. So, though it
may be a commentary on human cynicism, the fact remains that
the famous death scene of Little Nell in *The Old Curiosity Shop*
evokes in most sophisticated readers today not tears but sniggers.[8]
The demise of the child seems more suited to a vulgar genre such
as soap opera than to high art.[9] However, it is one of the aspects of
genius to take inherently banal material and to reshape it in such a
fashion as to transcend its limitations. And so certain authors have
chosen this essentially lachrymose topic and employed it for purposes more serious than merely to provide a good cry for those in
need of instant catharsis.

Sentimentalism is most easily and naturally avoided by writers whose religious faith is deep enough to mute whatever grief
they may feel at the loss of a child. For Eichendorff, the devout
Catholic, death is a natural event, and the sorrow he expresses in
"Auf meines Kindes Tod" ("At the Death of My Child") (1832) is
attenuated by the certainty that his child has found a far more
beautiful garden to inhabit than the terrestrial one and by the
knowledge that he will act as an intercessor for his parents. Unlike
such untroubled belief, pious fanaticism can, in extreme cases,
even lead to rejoicing in death. A terrifyingly effective instance of

such perverse jubilation is found in the diary of James Whistler's puritanical mother, who goes so far as to express pleasure at watching one of her sick children "ripening for the skies." [10] Most writers are less callous and try, like Shakespeare in *King John*, to master an overpowering sorrow through its powerful expression:

> Grief fills the room up of my absent child,
> Lies in his bed, walks up and down with me,
> Puts on his pretty looks, repeats his words,
> Remembers me of all his gracious parts,
> Stuffs out his vacant garments with his form.
>
> (act 3, scene 4)

This lament is rendered effective by the substanceless plenitude that in vain tries to fill the emptiness left by the absent child and by the juxtaposition of grandiloquence with familial and domestic details. As such, it is more than a mother's overwhelming outpouring of personal grief. It gives expression to the realization that the death of the child is an unbearable event, as necessary as it is impossible. By murdering him in the realm of the imaginary an author fulfills an unspeakable but universal wish. The child must be killed and yet remain a continuous presence. The constant reproach of his existence is intolerable, for it undermines any confidence in the reality of the adult world. So the threat which he incarnates must be eliminated. On the other hand, it is only his presence that accounts for whatever is transcendental in the human experience, and so he must be preserved at all costs. This is the paradox expressed in appropriately elliptical terms by Serge Leclaire:

There is, for each of us, always a child to be killed; the funeral of a representation of plenitude, of immobile ecstasy must be enacted and reenacted continuously, a light blinding so that it might shine and extinguish itself in the depths of the night. Whoever does not enact and reenact this funeral of the marvelous child he would have been remains in limbo and in the murky clarity of expectation without shadow or hope. But whoever thinks once and for all to have liquidated the figure of the tyrant is exiled from the sources of his genius. [11]

Abraham's knife must not remain suspended above the breast of Isaac forever. Adhering to an archaic subconscious logic, the ritual sacrifice must be consummated, even if through the medium of a surrogate, so that it can be constantly reenacted. For everyone there is always a child to be assassinated, to be mourned, and to be resurrected.

The Expiatory Child

> The false situations to which the young are condemned imply a terrible expiation.
>
> Sainte-Beuve

Certainly not all authors have been conscious of the implications of the cataclysmic event represented by the death of the child. If the child's identity is not clearly established, it loses its uniqueness, and its individual fate, no matter how horrendous, is emptied of emotional content. In such cases one child can replace another and adequately compensate the loss occasioned by death. Such interchangeability is a recurrent motif in the novellas of Heinrich von Kleist. In *The Foundling* (1811) the bereaved parents of Paolo adopt the little survivor of the plague who infected their only son with the mortal malady. The consequences of this substitution are catastrophic: when he reaches adolescence, the foundling attempts to rape his stepmother, dispossesses his benefactor, and causes both their deaths. And yet this tragic aftermath cannot be interpreted as a punishment or condemnation of the well-intentioned stepparents. In *The Earthquake in Chile* a similar exchange occurs with beneficent results. Don Fernando's son, Juan, is smashed to death against a church pillar by an enraged fanatic while his father is saving the intended victim whom he shortly thereafter adopts, much to the future satisfaction of himself and his wife. The subordination of natural parental affection to a higher principle can also deprive the death of the child of its significance. In Prosper Mérimée's *Mateo Falcone* (1829) the ten-year-old Fortunato succumbs to the temptation of a bribe and betrays the tracked-down outlaw who has sought his protection. For this infraction of the code of honor Mateo Falcone leads his son into the forest, makes him kneel down to say his prayers, and shoots him. The emotional and practical consequences of the execution of his only male heir are minimal. Before proceeding to bury the corpse, Falcone orders his wife to have a mass said for his soul and to send for one of their sons-in-law to take the place of the victim. The sacrifice of a child to an abstract ethical system is made possible through the ready availability of surrogates.

Such compassionless lack of involvement is an attitude portrayed by many writers who have used the death of the child simply as an appropriate vehicle for social criticism. Although Mérimée in his objectivity scrupulously avoided moral judgment, most authors interpret the expiration of the child as a punishment of its parents as representatives of a social order who have abused their privileges. But even on such a superficial level there are deeper implications. In D. H. Lawrence's *The Rainbow* (1915) a father looks at his child: "As the newly-opened, newly-dawned eyes looked at him, he wanted them to perceive him, to recognise him. Then he was verified." [12] The child is the verification of the adult; hence its destruction represents the annihilation of its progenitor. Thus, in Thackeray's *Barry Lyndon* (1844) little Bryan is the incarnation of all of the possibilities that his profligate father has been unable to realize. It is expected that the young scion, by inheriting a title and regaining the long-lost properties of the family, will attain the legitimacy that is lacking in Barry Lyndon's boastful accounts of his ancestry. But just before his ninth birthday, Bryan is thrown from the horse his father has just acquired for him and never regains consciousness. His demise is the undoing of Barry Lyndon, whose precarious prosperity depended entirely on his offspring's continued existence. This dependency is not merely material in nature: with the death of the child the dreams of the father become what they had been all along, the unreal fictions of a coarse braggart given to drink, dreams that served temporarily to veil the sordid reality of an egocentric existence. Barry Lyndon is punished for his violation of the social code, for his crude attempt to impersonate a gentleman.

The punishment that Pérez Galdós metes out to Torquemada, the central figure in a series of novels bearing his name (1889–95), is even greater. The miserly moneylender's son, Valentín, is a potential genius with a special gift for mathematics. His father sees in him a means of attaining glory and a fortune. But Valentín wastes away and, despite Torquemada's attempts to placate God, dies. The cult which the bereaved father subsequently devotes to the child has but one purpose: the reincarnation of Valentín. When Torquemada's second wife (whom he has married in order to gain entry into the world of the nobility) gives birth on Christmas Eve to a male infant, it seems that Torquemada's prayers are answered. But this resurrection is a cruelly deceptive one, for the surrogate turns out to be an imbecile. Both children are the sacrificial victims of the materialism of the adult. The death of the one and the mental deficiency of the other are expiations for Torquemada's greed and social pretensions.

Like Barry Lyndon's son, the young protagonist of D. H. Lawrence's "The Rocking-Horse Winner" (1933) also comes to grief because of a steed, even though only a wooden one. Unlike Bryan, who is a passive and unwitting victim of the horse as agent of destruction, Paul courts disaster by actively playing the role of redeemer. Like Barry Lyndon, his parents have squandered their heritage and continue to live beyond their means. The result is that the family house is haunted by voices crying for more money, and Paul's ambitious project is to stifle them. It is his demonic rocking-horse that leads him to the luck (lucre) whose lack his mother sees as a curse. His furious gallops transport him into a new realm, and in this state of ecstasy the names of racehorses destined to win flash through his mind. With the help of the family gardener he places money on them and begins in secret to provide for the needs of his mother. The eerie voices only become shriller, and Paul's efforts more frenetic, as he slashes the wooden courser with a whip in order to discover the future winner of the Derby. He succeeds, but his culminating charge brings on a brain fever to which he succumbs. His death is a reproach to his mother, whose greed was responsible for the impoverishment of the family and whose neglect was indirectly responsible for his fatal ride. It is also a reproach to a social caste whose members have abdicated their duties in their selfish dedication to self-gratification.

A dimension is lacking not only in these three stories but in many others like them. The compassion that doomed children in both literature and life evoke in adults is totally absent. This indifference is epitomized in Stendhal's *The Charterhouse of Parma* (1839). The mysterious demise of Sandrino, the illegitimate son of Fabrice and Clélia, is certainly expiatory in nature, and the guilt-ridden mother sees in it a divine rebuke. However, her interpretation does not lead to atonement, nor does it prevent her from ultimately dying in the arms of her lover. Even when apparently overwhelmed by the death of an offspring, adults frequently use the occasion to wallow in their own emotions. In one of the many grotesque incidents in Flaubert's *Sentimental Education* (1869), the apparently distraught Rosanette wants to embalm her child, but Frédéric talks his mistress into having one of their friends do a portrait of him instead. While carrying out his morbid commission, the artist discusses the aesthetics of still lifes with the bereaved parents. The painter and father demonstrate their total detachment while the courtesan plays the role of a despairing mother. Some grown-ups go even further in their disinterest by callously exploiting their loss. In Zola's *The Masterpiece* (1886) the avant-garde artist Claude Lantier, completely unmoved by the expiration of the son whom he has consistently neglected, looks at him carefully for the first time. Suddenly inspired, he takes advantage of the opportunity to do a portrait of the corpse and at once submits the result for an exhibit. Most adults do not even have the excuse of the compulsive creative urge that might justify Lantier's monstrous selfishness. Immured in their egocentrism, they remain unconcerned with anything but the practical import of the loss of their offspring. Barry Lyndon made an ostentatious show of affection for his son, but in his bereavement he is mainly concerned with the material loss that the child's death entails. Immediately after the pompous burial, he schemes unsuccessfully to replace him by finding a substitute heir for the estate among his illegitimate offspring. Torquemada, in his cynical attempt at self-reform, tries to buy off God so that his child may live and provide for his future. The same cold, calculating attitude characterizes Paul's family. His mother is incapable of love, and his uncle, who has profited immensely through Paul's uncanny prescience, shrugs off his death and consoles the mother by explaining to her that she is now eighty thousand pounds to the good "and a poor devil of a son to the bad." [13] In *Les Misérables* Hugo condemned the cynicism of adults responsible for the death of children in his depiction of the execution of Gavroche. The soldiers, preparing to gun down the urchin, smile as they take aim.

The Metaphysical Death of the Child

> Since we have been children before being men. . . .
> Descartes

It is compassion that distinguishes Dostoevski's treatment of children from those of Thackeray, Galdós, and Lawrence. In *The Brothers Karamazov* (1879–80) Ivan describes to his brother Alyosha the atrocities to which children have been subjected and in doing so insists on the most ghastly details imaginable.[14] He tells of parents who, after beating her black and blue, lock their little daughter into the outdoor privy all night in the middle of winter and then force her to eat her own excrement. Further, he recounts the story of a general who punishes an eight-year-old serf for having accidentally wounded one of his hounds. He has the child stripped and then incites his vicious hunting dogs to tear him to pieces. There are other horror stories concerning the unmitigated suffering of children in this novel, but of a different type. Lisa depicts with complicitous relish her vision of herself eating pineapple jam while watching a child being crucified. Her neurotic delectation of evil is the manifestation of a deep inner sickness. Ivan's recitals, on the other hand, are not the products of a perverse imagination but of the overwhelming sense of injustice that his solidarity with the innocents who suffer inspires in him.[15] His stance is that of revolt: he will refuse admission to paradise if it must be purchased at the cost of children's tears. Whereas in Thackeray, Galdós, and Lawrence the death of a child is primarily a reproach against human society, here it is a protest against the divine order. And so *The Brothers Karamazov* transcends social criticism in order to make a metaphysical statement.

Despite its dramatic impact, it is not Ivan's cry of outrage that dominates *The Brothers Karamazov*. His two brothers are equally obsessed with children, and their reactions to their death and suffering is intertwined with that of Ivan. Dmitri, when he is arrested after his night of debauchery, has a dream of a little child whose hut has been burned down and who is now blue with cold and starving. This vision of the suffering infant continues to haunt him throughout his trial and almost enables him to reconcile himself to his fate. Ivan's and Dmitri's thoughts are fixed on children of history or of dreams. Alyosha's thoughts, in contrast, are preoccupied with a real child, the young schoolboy Ilyousha, whose stoning triggers a fatal malady. But it is his agony that provides the necessary pretext for reconciliation, and the bed from which he will never arise becomes the focal point for the reunion with the classmates who have taunted him. Finally, his funeral makes possible the feast of communion with which the novel closes. The death of the child cannot be the cornerstone of a paradise acceptable to Ivan, nor can it justify or even bring about the salvation of an individual like Dmitri. It can, however, do more than that by consolidating the brotherhood of mankind into a community of sinner-saints.[16]

The influence of Dostoevski on Camus is unquestionable and particularly obvious in the latter's exploitation of the death of the child in *The Plague* (1947). In some respects very similar to Manzoni's imaginative reconstruction of the plague that really did ravage Milan in 1630, this fictitious chronicle of the outbreak of the bubonic plague in a North African city is replete with macabre and sometimes melodramatic tableaux depicting the death of guilt-ridden grown-ups. But none surpasses in horror the minute description of the agony of an innocent child, whose physical suffering is greater than that of any of the adult victims. Because the boy is condemned anyway, Dr. Rieux decides to try out a newly developed, untested serum on him. The fate of the child, in the doctor's eyes, will determine whether the plague can be contained or whether it must be left to run its own capricious course. Although inconclusive, the results of the experiment are not entirely devoid of hopeful signs. The inoculation gives the child sufficient strength to fight the infection, but not enough to vanquish it. In other words, man is not entirely impotent, and the quest for a remedy may not be entirely absurd. But on the individual level there is something monstrous about this attempt. The medication serves merely to prolong the agony and intensify the pain of the child. It also inspires in the innocent victim the power and instinctive need to protest for all of mankind:

In the hollow of his face, now frozen into a gray mass of clay, his mouth opened and almost immediately there emerged from it a continuous cry, barely modulated by his breathing, a cry which suddenly filled the entire ward with a monstrous and discordant protest, which had so little of the human about it that it seemed to come simultaneously from all men.[17]

When the child finally expires, the normally self-possessed Rieux directs a violent outburst of anger at the representative of God, Father Paneloux. Despite the initially hostile confrontation provoked by failure, something positive emerges out of this death. Before going their separate ways, the two natural antagonists, the priest and the doctor, come to an understanding:

Paneloux held out his hand and sorrowfully said, "So, despite everything, I haven't convinced you." "What difference does that make?" said Rieux.

"What I hate is death and evil, as you well know. And, whether you like it or not, we are united in suffering them and in combatting them."

Rieux held onto the hand of Paneloux.

"You see," he said, avoiding looking at him, "Now even God cannot separate us." (p. 1396)

The function of the death of the child within the framework of Camus's allegorical recital is a conciliatory one. As in *The Brothers Karamazov*, it serves as a vehicle of expression for outrage and for a defiance of divinity, but it also cements an alliance between men and creates the human solidarity that Camus celebrates in his novel.

Dostoevski and Camus succeed in maintaining the precarious balance between sentimentalism and a Kantian schematism. Theirs is a passionately involved mediation between an abstract concept and the particular content of sensory experience. Compassion prevents them from simply exploiting the death of the child to reinforce a philosophical point, and their intellectual concerns place strict limits on the emotionalism inherent in their subject matter. Compassion unchecked by metaphysical considerations can lead beyond bathos to untrammeled sensationalism. In Gerhart Hauptmann's *Bahnwärter Thiel* (1887), which can be considered one of the first works of German expressionism, the violent death of the signalman's first child certainly does not fall into the category of the expiatory. It is the direct result of the father's paralyzing passivity and the stepmother's callous lack of concern, but neither of the guilty parties is redeemed or even chastened by the mortal accident they have provoked. Immediately after the fatal accident, while Lene attempts feebly to exculpate herself, her husband abandons himself completely to his emotions. Both abdicate all sense of responsibility. And in one respect the parents are indeed innocent. Thiel, whose obsession with the memory of his deceased first wife has cut him off from the reality of his offspring, and Lene, whose devotion to her own child has provoked her hatred for his rival, are actually only the instruments of fatality. For little Tobias is the victim of the powerful and unsublimated passion represented by the onrushing train which smashes his fragile body already weakened by hydrocephalia and calcium poisoning. It is the same force expressed in Lene's domineering sexual drive which drains Thiel of his energy. There is nothing redemptive about the bloody episode with which the novella ends. Far from bringing about a reconciliation, the death of Tobias loosens chaos upon the world. It unfetters the violence that Thiel has suppressed all his life. The outraged guardian of the railroad crossing, ignoring the signals he has always dutifully heeded and jumping the tracks he has so carefully maintained, goes on a rampage; after battering his wife to death and slitting the throat of their baby, he lapses into total madness.

In *The Rebel* Camus wrote, "It is not the suffering of the child in itself which is revolting, but the fact that this suffering is not justified."[18] The deaths of Tobias and his half-brother are indeed revolting. They are as senseless as that of Ilyousha, but the fact that they occur in a senseless world deprives them of the transcendence that informs the vision of Dostoevski. The fact that they do not even serve as a protest against the absurdity of the universe deprives them of the tragic resonance evoked by the agony of the child in *The Plague*. Unlike his biblical namesake, Tobias does not cure his father of blindness but plunges him into the sightlessness of despair. He is not a witness against injustice but merely its victim. Unlike his eloquent counterparts, he dies in silence in a world deafened by the roaring of trains and the howls of the insane.

Beyond the Death of the Child

> The child is a god for the child.
> Alain

The death of the child is a commentary on the state of man or the state of God. It can also be a commentary on the state of childhood itself. This solipsistic stance, as distinct from the social and metaphysical one, is first exemplified in Goethe's *Wilhelm Meister's Apprenticeship* (1795). Unlike Bryan, Paul, and Ilyousha, whose existences are firmly grounded in their individual novelistic universes, Mignon transcends the fiction that gave birth to her. She is as independent of the novel as of its author. She is one of those rare fictitious characters (like Falstaff, Don Quixote, or Ubu Roi) who have attained autonomy. She has escaped the confines of the book because she is the quintessential child. The young personages of Thackeray, Dostoevski, and Lawrence possess only the reality their creators could give them. They have the clearly determined sex, age, psychological makeup, and status in society with which the authors saw fit to endow them. Above all, they have names that clearly identify them. In other words, they do not form a race apart, but are children only as adults see them. Mignon, on the contrary, is the child as it is, that is to say a pure enigma. When Mignon is initially presented to Wilhelm Meister, Philine's only words of introduction are, "Here is the enigma." Further questioning elicits little additional information. Her age is indeterminate (from her physical appearance it seems that she is twelve or thirteen), and she is even uncertain about her name ("They call me Mignon" is her answer to a direct query). Doubt is cast even upon her sex. She appears in boy's garb, which she casts off only at the end in favor of the costume of an angel. Unlike Marianne, who enters Wilhelm's life dressed as an officer before revealing her total femininity to him, Mignon retains her androgynous character until her death. Her aura of mystery is heightened by the fact that she is practically inarticulate. Nor, as the reader is led to believe at first, can her broken speech be attributed to the fact that she is a stranger who cannot master a foreign tongue. When, at the end of the novel, her entire history is at last revealed, we learn that, even as a child in her native land, she could not express herself in a human language: "With words alone she could not express herself, and this seemed to be due more to an impediment in her way of thinking than in her vocal chords."[19] Words fail her, but she can play the zither and sing. Like Dona Musique of Claudel's *The Satin Slipper*, she is a creature of music: "Celui qui ne sait plus parler, qu'il chante" ("Whoever no longer knows how to speak, let him sing").[20] The enigmatic child is the bearer of a message that cannot be spoken.

This other-worldly creature exerts on Wilhelm Meister an extraordinary fascination very different from the normal parental affection that his young son Felix, whose name, age, and condition are known, inspires in him. When he first lays eyes on her, it is with wonderment and he is almost mesmerized. In fact, when Philine talks to him she interrupts his reverie and awakens him from a hypnotic trance that he describes as a half-dream. It is certainly not Mignon's beauty or grace that produces this powerful effect on him. Indeed, the dark-haired, olive-skinned child, whose face is smeared with cosmetics, is not extraordinarily handsome: "Her physical conformation was irregular" (15, 1:93). Even her rapid movements have something abrupt and unquiet about them—and yet she is a consummate dancer. It is her secretive presence and not her physical attributes that entrances Wilhelm.

This prepubescent enchantress who sings of the land where the lemon trees blossom and where the blood oranges glow in dark groves must die. She stands at the threshhold of maturity, and her innocent devotion to her master is on the verge of corruption. The loss of innocence is tantamount to the undoing of her existence, and so she is doomed:

It is not only the first blossoms that fall, but also the fruit, hanging from the branches and which for a long time still hold out the most beautiful promises, while a secret worm prepares this early maturity and destruction. (15, 2:264)

Here Goethe anticipates a basic Victorian pattern which is prevalent in Dickens, the early Dostoevski, and James. The secret worm that undermines her existence is sex. Mignon is the incarnation of yearning, and, when fulfillment is at hand, all longing is of necessity destroyed. Thanatos follows ineluctably on the heels of Eros. It is an omen that Mignon's first movement of voluptuousness triggers an attack from which she nearly dies. So it is only natural that she expires so suddenly when Wilhelm offers his hand to Therese, for in Therese, the practical and earthbound mother figure, Mignon must recognize what she would become were her existence prolonged. And so Mignon passes away and is buried in state while an invisible choir of youths intones: "Well preserved now is the treasure, the beautiful image of the past. Here within the marble it reposes incorruptible; and in your hearts too does it live and continue efficacious" (15, 2:300). While Felix lives in order to become an adult, the enigmatic child must die because it is an evanescent, passing phenomenon. So Mignon, the well-protected treasure, in her death lives on forever, preserved in the marble crypt of the room of the past.

Like Goethe, Thomas Mann in *Dr. Faustus* (1947) employs the theme of the death of the child to make a philosophical statement that illuminates the human condition of both child and adult. At the same time, he enlarges the scope of his enterprise by using it to make not only a social protest but a metaphysical one much in the manner of Dostoevski. It is almost impossible to limit to a single novel an analysis of the significance of the child in Mann's work. The theme is omnipresent from first to last, from

Buddenbrooks to *The Holy Sinner*. The former opens with a dialogue in which the babbling of young Tony is musically interwoven with the simple dialect of her grandfather and culminates with the death of the fragile Hanno, which marks the nadir in the decline and downfall of the Buddenbrooks family. Among the other works anterior to *Dr. Faustus*, one of the most provocative is *Tristan*, in which a sullen infant, Anton Klöterjahn, is depicted as the frightful harbinger of a new world order inimical to all aesthetic values. Nor can we fail to mention in this context the incomprehensible Tadzio of *Death in Venice*, the ultimate incarnation of the child who holds out the promise of salvation through death. Nepomuk Schneidewein, in *Dr. Faustus* (1947), is as enigmatic as any of his predecessors. He is also quite obviously a symbol of possible redemption through innocence, and far less obviously the personification of a future that is more uncertain and that lies beyond the one announced by young Klöterjahn. The symbolic import of this subject is further complicated by the fact that in his case innocence proves impotent when confronted with the powers of the demonic. The young Nepomuk is doomed from the outset to be destroyed by the forces of evil with whom his uncle, Adrian Leverkühn, has made a fateful pact. Nepomuk arrives at the country home of the composer after a series of catastrophes culminating in the disintegration of Leverkühn's marriage plans and in the melodramatic death of his closest friend, Rudolph Schwerdtfeger. The life of the musician, plagued by ever-worsening migraine headaches, has reached a low point just before his five-year-old nephew comes to live with him. Nepomuk's appearance at Pfeiffering has an immediate impact, and everyone, including the menials and the farmers greet him with delight and with cries of astonishment. There is something of the miracle in his advent. There is also something magical in his restrained smile, which gives promise of a precious lesson and message.[21] The Klöterjahn baby had not yet attained the powers of articulation, and Tadzio conversed only in Polish, which Aschenbach could not comprehend. The enigma of Nepomuk is heightened by the strange speech he employs. It is accented and contains many colloquialisms and unusual dialectical expressions, as well as archaic words from a long-forgotten language. This unique composite tongue makes him difficult to comprehend. As if aware of his very special nature, like the young Joseph, he refers to himself always in the third person, and usually as "Echo." This self-consciousness adds another element of artificiality to his language. But the overall effect of such precocious preciosity is an enchanting one, and no one is immune to the charm of the ethereal child. Only the pedagogically inclined narrator, Zeitblom, momentarily attempts to deal with him as he would with one of his ordinary pupils. But when he speaks rather gruffly and condescendingly to Nepomuk, the child makes an engaging attempt to suppress his laughter. The confrontation between candor and pomposity causes the adult to feel extremely foolish. So Zeitblom, sensitive to the absurdity of his attitude, gives up his halfhearted attempts at sternness and recognizes Nepomuk for what he is, "a little emissary from the realm of children and elves" (p. 618).

Zeitblom is fully conscious both of the child's extraordinary quality and of the transient nature of the enchantment Nepomuk embodies. As an educator, Zeitblom is concerned because he knows what the effects of time will be on the child: he is, like all mortals, destined to mature and to fall prey to the earthly. The innocence of his blue eyes will become clouded by impurity and all too soon the poetry of his being will be transmogrified into prose before his elfin essence assumes the form of a more or less ordinary boy. Even the down-to-earth Zeitblom revolts against the tyranny of the temporal and tries to justify his refusal to accept the brutal power of time over "this blessed apparition" by an explanation of what Nepomuk represents:

. . . his rare quality of being self-enclosed, his validity as a representative of *the child* on earth, the feeling he inspired of having descended from on high (and I repeat myself) in order to deliver a precious message. . . . His character could not deny the inevitability of growth, but took refuge in an imaginary sphere of the mythic-atemporal, of simultaneity and existence in a continuum in which the adult form of man is not in contradiction with the child in the arms of the mother. (p. 619)

The presence of Nepomuk has transformed the practical and sober Zeitblom into an enthusiast.

It is on Leverkühn that Nepomuk exerts the greatest influence. The cold and in many respects inhuman composer is transformed into the stereotype of the adoring uncle who tells the child stories, buys him toys, lets him look at his work, and with touching admiration repeats to his acquaintances every one of his infantile sayings. Nepomuk's sojourn represents for Leverkühn an interlude, a charming domestic respite within his tormented existence. However, there is far more to Leverkühn's feelings than the pure enjoyment of a familial idyll. The man who knows he is cursed is especially fond of the moments when Nepomuk says his evening prayers. After one such session, he and Zeitblom analyze the child's orison:

> "You are right," I replied. "He keeps his prayers in the realm of the selfless because he does not plead merely for himself, but rather for all of us."
> "Yes, for all of us," said Adrian quietly. (p. 626)

Leverkühn sees in Nepomuk a figure who might save him from damnation, who might absolve him of his pact with the devil. But Leverkühn's hopes are illusory, and it is he who will be the cause of the child's destruction.

Nepomuk, after having captivated the hearts of all who surround him, falls victim to cerebral meningitis. The unacceptable atrocity represented by the horrible death of the guiltless child and its very senselessness arouse indignation. The reader (and the author) are revolted by a system in which innocence is sacrificed needlessly and capriciously. Aldous Huxley, in *Point Counter Point* (1928), inflicted the same malady on little Phil and brilliantly played on the reader's hopes and fears by his masterful depiction of the disintegration of the child and by his clever manipulation of the course of the malady. It is only after a suspenseful respite and a dreadful relapse that the author finally allows Phil to succumb. His death has conveniently prevented his mother from committing adultery, but the price for her continued chastity seems high. With Nepomuk, however, it is not marital fidelity that is at stake, but salvation itself, and the awfulness of his agony is enhanced by the fact that his death is inevitable from the moment when Leverkühn first lays eyes on him. The delicacy of his physical system is no match for the infectious venereal disease that is ravaging his uncle's body, just as the fragility of his spiritual system is incapable of resisting the demonic powers that Leverkühn has purchased from the devil at the price of his soul. Like Mignon, Nepomuk must die, and Leverkühn is perfectly aware of his responsibility for this death. To Zeitblom he explains:

"... what guilt, what a sin, what a crime ... to have let him come here, to have left him in my vicinity, to have let me feast my eyes on him! You must know that children are delicate creatures, all too susceptible to poisonous influences." (p. 633)

Shortly after Nepomuk's death, Leverkühn plunges into the composition of his last work, the monstrous and despairing "Lamentation of Dr. Faustus," a composition whose fundamental theme is constructed out of the letters forming the name of the woman who has infected him. The first audition of this apocalyptic oratorium is a disaster, and soon thereafter Leverkühn lapses into the imbecility in which he lives out the remainder of his days. In an ironic counterpoint typical of the entire novel, Zeitblom's depiction of Nepomuk's death is contemporaneous with the Wagnerian disintegration of the Third Reich.

Music is the key to everything in *Dr. Faustus*, and it is Zeitblom's description of the chorus in Leverkühn's "Apocalypsis cum Figuris," the last work the composer writes before his encounter with Nepomuk, that helps to explain the role of the enigmatic child in the novel:

The infernal laughter with which the first part ends has its counterpart in the wondrously supernatural chlildren's chorus . . . that opens the second part, a piece of cosmic music of the spheres, icy, clear, transparent as glass, astringently dissonant and yet imbued with a tonal sweetness that, so to speak, is unattainable and supernatural, foreign, filling the heart with a longing without hope. (pp. 502–3)

What Zeitblom finds truly astonishing in this children's chorus is that it is formed out of exactly the same notes as the laughter that arose from hell. The angelic tones are those of Satan, only they have been orchestrated differently and given a new rhythm. The enigmatic child in Mann's masterpiece is the ultimate in complexity and ambiguity. The angelic being is of the same material as his infernal counterpart. Though unable to stand up to the demonic, he is, even in his death, the harbinger of the end of the epoch of bourgeois humanism and the herald of the advent of a new stage in life, a stage when it seems as if "a mutation would take place during which the world would find itself under a new, still nameless constellation" (p. 469). After the era of art promised by Tadzio's gesture and after the age of commercialism announced by the Klöterjahn baby will come the unknown and unnamed epoch heralded by the death of Nepomuk.

Conclusion

> All children are mirrors of death.
>
> Jean-Paul Sartre

The implications of the death of the child are as complex and varied as the many forms it takes, and the attempts of grown-ups to come to terms with them are often characterized by the uncertainty arising from incomprehension. The little victim is often less horrified by his fate than the adult who witnesses and survives his demise. In fact, for the child death occasionally represents an escape from an intolerable reality. Even more positively, it can sometimes even be a longed-for condition that transcends reality. Thus, in Conrad Aiken's "Silent Snow, Secret Snow," the child's yearning for oblivion proves irresistible. This theme is sensitively developed in Colette's "The Sick Child" (1943), the story of "a child who had to die"[22] and who throughout his long malady flirts with death, whose attractions are depicted in sensuous detail. Jean literally savors death with his mouth, eyes, and ears. But the condemned child, thanks to the care of the doctor, is saved and, "cut off from miracles, he falls asleep, consenting, cured, and disappointed" (p. 96). Unlike Aiken's child, Jean does not succumb to the seduction of the ultimate temptress, but he loses the magic universe he had been constructing in collaboration with her.

Most authors have avoided looking at the voluptuous traits of death to which some children are so sensitive, and have preferred a teleological approach to the theme. In general, since the eighteenth century they have used the death of the child for three purposes: to register a social protest, as did Thackeray, Pérez Galdós, and Lawrence; to express a metaphysical revolt, as did Dostoevski and Camus; or to make a comment on the precarious condition of childhood itself, as did Goethe and Mann. The last category is the richest in significance, for it subsumes the other two. Mignon and Nepomuk demonstrated the impossibility of a certain type of existence. They cannot live, for if they did the purity which is their very essence would be tainted by sexuality, and only through death can they achieve immortality. Vladimir Nabokov's *Lolita* (1955) is a protest, but an ineffectual one, against this paradox. Humbert Humbert longs to eternalize childhood; sitting on a park bench next to an old hag dressed in black with children playing around them, he utters to himself a wish that is addressed to his neighbor: "Ah, leave me alone in my pubescent park, in my mossy garden. Let them play around me forever. Never grow up."[23] The fulfillment of this wish is possible only within the realm of absolute fantasy in which Peter Pan never grows up, or of death, which is the natural habitat of the *puer aeternus*. In the real world, however, the dream of arresting time has always been an impossible one. Lolita, the enticing nymphet, will grow up into a vulgar, hugely pregnant housewife "with her ruined looks and her adult, rope-veined narrow hands and her goose-flesh white arms, and her shallow ears, and her unkempt arm-pits" (p. 279). But even for the maniacal narrator there remains the possibility of recreating Lolita through the Proustian memory evoked by the sounds of children at play. When all is lost, he hears the magic tones again: "What I heard was but the melody of children at play, nothing but that, and so limpid was the air within this vapor of blended voices, majestic and minute, remote and magically near, frank and divinely enigmatic" (p. 310).

But there is a fundamental difference between this concert and the chorus of youths that accompanies Mignon to her grave. Whereas Mignon's presence is at the very center of the chorale, there is a terrible void in the melody that Humbert Humbert hears:

I stood listening to that musical vibration from my lofty slope, to those flashes of separate cries with a kind of demure murmur for background, and then I knew that the hopelessly poignant thing was not Lolita's absence from my side, but the absence of her voice from that concord. (p. 310)

It is on this note of profound disillusionment that the novel ends. This emptiness could never have been felt by Barry Lyndon, Torquemada, or the relatives of little Paul; having always lived in a vacuum, they had become insensible to the loss of a child. Ilyousha's father, as well as Rieux and Paneloux, are immune to such suffering because for them the death of the child brings about a higher form of communion. Wilhelm Meister and Leverkühn do indeed feel the misery of deprivation, but their anguish is relegated to the background. Their loss is as nothing in comparison to the triumph of the child in death. Although Mignon and Nepomuk are both siblings of Lolita, they will never know the same fate to which she is condemned, for they die before being incarcerated in "the coffin of coarse female flesh within which my nymphets are buried alive" (p. 177). Lolita is condemned to a sordid existence of flesh-bound reality from which she escapes only through a death brought on, ironically, by her giving birth to a child. Mignon and Nepomuk, on the other hand, are royally entombed in the crypt of the past. For them, after the first death there is indeed no other.

CHAPTER FIVE

Voci Puerili: A Resonance in Modern Poetry

Do you know the sweetest dream which I dream many
thousand times? It is the one of pre-eminence and childhood.
Thomas Mann

The Redemptive Song

Childhood is a forgotten voyage.
Jean de la Varende

"From the depths of time emerges a cradle song."[1] With these
opening words of his radio broadcast of 4 November 1949, Paul
Eluard refers not to a lullaby composed to soothe an infant but to
a song which captures the essence of the earliest stages of life. In so
doing it becomes a chant which can alleviate suffering even as it
expresses it, which can render habitable the inferno to which some
children are condemned, and which can even abolish death to
which they are all subject. It is the ultimate expression of the
enigma represented by the child.

The voices of children have always been audible in poetry and
infinite in their modulations. Their plaints can be heartrending, as
in the fifth epode of Horace when the unnamed boy, tortured by
the witch Canidia and her fellow crones, pleads with the gods,
"Per hoc inane purpurae decus precor" ("By this poor helpless
childhood's dress, I pray"). Their songs can be ethereal, as in the
tones of "la gente festinata" ("the fleeting people") accompanying
Dante's ascent in the *Paradiso.* Or they can express ecstasy, as in
Henry Vaughan's "The Retreate" from his collection of mystic
verse *Silex Scintillans* (1650), in which the poet, in his opening
evocation of the bliss of childhood, anticipates Wordsworth by almost two centuries:

196

Happy those early dayes! when I
Shin'd in my Angell-infancy!
Before I understood this place
Appointed for my second race . . .

The child is closer to celestial creatures than to adults, who constitute an entirely different order of mortals. And the world, incomprehensible to the child exiled from a heavenly preexistence, is
nonetheless the natural habitat for this second race. What gives
childhood its particular grace, according to the poet, are the intimations of immortality to which the young, still untarnished by
reality, are particularly susceptible. For it is a time of reverie in
which they live, a wistful age when the spirit is still capable of es-
pying through the beauties of nature a greater glory:

When on some *gilded Cloud*, or *flowre*
My gazing soul would dwell an houre,
And in those weaker glories spy
Some shadows of eternity. . .
(lines 11–14)

Early in life the fleshly envelope can still be penetrated by "Bright
shootes of everlastingnesse" (line 20) from another realm. The
poet expresses his profound yearning for what seems unattainable,
namely a return to a stage of innocence that now seems so remote
as to belong to another era of history:

O how I long to travell back
And tread again that ancient track!
That I might once more reach that plaine
Where first I left my glorious traine.
(lines 21–24)

In another poem on the same subject, "Childe-hood," Vaughan acknowledges the impossibility of returning to this Eden despite all
his efforts. Nonetheless, the inaccessible kingdom of childhood
still illumines the present of the seeker after the impossible:

I cannot reach it; and my striving eye
Dazles at it, as at eternity.

In an eloquently simple plea for the prelapsarian state, the poet
proceeds to assert that it is knowledge that undermines the foundations of the childhood paradise:

> If seeing much should make staid eyes,
> And long experience should make wise;
> Since all that age doth teach, is ill,
> Why should I not love childe-hood still?
> (lines 17–20)

This anti-intellectual posture, despite its mystical underpinnings, betrays a curiously modern bias. The child portrayed in Vaughan's verses is the noble savage whose simplicity is corrupted by civilization and whose innocence is ravished by an egotism which is linked with sex. This Rousseauistic vision is expressed in an elegiac stanza which simultaneously laments the fleeting nature of childhood:

> Dear, harmless age! the short, swift span,
> Where weeping virtue parts with man;
> Where love without lust dwells, and bends
> What way we please, without self-ends.
> (lines 31–34)

The all-too-brief "harmless age" is an enigmatic one which, despite its apparent elusiveness, must be recaptured, for it contains the possibility of salvation:

> An age of mysteries! which he
> Must live twice, that would God's face see;
> Which *Angels* guard, and with it play,
> Angels! which foul men drive away.
> (lines 35–39)

Not only does the heaven of childhood precede the age of man, but it is also the heaven that he must regain. It can be found again through the song of the child which poets like Marvell and Traherne tried to intone. Despite their diversity, however, these early voices are isolated ones, and it is only toward the end of the eighteenth century that they swell into that chorus which Blake announced in "Holy Thursday": "Now like a mighty wind they raise to heaven the voice of song."

To analyze this celestial chorus systematically is impossible within any framework, for we lack the ability to conceptualize its nature. Its beauty lies in a wholeness which cannot be articulated. In *Hyperion* (1797) Hölderlin, referring to childhood, says "Es ist ganz was es ist, und darum ist es so schön" ("It is wholly what it is, and therefore it is so beautiful").[2] He goes on to acknowledge the impossibility of expressing a condition for which we have no terms when he attempts to intone his "Hymn to Childhood":

Ruhe der Kindheit! Himmlische Ruhe! Wie oft steh' ich stille vor dir in liebender Betrachtung, und möchte dich denken! Aber wir haben ja nur Begriffe von dem, was einmal schlecht gewesen, und wieder gut gemacht ist; von Kindheit, Unschuld haben wir keine Begriffe.

Peace of Childhood! Heavenly peace! So often do I stand quietly before you in loving contemplation and would like to think you! But we have concepts only of what was once bad and has been redeemed; we have no concepts of childhood, of innocence.

In view of the lack of a rational context in which to situate much less to analyze the children's chorus, I shall comment on some dominant melodies chosen almost at random. These examples may help us to contemplate childhood more sympathetically.

Inflections for the Inspired

Cette naissance
Perpétuelle.
Cette enfance
Perpétuelle. Qu'est-ce que l'on ferait,
qu'est-ce que l'on serait, mon Dieu, sans
les enfants. Qu'est-ce que l'on deviendrait.

This perpetual
Birth.
This perpetual
Childhood. What would one do,
what would one be, my God, without
children. What would one become.
Charles Péguy

The keynote of the children's song in its modern setting was sounded by Novalis. In the dedicatory poem to *Heinrich von Ofterdingen*, he addresses his muse and explains her relationship to the child:

Mit Ahndungen hast du das Kind gepflegt,
Und zogst mit ihm durch fabelhafte Auen.

With presentiments you have fostered the child,
And wandered with him through fabulous meadows.

The child, carefully nurtured by the poet who senses its potential for his art, will lead him through the marvelous zones which he is to explore. The voice of this "miraculous child" is omnipresent in the works of Novalis. Of divine origin, it is both unfathomable and joyful. So in *Hymns to the Night* (1799) the divine youngster's salutatory message, formed of incomprehensible fragments, is an ecstatic one:

Unerschöpfliche Worte und der Botschaften fröhlichste fielen wie Funken eines göttlichen Geistes von seinen freundlichen Lippen.[3]

Unfathomable words and the most joyful of messages fell like the sparks of a divine spirit from his amiable lips.

Novalis's major attempt simultaneously to capture the voice of the child and to explain its function is found in an isolated and hermetic dedicatory poem addressed to his fellow poet, Ludwig Tieck. Its simple title, "An Tieck," contains a play on the word "antique" that evokes for the reader, whether consciously or unconsciously, the ancient lore underlying the mystic verses. The poem opens with the description of a melancholy and faithful child ("Ein Kind voll Wehmut und voll Treue") ("A Child Full of Melancholy and Loyalty") who has been exiled to a foreign country. After a long quest, a long period of waiting and painful wandering, he comes upon a desolate garden and there he finds a book that prefigures the one that Mallarmé was to search for in vain:

Ein altes Buch mit Gold verschlossen
Und nie gehörte Worte drin;
Und wie des Frühlings zarte Sprossen,
So wuchs in ihm ein innrer Sinn.

An old book enclosed by golden hasps
Containing words never before heard;
And like Spring's delicate buds
There grew in him an inner sense.

This arcane tome is a relic of that time immemorial from which the child has been expelled and for which he retains a deep nostalgia. As the child pores over the volume, there appears an old man described as "so childlike and so marvelous" ("so kindlich und so wunderbar") and whose silver hair is gently blown by "the cradle's spring breeze" ("die Frühlingsluft der Wiege"). The child now realizes that he has come to the end of his bitter pilgrimage, for he recognizes in the seer the spirit of the book he has been perusing. This mysterious encounter is a recurrent moment in the cyclical process of birth and death, an evocative symbol of eternal renewal. The vision is similar to the one evoked only a few years later by Blake in "The Mental Traveller." In both poems a wilfully naive mode of expression suggests a mystery that surpasses human understanding. The words and images, in their radical simplicity, are those of a child creating a fairy tale which adults can never comprehend but which can provide for their salvation. The child can do so because his is a different relationship to language, one which Novalis explained in *The Novices of Sais* in a passage that provides the key not only to the child's language but to many modern linguistic concerns:

Man verstehe die Sprache nicht, weil sich die Sprache selber nicht verstehe, verstehen wolle; die echte Sanskrit spräche, um zu sprechen, weil Sprechen ihre Lust und ihr Wesen sei. (pp. 233–34)

We cannot understand language, because language does not understand itself, does not want to understand itself; authentic Sanskrit spoke in order to speak, because speech was its joy and essence.

This naive relationship between the articulator and the articulated is the same archetypal one imagined by Rousseau. In his "Essay on the Origin of Languages" he claims that the primitive language of mankind's childhood, whose "seductive accents" are no longer comprehensible to a civilized humanity, were "daughters of pleasure and not of need."[4] In similar fashion, voices of children are not instruments of communication, but the very essence of their jubilant nature.

Clemens Brentano, like Novalis, questions the status of the word as a signifying element within a cohesive system of communication. In "Es ist der laute Tag hinabgesunken" ("The Noise-filled Day Has Descended") (1800), he signals the death of language and mourns the retarded divagation of the vestigial words which survive in meaningless isolation:

Erstorben ist die Sprache, wenige Worte
Durchirren, sich verspätend, meine Welt.
                    (lines 43–44)

Language has died out, a few words
Drift, with delay, through my world.

The child as child does not survive to learn this meaningless tongue, but its incoherent babbling forms the basis of a far more precious orison. So, in a reversal of the traditional roles, it is the babe who intones a moving lullaby "Gesang der Liebe als sie geboren war" ("The Song of Love As It Was Born") (1817)[5] addressed to the mother from whom it will be separated:

> O Mutter halte dein Kindlein warm
> Die Welt ist kalt und helle,
> > (lines 1–2)

> Oh mother, hold your little child warm,
> The world is cold and clear.

The fragility of the child demands that infinite care which Gerard Manley Hopkins was to express in "The Blessed Virgin Compared to the Air We Breathe":

> World-mothering air, air wild,
> Wound with thee, in thee isled,
> Fold home, fast hold thy child.
> > (lines 124–26)

But for Brentano such tender precautions are ultimately of no avail for the preservation of the child. They can, however, lead to the sanctification of the parent. This required protection evokes compassion and thus serves to bestow grace on the adult, who otherwise is lost in the maze of the world. In an untitled poem Brentano demands the death of the child as a price for this salvation:

> Ich nahm das Kreuz und zog durchs Labyrinth,
> Das wie ein Garten voll von Dornen war,
> Drin sass das Mitleid, ein verschleiert Kind,
> Und weihte sich als Opfer am Altar,[6]

> I took the cross and went through the labyrinth,
> That like a garden was full of thorns;
> Within sat compassion, a veiled child,
> Who consecrated himself as a sacrifice at the altar,

The pious vision of the Catholic poet centers on the emblematic figure of the sacrificial child.

Brentano's child must die, but the song with which it was born remains forever. In "Die grünen Blätter sind gefallen" ("The

Green Leaves Have Fallen") (1802) a child, led by a butterfly, returns home to expire. In the garden, where he calls in vain for his mother, a bird says to him:

> Im Maie, da du hier geboren,
> Da lernte ich ein Lied von dir,
> Ist Mai und Jugend auch verloren,
> Dein süsses Lied, das bleibet mir.

> In May, when you were born here,
> I learned a song from you;
> Although May and youth have been lost,
> Your sweet song remains to me.

This eternal song contains the cryptic message carried by the child and which makes of him an emissary from another world. In the circumstantial "Ermunterung zur Kinderliebe und zum Kindersinne" ("Encouragement to Child's Love and Mind") (1822) we are given some indications as to the structure of this communication but nothing as to what it contains:

> Welch ein Bote ist ein Kind!
> Denn das Wort, das es erquicket,
> Bis zum Himmelsgarten rinnt,
> Wo das Wort ward ausgeschicket,
> Welch ein Bote ist ein Kind!

> What a messenger is the child!
> For the word which it revives
> Flows to the garden of heaven
> From which the word had been sent out.
> What a messenger is the child!

This is a circular message without a recipient, flowing from its origins to its source via a reanimating transmitter, and it has no content that can be expressed through language. But it is this jubilant song which, as an empty medium, encompasses man and whose inspirational inflections make possible his salvation.

Francis Thompson sounds this same triumphal note in a pursuit of the child which is as persistent as that of the Hound of Heaven on the traces of the human soul. In his posthumous essay on Shelley, he tries to come to terms with a question that is intimately linked with his unremitting search for grace: "Know you what it is to be a child? It is to be something very different from the man of to-day. . . . it is to turn . . . nothing into everything."[7]

To perform this operation (which is the divine one of the *creatio ex nihilo*) the child distills from ordinary words "their lovely languid language," that is, their divine essence:

> When from the common sands
> Of poorest common speech of common day
> Thine accents sift the golden music out![8]
> ("Sister Songs")

These tones are not of this world; they are "murmurous with music not their own." When the poet addresses his godchild, it is to a solar stranger consecrated to the divinity that he speaks:

> To the Sun, stranger, surely you belong,
> Giver of golden days and golden song;
> (lines 10–11)

The chant of the child can have the same conciliatory effect as its death and bring about the community of mankind:

> The man at feud with the perduring child
> In you before Song's altar nobly reconciled;
> ("To My Godchild," lines 38–39)

Although the child is eternal, his presence is a fleeting one which can never be recaptured. After his redemptive encounter with man he disappears irrevocably: "Then fled, a swift and trackless fugitive." Thompson's religiosity may be out of favor and his intricate style denigrated as florid. Readers no longer seem to have an ear for

> The subtle sanctities which dart
> From childish lips' unvalued brush.[9]
> ("Sister Songs")

Nonetheless, the canticle of praise the poet intones can be as simple and as subtle as the one which in "Sister Songs" (1895) he urges his children to sing: "Then, Spring's little children, your lauds do ye upraise. . ."

According to Rousseau, whereas our sophisticated modern languages are "the sad daughters of necessity" consisting only of "cries for those possessed of the devil," the childish tongues, which are also those of the great prophets, are constituted of "inflections for the inspired."[10] So the function of the latter as illustrated in the mystic verses of Novalis, Brentano, and Thompson is evidently a redemptive one. This is the case even of songs that are not joyful. In Coleridge's "Dejection: an Ode" (1802), the poet whose "genial spirits fail" is revived by the tale of a child:

> 'Tis of a little child
> Upon a lonesome wild,
> Not far from home, but she hath lost her way:
> And now moans low in bitter grief and fear,
> And now screams loud, and hopes to make her mother hear.

This is, in its brevity and simplicity, a heartrending story of an innocent being lost and isolated. The image of a fearful child lamenting the loss of contact with a familiar world on which is superimposed the picture of the same child shrieking in the forlorn hope of reestablishing communication with that world contains all of the terror of childhood nightmares. And yet this unresolved drama is described by Coleridge as "A tale of less affright / And tempered with delight." And it is this never-concluded tale that directly precedes and makes possible the poet's conversion from dejection to jubilation. It is thanks to the child's song, compounded of moans and screams, that the poet awakens from "reality's dark dream" to the joy that lifts his soul.

The perplexing paradox which lies at the core of Coleridge's "Dejection" is absent from what is without a doubt the best known of the many evocations of an idyllic childhood, Wordsworth's *The Prelude* (1799–1805). Unlike Bernardin de Saint-Pierre's tropical isle from which all sorrows are banned, the "beloved Vale" of the British poet's childhood does not preclude negative emotions. Indeed, some of them, like terror, represent integral components of early age:

> Fair seed-time had my soul, and I grew up
> Fostered alike by beauty and by fear:
>   (lines 301–2, 1850 version)

It is the extraordinary merging of all human emotions, as contradictory as they may be, that gives Wordsworth's childhood para-

dise its very particular quality and that makes its principal inhabitant less vulnerable to the uncertainties of the future:

> . . . there is a dark
> Inscrutable workmanship that reconciles
> Discordant elements, makes them cling together
> In one society.
>   (1.341–44)

Bernardin de Saint-Pierre's Paul was incapable of dealing with the
realities of manhood because he had been overly sheltered in his
sorrow-free youthful existence. The young poet, on the contrary, is
prepared for the rigors he will eventually have to face because of
the very nature of his paradise. Indeed, the early miseries that are a
part of it ensure a richer stage to come:

> How strange that all
> The terrors, pains and early miseries,
> Regrets, vexations, lassitudes interfused
> Within my mind, should e'er have borne a part,
> And that a needful part, in making up
> The calm existence that is mine when I
> Am worthy of myself!
>   (1.344–50)

There is another essential difference between this child and his
predecessors. Despite their close ties with nature, Emile, Paul, and
Virginia were outcasts, exiled from the civilized world that surrounded them and that constantly threatened to encroach upon
their freedom. In *The Prelude*, nature serves as the bond that ties
the child to the world:

> No outcast he, bewildered and depressed:
> Along his infant veins are interfused
> The gravitation and the filial bond
> Of nature that connect him with the world.
>   (2.241–44)

Unlike the ideal but unstable dreamworlds of Rousseau and Bernardin de Saint-Pierre, the childhood paradise is not in danger of
constant disintegration because it is an inseparable part of the real
world.

Wordsworth's blissful realm is as innocent as the preromantic one, but its simplicity is based on the very complexity of harmonious interrelations. The calm delight of early age is attributed:

> To those first-born affinities that fit
> Our new existence to existing things,
> And, in our dawn of being, constitute
> The bond of union between life and joy.
>   (1.555–58)

Wordsworth finds two types of bliss in the childhood paradise. The first is ordinary joy, which, though not to be disdained, is soon forgotten:

> Thus oft amid those fits of vulgar joy
> Which, through all seasons, on a child's pursuits
> Are prompt attendants, 'mid that giddy bliss
> Which, like a tempest, works along the blood
> And is forgotten;
>   (1.581–85)

But there is a more sublime joy, "gleams like the flashing of a shield," an almost inexpressible form of ecstasy. Unlike its more common counterpart, this sacred joy remains forever embedded in the memory:

> —And if the vulgar joy by its own weight
> Wearied itself out of the memory,
> The scenes which were a witness of that joy
> Remained in their substantial lineaments
> Depicted on the brain, and to the eye
> Were visible, a daily sight;
>   (1.597–602)

This supranatural bliss is intimately connected with the privileged instances of the recollection of years gone by. Through the involuntary memory, "by chance collisions and quaint accidents," the reality of the childhood past can be invoked. When, as an adult, the poet feels that he has gone astray, his temporary despondency can be quickly dissipated because he can find "in simple childhood" something of the base upon which his entire existence and his present stature as a writer rest. In a Proustian stanza, Wordsworth maintains that there is a redemptive quality in the recollection of the past Eden:

There are in our existence spots of time,
That with distinct pre-eminence retain
A renovating virtue,
    (12.208–10)

These remembrances of things past are retrospective visions that justify existence by imparting a special grace to what would otherwise be a dreary present. Thus their charm is a magical one:

Those recollected hours that have the charm
Of visionary things, those lovely forms
And sweet sensations that throw back our life,
And almost make remotest infancy
A visible scene, on which the sun is shining.
    (1.631–35)

The childhood paradise is no longer a transient phase through which one passes on the way to the miseries or to the joys of adulthood. It is an omnipresent reality that can shape our whole existence and that makes possible the poetic act. Wordsworth's enterprise is to demonstrate the lasting and ever-augmented impact of childhood upon the present and the future:

I have endeavored to display the means
Whereby this infant sensibility,
Great birthright of our being, was in me
Augmented and sustained.
    (2.269–72)

The foundations of an aesthetic eternity, of the religion of art, are grounded in the childhood paradise.[11]

The salutary effect of the child's song becomes, of course, a favorite theme of the romantics and finds its most eloquent expression in the works of Victor Hugo. All too often his verses are denigrated as being too grandiloquent and sentimental; his depictions of domesticity are decried as tasteless. The mystical subtleties of Novalis and the philosophical intimations of Coleridge are usually considered as foreign to the comforting and reassuring qualities associated with Hugo and which he himself ascribes to his children in the poems of *Interior Voices* (1837) and *Leaves of Autumn* (1831). And yet there are unsuspected depths beneath the.surface of even his apparently simple works. The opening words of one of his most familiar and familial poems, "Lorsque l'enfant paraît. . ."

("When the child appears. . ."), have an incantatory quality that evokes the apparition of the mysterious child. It is an invocation that gains in power thanks to the abrupt contrast with the hemistich that completes the verse: "le cercle de la famille" ("the family circle"). On the one hand there is a wondrous intrusion, on the other the closed circularity of domesticity. The concluding episode of a less well-known work, the wilfully naive "Epopée du lion" ("Epic of the Lion"), despite its unpromisingly banal subject matter achieves a similar effect through the juxtaposition of two modes of discourse. A horde of hunters has failed to save the little prince, whom the lion is holding between his jaws. Where the adults are impotent, a naked little girl, who sings with "une ineffable voix, plus tendre qu'une lyre" ("with an ineffable voice, more tender than a lyre"), succeeds. She falls silent when she perceives the lion, and it is her mere presence and the simple gesture of her arm that tame the beast, who gently deposes the boy at her feet. As in Goethe's *The Novella*, the child triumphs over savagery.

In other poems from *L'Art d'être grand-père* (*The Art of Being Grandfather*) (1877) Hugo explains what it is that gives a little girl the powers that adults do not possess. In "Le Syllabus" the poet listens to children:

> Et je crois entrevoir une vague ouverture
> Des grands cieux étoilés.
> Car vous étiez hier, ô doux parleurs étranges,
> Les interlocuteurs des astres et des anges.

> And I believe I can perceive a vague opening
> In the spacious starry skies
> For yesterday you were, oh sweet strange speakers,
> The interlocutors of stars and angels.

In "Encore une Immaculée Conception" ("One More Immaculate Conception") Hugo goes on to indicate that such gentle creatures are the bearers of significant tidings. Even the babbling of three-year-olds is fraught with meaning, and the poet opens each one of their words like a book and in them discovers "un sens profond et grand, sévère quelquefois" ("A great and profound, sometimes severe meaning"). Not only are Hugo's "strange speakers" emanations of extraterrestrial regions, they are the abodes of divinity. So, above all, these celestial creatures are agents of salvation, bringing the poet the light of some indefinable "ray from an unknown dawn." Their role is defined in a poem explicitly entitled "Fonction de l'enfant" ("Function of the Child"): it is to effect that "sainte intervention" which will assure the dominance of justice and goodness. For "Les hommes sont victorieux, formidables, terribles; / Mais les petits enfants viennent à leur secours" ("Men are victorious, formidable, and terrible / But little children come to their rescue"). Thus for Hugo the sanctified child comes from on high to save man through his song, not from defeat, but from the very triumph that spells spiritual disaster.

The motif that recurs most often in the children's music is the redemptive aspect of the past in which they are memorialized. Although Wordsworth has provided the most extensive treatment of this theme, its most poignant and concentrated expression is found in a poem by Chamisso, "The Castle Boncourt" (1827). In the opening stanza, the poet sounds the familiar theme of an old man reminiscing on his early years:

> Ich träum' als Kind mich zurücke
>   Und schüttle mein greises Haupt;
> Wie sucht ihr mich heim, ihr Bilder,
>   Die lang ich vergessen geglaubt?

> I dream myself back as a child
>   And shake my grey head;
> How you do search me out, you images,
>   Which I had long thought forgotten?

The simplicity of these words and images seems to belie their ambiguity. On an obvious level, we have the poet as an old man who, through the medium of a dream, forces himself back into childhood. But a more subtle interpretation is possible. The old man, as a child, dreams himself and his past simultaneously. And it is the images of the past that search him out, that visit him in the biblical sense. In any case, the following stanzas are an evocation of the castle of his childhood, with all the accoutrements of a fairy tale, with its moat, its stone bridge, its turrets and statues. In the very center of this visionary fortress, in the chapel of the castle, lies the incomprehensible mystery of childhood: an inscription that remains indecipherable. Although illuminated by the bright light that passes through the stained-glass windows, it cannot be seen by the poet's tear-veiled eyes. As dreamlike as all these images are, the poet imparts to his homestead a solid reality—and at the same time denies its existence. The massive castle of his fathers stands firm and true in the poet's mind and yet it has disappeared from the earth. Despite this negation, the enigmatic message that lies at the core of childhood serves as a benediction which makes it possible for the poet to resume his triumphant song.

Not all castles are constructed on as solid a fundament of memory as the Chateau Boncourt. The ruins of Joseph von Eichendorff's ancestral estate cannot be restored, and the secret of the childhood song is no longer contained within its crumbling walls. In "Heimkehr" ("Homecoming") (1810) the wanderer who traverses Eichendorff's entire work returns home to find the portal solidly locked and breaks it down with his sword. Behind the smashed gates he finds a terrible void. All that remains is the abandoned shell of the mansion, through whose deserted corridors the wind howls. In the courtyard lie the fragments of the statues of his forefathers, and on this rubble heap of the past he comes upon the shattered zither on which he had played as a child while his now deceased mother read him fairy tales. We can still hear faint echoes of this forever stilled music in other poems such as "An die Dichter" ("To the Poets") (1815), but only through retrospection and even then only in an interrogative mode:

> Wo findest du den alten Garten,
> Dein Spielzeug, wunderbares Kind,
> Der Sterne heilge Redensarten,
> Das Morgenrot, den frischen Wind?

> Where do you find the old garden,
> Your toys, wondrous child,
> The sacred astral accents,
> The dawn, the fresh wind?

The discouraging answer to this question, a response already implicit in "Heimkehr" ("The Homecoming"), is unambiguously repeated in "Der irre Spielmann" ("The Mad Street-player") (1837), the penultimate poem of the cycle of *Wanderlieder*, which is followed by the poet's encounter with death:

> Aus stiller Kindheit unschuldiger Hut
> Trieb mich der tolle, frevelnde Mut.
> Seit ich da draussen so frei nun bin,
> Finde ich nicht wieder nach Hause mich hin.

From the innocent shelter of childhood
Mad, outrageous mettle drove me.
Since outside I am now so free,
I cannot find my way back home.

The poet can never recapture the magic language of the past, for it is spoken only in the place of his birth, to which he can never return.

The plaints lamenting the irremediable divorce from childhood belie the reassuring image of Eichendorff as the carefree bard of a cheerful youth whose minstrels roam over hill and dale, playing their fiddles and stopping off to dance at village taverns and country inns, an image which in any case is in contradiction to the complex reality of his entire work. His favorite protagonist is indeed a thing of threads and patches, but then so are those of Samuel Beckett. In a way that anticipates the latter's "L'Expulsé," the familiar and exuberant novella *Memoirs of a Good-for-nothing* (1826) opens with the brutal expulsion of the narrator from the world of childhood. The father sees the son lazily sitting against the door and exclaims.

"You good-for-nothing! There you are again sunning yourself, yawning, and exhausting yourself by stretching your limbs, while you let me do all the work alone. I can't feed you here any longer. Spring is at hand; get out in the world and earn your own bread."[12]

This violent eviction is reenacted many years later in the conclusion to Maxim Gorki's *My Childhood* (1913) when the narrator's grandfather propulses his young charge into the world with the words: "Alexei, you're not a medal, you're only hanging round my neck. There's no room for you here. You must go out into the world."[13]

Gorki's childhood was embittered by the misery of indigence, death, and sadistic cruelty, whereas Eichendorff's was an idyllic one, and this difference is reflected in the attitudes of their respective autobiographic narrators. Nonetheless, in addition to the fact that both are equally unprepared for the reality into which they are so rudely thrust, there is one similarity so fundamental that it obliterates all the surface disparities. Alexis's expulsion separates him forever from an anterior universe that has been colored by the ancient Slavonic myths and legends recounted by his grandmother and whose resonances resounding through the work are foreign to both narrators. Eichendorff's wanderer is cut off forever from a world shaped by his mother's recitals of fairy tales whose accents mark a poetry which, likewise, is estranged from them.

Nostalgia for the security of this lost domain of a childhood unsullied by evil is a dominant theme in Eichendorff's poetry. In some untitled, posthumously published verses (c. 1809) he writes:

> Bin ich denn nicht auch ein Kind gewesen?—
> Spielte goldne, goldne Stunden,
> Unbekannt noch mit dem Bösen,
> Furchtlos an den finstern Schlunde.

> For had I too not been a child?—
> Played golden, golden hours,
> Still unacquainted with evil,
> Fearless by the somber abyss?

Along with this wistful longing, there is also resentment against those who lure the child into leaving his home voluntarily. In "Der Schnee" ("The Snow") (1815) a wandering child urges the one who has stayed home to explore the world with him. Despite the poet's warning, "Glaub dem falschen Herzen nicht" ("Do not believe the false heart"), the child is seduced by the vagabond, "Denn so schön klingt, was er spricht" ("For what he says sounds so beautiful"). The beauty of the song of the tempter is stronger than the admonitions of the poet who concludes sadly, "Armes Kind, ach wärst du tot" ("Poor child, would you were dead").

Despite these recurrent expressions of yearning for the garden of innocence, Eichendorff's conception of childhood is far more ambiguous than that of Brentano. In a striking reversal of the romantic faith in reveries, the poet asserts in "Die Freunde" ("Friends") (1837) that the homebound child's vision is limited rather than expanded by dreams and hence its song lacks depth:

> Wer auf dem Wogen schliefe,
> Ein sanft gewiegtes Kind,
> Kennt nicht des Lebens Tiefe,
> Vor süssen Träumen blind.

> Whoever sleeps on the waves,
> A softly cradled child,
> Does not know life's depth,
> Blinded by sweet dreaming.

In contrast to this slumbering infant is the child seized by the storms who leaves the false world of innocence to wander along the dark streets which lead him "zu wildem Tanz und Fest" ("to the wild dance and feast"). It is the latter child whose joyful voice is inspired by his faith in God and in the stars and whom the poet would choose as his guide. In "Die falsche Schwester" ("The False sister") (1837), a late poem included in the *Romanzen*, the poet renounces the childhood world of passivity for which he continues to long. The poem opens with a nostalgia-charged evocation of a naively simple scene:

> Meine Schwester, die spielt' an der Linde—
> Stille Zeit, wie so weit, so weit!
> Da spielten so schöne Kinder
> Mit ihr in der Einsamkeit.

> My sister she played by the lime tree—
> Silent time, so far off, far off!
> There played such beautiful children
> With her in loneliness.

This matinal stanza is followed by a nocturnal one in which the sister, with a smile playing over her features, sleeps in her chamber, lulled by the songs which the children continue to sing the whole night through in the garden. This gentle idyll, so characteristic in its simple charm of a certain strain in German romanticism, is interrupted by its vehement denunciation:

> Die ganze Nacht hat gelogen,
> Sie hat mich so falsch gegrüsst,
> Die Engel sind fortgeflogen,
> Und Haus und Garten stehn wüst.

> The whole night was a lie,
> She greeted me so falsely,
> The angels have flown away,
> And house and garden are desolate.

The wasted castle and garden will never be restored, for they represent a falsehood, an artificial construct cut off from the reality of a passionate faith. The passivity of the cradled child is rejected in favor of a more forceful activity. With Eichendorff the innocent child's voice begins to be muted, almost drowned out by the more powerful one of the adolescent wanderer who will reappear in the bohemian guise of Rimbaud's unbridled youth.

The Reverberation in a Void

Le ventre obscure s'entr'ouvre à la lumière
Un enfant vient de naître. . .

The dark womb opens up to light
A child has just been born. . .

Paul Eluard

There are, of course, more false notes in the divine symphony of childhood than the ones which occasionally intrude as dissonances in the lyrics of Eichendorff. One of the most discordant is sounded by Heinrich Heine. The promising first verse of one poem, "Mein Kind, wir waren Kinder" ("My Child, We Were Children") (1824), is followed by a sarcastic depiction of children acting like little adults. The ludic strain is disrupted by the sardonic disillusionment of the grown-up. A banal materialism negates the values that earlier romantics perceived in the child. The poem ends on a mordant note:

Vorbei sind die Kinderspiele,
Und alles rollt vorbei—
Das Geld und die Welt und die Zeiten
Und Glaube und Liebe und Treu'.[14]

Children's games are over,
And everything rolls past
Money and the world and the times
And faith and love and trust.

The end of children's games marks the end of faith.

Later on in the century, there are other signs that the child's voice is growing harsh, or even failing. Rimbaud's "seven-year-old poet," who can find peace only in the latrine, intones a song of violence. His postdiluvian children have been divorced from a higher reality. They can no longer experience wonderment directly. At best, they can perceive it only through windowpanes. This is the meaning of the evocative lines which create the central image of "Après le Déluge" ("After the Flood") (1875?):

Dans la grande maison de vitres encore ruisselante les enfants en deuil regardèrent les merveilleuses images.[15]

In the large house of panes, still dripping, children in mourning were looking at the marvelous images.

Such a glass partition does not always prevent the child-spectator from becoming child-participant. In "Les Effarés" ("The Frightened Ones") (1870) impoverished urchins in rags press their faces against the window of a bakery. While the baker with his greasy smile hums an old tune, they take part vicariously in the miraculous baking of bread. Inspired, they, too, sing, and their song is like a prayer. It is this orison that eventually, in the midst of physical and spiritual indigence, will permit the child-poet to give a raucous expression to his intoxication as he does in the violently ecstatic "Ma Bohème" and "Roman." And in *Les Illuminations* (1875?) Rimbaud can even become jubilant:

J'ai tendu des cordes de clocher à clocher; des guirlandes de fenêtre à fenêtre; des chaînes d'or d'étoile à étoile, et je danse. (p. 132)

I have attached ropes from bell tower to bell tower; garlands from window to window; chains of gold from star to star, and I dance.

This wild jubilation, barely contained by the strictures of music, is echoed later by W. B. Yeats, whose crazed girl dances upon the shore intoning an incomprehensible song:

> No matter what disaster occurred
> She stood in desperate music wound,
> Wound, wound, and she made in her triumph
> Where the bales and the baskets lay
> No common intelligible sound
> But sang, "O sea-starved, hungry sea."[16]

Such exaltation is in striking contrast to the gentle voluptuousness of Rimbaud's "companion in hell," Paul Verlaine, and to the childish vision expressed in such simple but carefully wrought lyrics as "Green." The dangers inherent in Verlaine's wilful naiveté become manifest in the works of the many symbolists whose effete tones are incompatible with any authentic rendition of childhood. At approximately the same time that Rimbaud's vagabond treads the fields and Verlaine's child is lying in the lap of his beloved, Laforgue's simpering hypertrophic child longs plaintively to go bye-bye with his mommy. His mawkishly sentimental refrain, "Dis, maman, tu m'appelles?" ("Say, mommy, are you calling me?"), is a far cry from the vigorous tone Rimbaud adopts in his sacramental celebration of childhood.

Although the infant's voice cannot be stifled either by the bitter tones of Heine or the dulcet ones of Laforgue, it does become muted. This new song, hovering as it does between silence and barely voiced melodies, contains previously unheard harmonies which suffuse the entire work of Rainer Maria Rilke. In the essay *About Art* he admits that his aesthetics are based on a careful exploitation of the childhood theme, and *The Notebooks of Malte Laurids Brigge* represents a practical demonstration of this *ars poetica*. The relationship of the poet and the child as analyzed in Rilke's works is far more complex than in the works of Novalis, in which the simple inspirational role of the child is posited. For the romantics the fundamental question was that of the influence of the child on the poet. The reverse is equally important for Rilke, who constantly demonstrates his concern for the effect of the poet on the child. So in the poem "Ich war ein Kind und träumte viel" ("I Was a Child and Dreamt a Lot"), the poet steals the child's song and, in doing so, robs him of his very existence:

Er sang. Und dann verklang sein Schritt,—
er musste weiterziehn;
und sang mein Leid, das ich nie litt,
und sang mein Glück, das mir entglitt,
und nahm mich mit und nahm mich mit—
und keiner weiss wohin. . .[17]

He sang. And then the sound of his steps died out,
he had to move on;
and sang my suffering that I never suffered
and sang my fortune that escaped me
and took me along and took me along—
and no one knows where. . .

The appropriation by the adult of the child's music is a necessary act which makes possible the full expression of the infantile voice but simultaneously leads to the disappearance of its bearer. The ambiguity of this emerging song is hinted at by the paradox represented by the provenance of the voice itself. For the song is sounded not by the poet (who has also disappeared) but by the vanished child. It arises as the result of a dual absence.

The inherent difficulty in recreating the music of childhood without an irreparable loss is the subject of another Rilke poem, which opens with the query, "Was war denn das in Kindertagen?" ("What was it then in childhood days?"). This is followed by what appears to be an answer: an extraordinary impressionistic recital suggestive of the sensations evoked by the Christmas feast. But the stanza closes with the implied admission of failure inherent in the expanded repetition of the original question: "Was war es denn in Kindertagen, / das sich nicht wiederleben lässt?" ("What was it then in childhood days, / that can never be relived?"). The following quatrain is an attempt to recreate that which cannot be relieved:

> So muss es das Wehen im Wind sein—
> weils nichtmehr unheimlich hallt
> oder das Traurig—und Blindsein,
> oder der Wünsche Gestalt:

> It must be the fluttering in the wind—
> because it no longer echoes in unearthly fashion
> or mournfulness and blindness
> or the configuration of wishes:

The complex nature of this evocation is epitomized in the metaphor of "Das Wehen im Wind." The fluttering of the wind is indeed joyful, and yet the word *Wehen* contains *Weh*, which means "woe," and *Wehe*, which implies suffering. A sinister resonance belies the pure joy of childhood. The poem ends with an ambiguous couplet: "Jeder will wieder Kind sein, / und doch sind die Wünsche so alt" ("Everyone wants to be a child again / and yet wishes are so old"). Longing after childhood is universal, but has this age-old wish ever been fulfilled?

This ever-unresolved quality of the child's voice finds its fullest expression in yet another of Rilke's poems, "Kindheit." It consists of four stanzas, each of which conjures up a different situation within childhood and each of which ends with a pair of verses that summarizes a complex emotional state. The first of these closing couplets expresses simultaneously wonderment and a sense of futility within solitude: "O wunderliche Zeit, o Zeitverbringen, / o Einsamkeit" ("Oh marvelous time, oh wasted time / oh loneliness"). The second begins with a dreamlike, nameless sorrow reminiscent of Verlaine's wordless romances, yet very different in that the vague suffering implies a sense of horror evoked by a bottomless abyss: "O Trauer ohne Sinn, o Traum, o Grauen, / o Tiefe ohne Grund" ("Oh mourning without meaning, oh dream, oh horror, / oh bottomless abyss"). The third stanza concludes with the fearful expression of the vanishing powers of conceptualization: "O immer mehr entweichendes Begreifen, / o Angst, o Last" ("Oh ever more vanishing comprehension, / Oh fear, oh burden"). The giddiness evoked by this verse leads almost to a loss of consciousness.[18] The fainting motion is checked only by the weight of the last word, under which the poet bows. The fourth stanza, in its entirety, provides the ultimate vision of childhood:

> Und stundenlang am grossen grauen Teiche,
> mit einem kleinen Segelschiff zu knien;
> es zu vergessen, weil noch andre, gleiche
> und schönere Segel durch die Ringe ziehn,
> und denken müssen an das kleine bleiche
> Gesicht, das sinkend aus dem Teiche schien—;
> O Kindheit, o entgleitende Vergleiche.
> Wohin? Wohin?

> And to kneel with a small sailboat
> hours on end by the large gray pond;
> and to forget it, because still other, similar
> and more beautiful sails glide through the rings,
> and to have to think of the small pale
> face, that shone, sinking, from the pond—;
> Oh childhood, oh vanishing comparisons.
> Whither? Whither?

The central image seems to be drawn directly from the final section of Rimbaud's "Le Bateau ivre" ("The Drunken Boat"), in which a disconsolate boy squats by a puddle in whose cold gray waters he had just launched a toy boat. But there is an important difference. Whereas in the Rimbaud poem the boy is surrounded by menacing and imprisoning symbols of the adult world, Rilke's child is entranced by his own drowning image, and childhood itself becomes a series of evanescent comparisons. It is of such vanishing metaphors that the new music of childhood is composed.

Conclusion

> Voici pourtant l'enfant parfait
> Au sommet d'une aurore intime
>
> Here then is the perfect child
> At the summit of an intimate dawn
> Paul Eluard

A fish head lies grinning between the dugs of the swollen corpse of a cat. A prematurely old girl with leprous hands sucks a strand of her sticky hair. A fat, pink bitch taunts a hungry beggar with her flesh. A candy vendor is attacked by a swarm of bees. This is the sordid street scene which Saint-John Perse depicts in the opening verses of one of his poems from *Praises* (1908). But the child who is witness to this scene is so astonished by its beauty that he is almost paralyzed and cannot grasp it:

> . . . Un enfant voit cela,
> si beau
> qu'il ne peut plus fermer ses doigts.

> . . . A child sees that,
> so beautiful
> that he can no longer close his fingers.

The poet, however, can articulate this vision. In collaboration with the child, he can express wonderment at reality and discover beauty even in the detritus floating in an open sewer:

> Mais le coco que l'on a bu et lancé là,
> tête aveugle qui clame affranchie de l'épaule,
> détourne du dalot
> la splendeur des eaux pourpres lamées de graisses
> et d'urines, où trame le savon comme de la toile
> d'araignée.[19]

> But the coconut shell, drained and tossed away,
> a blind, indignant head severed from the shoulders,
> diverts from the culvert
> the splendor of purple waters striped with fat
> and urine, where the soap weaves like a spider
> web.

This power of transformation is the particular gift of the child which the poet must appropriate for himself and exploit in order to forge the new metaphors with which to celebrate the universe.

Perhaps no poet has been so aware as Paul Eluard of both the impossibility and the necessity of seizing these metaphors. "Le lieu de ma jeunesse m'est inaccessible" ("The place of my childhood is inaccessible to me"), he complains in a poem which nonetheless he entitled "Enfance maîtresse." In another poem he exclaims, "Enfant toujours blotti dans un temps inégal / Murs ensoleillés murs opaques." The child, hidden within a time that is foreign to us, is protected by sun-drenched but impenetrable walls. But this poem, too, has a title that belies the hopelessness of the task: "Deux Voix en une" ("Two Voices in One"). This implicit perfect joining of the adult and the child is expressed in the direct statement with which "Jeunesse engendre jeunesse" ("Youth Engenders Youth") opens:

> J'ai été comme un enfant
> Et comme un homme.
> J'ai conjugé passionément
> Le verbe être et ma jeunesse.

> I was like a child
> And like a man.
> With passion I conjugated
> The verb to be and my youth.

In *Hyperion* (1.3), Hölderlin sought to preserve the sanctity of childhood by positing a radical divorce between two separate races: "Ja! ein göttlich Wesen ist das Kind, solang es nicht in die Chämeleonesfarbe der Menschen getaucht ist" ("Verily, the child is a divine being as long as it has not been dipped into the chameleon dye of men"). Eluard refuses to accept such a separation.

The internal necessity of a marriage between man and child is a recurrent theme in Eluard's poems of *Le Dur Désir de durer* ("The Firm Desire to Last") (1946) and finds its most direct and eloquent expression in "Grandeur d'hier et d'aujourd'hui" ("Grandeur of Yesterday and Today"). The first three sections of the poem evoke a universe marked by the absence of children. They present a nightmare vision of disintegration and nausea, played out in a world in which the only audible word is an evil one. Without the child the desire to endure, no matter how persistent, is of no avail. The fourth and concluding section depicts the miraculous retrieval of the poetic word: "Mais soudain de parler je me sens conquérant" ("But suddenly I feel myself master of speech"). The recovery of language comes simultaneously with the birth of the child for whom the cradle song has been composed and whose intoning of the song ever emerges from the depths of time:

> Un enfant naît en moi qui n'est pas d'aujourd'hui
> Un enfant de toujours par un baiser unique

> A child who is not of today is born in me
> A child of all times by a unique kiss

The effects of the apparition of the unique and eternal child are instantaneous and dramatic, and the concluding verses of the poem are victorious ones:

> Et la mort est vaincue un enfant sort des ruines
> Derrière lui les ruines et la nuit's s'effacent

> And death is vanquished a child leaves the ruins
> Behind him the ruins and the night are effaced

The child makes it possible for man to triumph over the discouraging desolation of a disenchanted world and to survive even the destruction of the monuments of civilization. Conjoined with the child, the poet overcomes his aphasia. Eluard has rejected the cynical irony of Heine and at the same time refuses to revert to the mystic and sometimes excessively sentimental emotions of his romantic predecessors. Eluard merges the subdued tone of Rilke's children with the headily ecstatic realism of Rimbaud.

The poet's voice can and must merge with that of the child. Such a powerful conjugation is the key to the enigma posed by the four hermetic verses of "Toute la Vie" ("All of Life"):

> A l'origine de mes forces ma mémoire
> De tout son poids brille sur l'herbe de l'enfance
> Herbe déserte herbe d'azur sans un pas d'homme
> Où les jours moins les jours n'ont pas laissé de nuit.

> At the origin of my force my memory
> With all its weight shines on the grass of childhood
> Deserted grass grass of azure without a man's step
> Where days less days have not left night.

The voice of man and the voice of the child are blended into such a perfect unison that not a trace of either remains. We are left with a reverberation in a void, with the Mallarméan essence of poetry which is a sonorous inanity, with what Henri Michaux in "Paix dans les brisements" ("Peace in the Shattering") called "un écho d'un écho d'un écho." This is the resonance of which the music intoned by Dante's *voci puerili* is composed.

Children in Power

Any adult who begins to observe a child as a special being is
lost. The adoration of childhood is the worst heresy.

Giraudoux

A father, already well on in years, and his neighbor, both tapping
their well-made pipes, admire a pre-Columbian statuette as they
sip their after-dinner brandy. The children, physically exhausted
from a day spent fishing in the country, have politely excused
themselves and, while the adults are quietly conversing, retire to
the room upstairs to play a little before going to bed. The sound of
their clear, transparent laughter becomes audible in the living
room; the father falls silent, and his features are softened by a
tender expression tinged with melancholy. Raising his finger, he finally says, "You hear them? . . . They are cheerful, aren't they?
They're having fun."[1] The neighbor agrees, and a good-natured
smile wrinkles his cheeks. This touchingly reassuring miniature
scene provides the framework for Nathalie Sarraute's *Do You
Hear Them?* (1972) as well as the basic material for the variations
which form its substance. The narrative of this concentrated novella is equally limited in scope. When the children's laughter becomes too noisy, the father goes upstairs and talks to them for a
few moments before rejoining his guest. This rupture constitutes
the entire action of a recital which, through a series of speculative
modulations and elaborations by various narrative voices, achieves
a meticulous analysis of the fluctuating interrelationships between
adults and children. It gathers together the major themes we have
studied and simultaneously interjects a new element which points
to a radically new view of the implications of childhood.

Like the traces drawn in the sand by the children of Novalis,
Kafka, and Gide, the laughter of Sarraute's children is a fleeting
message so incomprehensible that it lends itself to a multiplicity of
contradictory interpretations. It is initially heard as a "fóu rire,"

one of those spontaneous and uncontrollable fits of laughter, devoid of significance, to which all children are subject. The innocence of these peals of laughter is infectious: as it evokes a host of simple images in its auditors, it transforms, though only momentarily, the adults, who, like the auditors of Brentano's fairy tale and the habitués of Grass's cabaret, themselves become childlike. This music is as evanescent as the enigmatic child itself and "the pure notes of their cristaline laughter are dispersed" (p. 10). Simultaneously, as if under the influence of Colette's Claudine, there emerges a not so innocent, flirtatious tone, barely verging on the erotic and hinting at a sexual awakening: "Their laughs, innocent, saucy, and just a trifle malicious, fuse and soar" (p. 10). Eventually, the father thinks to discern a mocking, ironic accent which calls into question all the cultural values, as represented by the statuette, that justify his existence. But who, in this laughter, "could have detected menace, danger, turmoil, disorderly flight?" (p. 14). The father's rhetorical question supposes suspicions that will be verified as the laughter becomes one of derision, prompted by the children's own cynical imitation of the admiring banalities which the adults employ to praise the statuette. The more the father reflects, the more sinister the tone becomes: like Blake's frowning babe, these children not only reject the norms of Western civilization but are a menace that can eventually destroy them. As well-treated children, they emulate Mishima's Noburu in their effort to take vengeance on the well-meaning progenitor who has imprisoned them in paradise. Their laughter is as meaningless and terrorizing as the gibberish songs of the children in Virginia Woolf's *The Years*. And its effect is similar to that produced by the children in Kafka's *The Trial*: it propels the father into a nightmare world in which, guilty of an unknown crime, he is subjected to interrogation by a social worker. With another modulation in the laughter a seductive note dominates, one which contains an irresistible invitation, one which urges the father to come up, not to scold a group of noisy, unruly children, but to participate in their innocent world of games. Like George Eliot's Eppie, they hold out the promise of redemption. But like a siren song, this laughter, too, is dangerous and the father is afraid: "They are calling me, casting a spell over me. . . . Hold me back" (p. 35). He knows that the enchantment of their laughter is so powerful that it can compel him to smash his statuette. So the children's laughter is made up of an infinite num-

ber of component parts. When reconstituted, its various contradictory elements form the same "sacred puzzle" which Stifter's
Abdias faced when he contemplated his daughter, Ditha. But it is a
puzzle which forces us, like Lévi-Strauss, to reverse the terms of its
definition. The enigma threatens to become a response to which
there are no questions.

Just as the laughter, in a process of continuous transformation, epitomizes the enigmatic child, so the playroom, as described
by Sarraute, represents the worlds of childhood in their various
configurations. It is a separate reality, physically close to the living
room which is the domain of the adults, and yet spiritually isolated. As soon as they pass into their realm, the children completely forget their elders. As for the grown-ups, they feel safe in
the apparent security of their seclusion:

But here they are protected. What powerful instruments it would take to
pierce, to crack these thick partitions behind which they are sheltered
with that [statuette] placed there, betwen them. . . . Nothing can attain
us and make us vacillate. (pp. 13–14)

The room of the children is a foreign country, and in many respects
a comfortable and protected paradise, a realm of oblivion. It is the
proper setting for children who have all the advantages of a comfortable upper-middle-class home and whose father has spared no
effort to inculcate in them the good taste that his parents have bequeathed to him. With its flowered curtains and white linens, it is a
setting as reassuring as the room which Hélène prepared with such
loving care for her daughter in Zola's *A Love Affair*. But, like the
magic chamber in Cocteau's *The Holy Terrors*, it contains the dis-
order of a different existence. It is littered with the vulgar detritus
of civilization; comic books, cheap magazines, and cigarette butts
are scattered all about. The room assumes as many forms as the
laughter, and its interior architecture is determined by the imagination of the children. When the father comes up to scold them,
he enters a well-ordered universe whose inhabitants treat him
gently. He is a benign if somewhat bumbling divinity in their
heaven who must be humored. And yet their indulgence is of a
condescending nature which implies a degree of hostility. This hostility becomes overt in another version of the father's unwarranted
intrusion. The room is now the filthy and disorderly domain of evil-
minded youngsters, and the father is transformed in their eyes into

the big black wolf, the evil ogre who has come to despoil their kingdom and to destroy their feast. Like Mr. Ramsay, in Virginia Woolf's *To the Lighthouse*, who constantly disappoints his son's longing for an excursion with the repeated phrase "There'll be no landing at the lighthouse tomorrow," this father is a spoilsport. In fact, he is worse than that. And in his rage at having been disturbed by their laughter and at having been misunderstood, he reveals his essential brutality. In an excess of rage, he turns on one of his daughters and, like an enraged dog, presumably bites her. He is a sadist, no better than the parents in Vallès's *Child* or in Renard's *Carrot Top* and the children suffer in the hell he has created for them. But not passively: the daughter takes her revenge by denouncing her father to a social worker (even though she bears no trace of an attack). Hers is the vengeance of both the mistreated and the well-treated child. As in so many hells created by adults for their children, psychological cruelty is more dreadful than physical torment. The father's attempts to raise his children with an appreciation for art are not as well-intentioned as they seem; they are vicious efforts to pervert the children's essentially innocent vision. The museums to which he drags them are torture chambers in which their aesthetic sensibilities are corrupted. So the heaven and hell he has created for them are equally noxious. Like Hugo's *comprachicos*, he is an evil surgeon who attempts to disfigure his offspring. His children must die so that they can become his image. But unlike Goethe's Mignon, they refuse to become entombed in the crypt of any past, no matter how splendid. They will emulate Lolita and shed their childhood to become modern adults divorced from the past.

The multiple versions of a minor episode contain in their ambiguity all the elements of the child and its world which we have discerned in Western literature. But Nathalie Sarraute goes further than her predecessors by drawing the inevitable conclusions from their premises. In his "Sister Songs," Francis Thompson delineated the traditionally subservient place of children while indicating their latent potential. By doing so, he perhaps unwittingly touched on the fundamental source of friction between generations:

Yea, ripe for kingship, yet must be
Captive in statuted minority!
So is all power fulfilled, as soul in thee.

As soon as the young become cognizant of the arbitrary nature of parental regulations and aware of their own maturity, a destructive irritation inspired by frustration sets in. Sarraute's children become resentful of their legislated status and unwilling to accept the mere virtuality of their power. They are ready to seize control immediately. So the song of their laughter no longer holds out a promise of redemption for the adult, but is the triumphant chant of the victorious child. The crushed father acknowledges the inevitability of their ascendance: "They are the strongest. They are invincible. Invulnerable" (p. 45). With these words he accepts the underlying thesis of Bernanos's *Les Grands Cimetières sous la lune* (*The Big Cemeteries in the Moonlight*) that the world will be judged by children.

The power the children wield is made manifest through the effect their actions have on their father. The multiple hypotheses he constructs are all the products of the guilty conscience which his children inspire in him, and the manifold versions range from the self-justificatory to the self-accusatory and culminate in a vision of abject self-humiliation. In a reversal of roles, he makes a supreme offering to the child-divinities, and it is no longer to chastise them that he goes upstairs. Instead, he humbly brings them the statuette, which he hopes they will deign to preserve in their sanctuary. The gesture entailed by this sacrifice in itself represents the defeat of the adult, and its consequences serve to confirm the extent of the disaster. The children do not enshrine the relic, which they have appropriated with reverence, but degrade it with an apparently innocent thoughtlessness. The statuette becomes a part of the rubble with which the room is filled and proves its utility only by serving as an ashtray. In an acknowledgment of his unconditional surrender, the father uses it to extinguish his own cigarette butt. Sure of their victory, the children now have no compunctions about returning the priceless objet d'art to their parent with the understanding that he will donate it to a museum. The children have obliged the adult to bury his fetish in the very mausoleum in which he has tried to suffocate them.

This victory of the weak over the powerful had already been foretold by Thomas Mann in his *Tristan* and is perhaps the logical, even inevitable, outcome of the idolatry of the child which Rousseau and Hölderlin inaugurated and which the romantics institutionalized. The eventual supremacy of the young is certainly implicit in the surrealist adventure and in Breton's dictum from his *First Manifesto of Surrealism* that "It is perhaps childhood which comes closest to 'true life.'" The implications of this dictum are exploited by writers of all persuasions. Even Giraudoux, in his *The Adventures of Jérôme Bardini*, envisages a future in which a triumphant childhood will be the model for life: "The feelings of the child were so spontaneous, so close to nature and to common sense that one could well imagine a humanity subjugated to this manner of being human" (p. 153).

Exactly as in the Rousseauistic vision, this utopia is based on the transparence of its inhabitants and the subsequent perfection of their interrelationships. This ideal harmony would make possible the abolition of the rules of civilization and would result in "a humanity without social and aesthetic laws, as free of its multiple codes as of those ties which produced glazed earthenware and Cordovan leather" (p. 154). Such a euphoric state assumes a universal concord without which the ascendancy of the child would lead to anarchy. Because Giraudoux is aware of the impossibility of establishing such an understanding, his child must return docilely to his family. Giraudoux is not yet ready to dispense with Sarraute's symbolic statuette.

Like so many liberation movements, the one for children culminates not in the re-creation of an innocent paradise but either in chaos or in the establishment of a new and equally repressive order marked by acrimonious recriminations. The children may indeed vanquish their elders in Vitrac's *Victor or Children to Power* but by humiliating their conquered parents they vitiate their own reign. And in Jean Varoujean's *Will There Be Another Summer?* the children choose as their allies Thanatos and Eros and thus assure the corruption of their kingdom before it can even be established. One of the most moving but delusory of the graffiti scrawled on the wall of a Parisian school in 1969 proclaimed: "Underneath the pavement there is the beach." The nostalgia for this unattainable strand is omnipresent in modern literature from Bernardin de Saint-Pierre to Eluard. However, only an unthinking emancipationist like Christiane Rochefort is naive enough to believe that a non-violent Children's Crusade can lead us to a strip of sand too fragile to support human habitation. So the platitudinous pieties of liberationism that characterize her puerile glorification of children's revolt in the novel *Encore heureux qu'on va vers l'été* (*It Is Fortunate*

We Can Look Forward to Another Summer) (1975) and the left-wing clichés of her hysterical diatribe *Les Enfants d'abord (Children First)* (1976) remain totally unconvincing. Golding, in *Lord of the Flies*, had already demythified puerile conquests by equating them with adult ones and George Bernard Shaw, in his preface to *Misalliance*, had already effectively railed against "the monstrous system of child imprisonment and torture which we disguise under such hypocrisies as education, training, formation of character and the rest of it." [2]

Nathalie Sarraute is far more realistic and subtle than Christiane Rochefort, and the triumph of her children is only transitory. The deflationary finale of *Do You Hear Them?* reduces the drama to its adult proportions, and, within these miniaturized proportions, the narrative resumes its simple functionality. The result is that in retrospect the entire recital becomes what, in a different context, Julia Kristeva has called "an analytical discourse which appropriates for itself a privileged foil, the nodal point of life and language (of the species and of society)—the child." [3] This transformation is brought about by the father's final meditation on the ambiguous scene which obsesses him. He envisions a future in which his children, as grown-ups, take out-of-town visitors to the Louvre to do obeisance to the statuette before going on to visit the cemetery of Père-Lachaise. This ironic undermining of the children's victory immediately precedes the ultimate silencing of their laughter with which the novel ends:

Their laughter is dispersed. . . . Carefree laughter. Innocent laughter. Laughter for nobody. Laughter in the void. Their voices make a confused sound which becomes weaker, which fades in the distance.

It is as if a door up there were being closed again. And then nothing. (p. 185)

We are left with the unanswered cry that resounds through the first chapter of Colette's *Claudine's House*: "Where are the children?" With the modern novel a door has indeed been closed on children, and the *voci puerili* seem, for the time being at least, to have been silenced. However, as Thomas Mann demonstrated in *Joseph and His Brothers*, their echo can impart new harmonies to the overwhelming concert of the adult orchestra. Even when carried away by his adulation of childhood, Hölderlin must confess that "The time of awakening, too, is beautiful," and in *Hyperion* he sings of the "sacred days" during which the child develops into an adult. In a similar but more sober vein Eluard praises the conjugation of the child and the man. It is in such hymns of joy that the echo of the voices of children is preserved and it is within this context that their language assumes its full significance.

Notes

Introduction

1. The English translation of his *L'Enfant et la vie familiale sous l'ancien régime* is appropriately entitled *Centuries of Childhood: A Social History of Family Life*, trans. Robert Baldick (New York: Random House, 1965).

2. *Collected Plays with Their Prefaces*, 2 vols. (London: Max Reinhardt, The Bodley Head, 1972), 2:18.

3. *Propos*, Bibliothèque de la Pléiade, 2 vols. (Paris: Gallimard, 1970), 2:785.

4. *The Collected Essays* (New York: Stein and Day, 1971), p. 471.

5. Jacques Lacan, *Ecrits* (Paris: Editions du Seuil, 1966), p. 652.

6. *Gesammelte Werke: Gedichte und lyrische Dramen* (Vienna: Fischer Verlag, 1952), p. 16.

7. *Oeuvres complètes*, Bibliothèque de la Pléiade, 2 vols. (Paris: Gallimard, 1968), 1:1199.

8. *Anthropologie structurale deux* (Paris: Librairie Plon, 1973), p. 33.

9. Quoted in Bertrand d'Astorg, "Enfance et littérature," *Esprit* 16 (July 1954): 13.

10. *De finibus* 2. 10. 32.

11. *La Poétique de la rêverie* (Paris: Presses Universitaires Françaises, 1961), p. 113.

12. *Phänomenologie des Geistes* (Hamburg: Felix Meiner Verlag, 1955), p. 11.

13. Ibid., p. 20.

14. Cf. François Chamoux, *L'Aurige de Delphe* (Paris: Editions de Boccard, 1955), pp. 47–49.

15. For an excellent analysis of the import of this garment see W. Warde Fowler, "On the Toga Praetexta of Roman Children," *Classical Review*, October 1896, pp. 317–19.

16. Emmanuel Le Roy Ladurie, *Montaillou, village occitan de 1294–1324* (Paris: Gallimard, 1975), p. 307.

17. *L'Escoufle, roman d'aventure*, ed. H. Michelant and P. Meyer, Société des Anciens Textes Français (Paris: Librairie de Firmin Didot et cie, 1894), p. 56.

18. *Jourdain de Blaye (Jordains de Blaivies)*, *Chanson de geste*, ed. Peter F. Dembowski (Chicago and London: University of Chicago Press, 1969), p. 109.

19. *Oeuvres complètes*, Bibliothèque de la Pléiade, 2 vols. (Paris: Gallimard, 1969), 1:535.

20. A provocative discussion of this phenomenon is found in Ernest G. Schachtel, "On Memory and Childhood Amnesia," in *The World of the Child: Birth to Adolescence from the Child's Viewpoint*, ed. Toby Talbot (New York: Doubleday, Anchor Books, 1968), pp. 11–51.

21. Cf. *Three Essays on the Theory of Sexuality*, trans. J. Strachey (New York: Basic Books, 1975).

22. Cf. *The Interpretation of Dreams*, trans. A. A. Brill (London: George Allen & Co., 1913).

23. *The Complete Works* (New York: Harper and Bros., 1871), 3:482.

24. Richard Howard, "Childhood Amnesia," ed. Peter Brooks, *Yale French Studies: The Child's Part*, 43 (1969): 168.

25. *The Interpretation of Dreams*, p. 107.

26. (New York: W. W. Norton, 1964), p. 76.

27. *Psychopathology of Everyday Life* (New York: New American Library, 1972), p. 34.

28. *Phänomenologie des Geistes*, p. 44.

29. As in the impressive though occasionally derivative study by Erna M. Johansen, *Betrogene Kinder: Eine Sozialgeschichte der Kindheit* (Frankfurt on the Main: Fischer Verlag, 1978).

30. This is the thesis of Pierre Leulliette, *Les Enfants martyrs* (Paris: Le Seuil, 1978), and of Leila Sebbar, *On tue les petites filles* (Paris: Stock, 1978).

31. *Répertoire* (Paris: Gallimard, 1967), p. 49.

Chapter One

1. *Oeuvres complètes*, Bibliothèque de la Pléiade, 2 vols. (Paris: Gallimard, 1967), 2:1508.

2. André Gide, *Romans*, Bibliothèque de la Pléiade (Paris: Gallimard, 1958), p. 31.

3. Cf. *Les Nourritures terrestres*: "My marvelous convalescence was a palingenesis. I was reborn with a new being, under a new sky, and in the midst of completely renewed things" (ibid., p. 161).

4. For a typical but brilliant interpretation of this sort, see Jean Delay, *La Jeunesse d'André Gide*, vol. 2 (Paris: Gallimard, 1957).

5. Franz Kafka, *Tagebücher (1910–1923)* (Frankfurt on the Main: Fischer Verlag, 1951), p. 633.

6. Henry James, *What Maisie Knew* (Garden City, N.Y.: Doubleday, 1954), p. 280.

7. *The Years* (New York: Harcourt, Brace & World, 1965), p. 68.

8. For examples see E. R. Curtius, *Europäische Literatur und Lateinisches Mittelalter* (Bern: A. Francke Verlag, 1958), pp. 106–8.

9. Adalbert Stifter, *Studien* (Munich: Winkler Verlag, 1966), p. 600.

10. J. W. von Goethe, *Werke*, Deutsche National Literatur (Stuttgart: Union Deutsche Verlagsgesellschaft, 1882–97), 14:188.

11. *Jude the Obscure* (New York: Airmont Publishing Co., 1966), p. 217.

12. The four extant letters to her all deal with the education of his ten-year-old nephew, Felix and, taken together, form a paradoxical essay on the role of the child.

13. A fact ignored by most Kafka critics. Cf. Gilles Deleuze and Félix Guattari, *Kafka: Pour une littérature mineure* (Paris: Editions de Minuit, 1975), pp. 141–44, for some fascinating suggestions concerning the interpenetration of "childhood blocks" with "adult blocks"; these concepts should be further developed.

14. Franz Kafka, *Erzählungen* (New York: Schocken Verlag, 1946), p. 153.

15. Franz Kafka, *Der Prozess* (Berlin: Schocken Verlag, 1955), p. 49.

16. Cf. James Gorden, "Demonic Children," in *New York Times Book Review*, 11 September 1977, pp. 3, 52–53 for a list and discussion of recent novels that exploit this theme.

17. *The Scarlet Letter* (New York: Hart Publishing Co., 1976), p. 243.

18. *Sämtliche Werke* (Berlin: v. Arnims Verlag, 1857), 20:10.

19. Friedrich von Hardenberg (Novalis), *Die Dichtungen*, 4 vols. (Heidelberg: Verlag Lambert Schneider, 1953), 1:408.

20. The name of this "chaste lamb" is also that of a plant reputed to have anaphrodisiac qualities, a significant detail in view of the importance of flower symbolism in Brentano's work.

21. In the paralipomena to the *Romanzen* Brentano equates Agnuscastus with the anti-Christ. Cf. *Werke*, 4 vols. (Munich: Carl Hanser Verlag, 1968), 1:992.

22. "To H. C." (1802), lines 11–14.

23. *Les Misérables*, Bibliothèque de la Pléiade (Paris: Gallimard, 1956), p. 182.

24. *Silas Marner* (New York: New American Library, 1960), p. 18.

25. *Aventures de Jérôme Bardini* (Paris: Grasset, 1966), pp. 155–57.

26. *Goodbye Columbus and Five Short Stories* (Boston: Houghton Mifflin, 1959), p. 158.

27. Thomas Mann, *Gesammelte Werke*, 13 vols. (Frankfurt on the Main: Fischer Verlag, 1974), 8:262.

28. The decline of Aschenbach is in many respects similar to that of the Baron de Charlus in Proust's *A La Recherche du temps perdu*. The latter also presents a pathetic figure when he makes himself up in order to please the young man he loves.

29. Leslie Fiedler, *The Collected Essays* (New York: Stein and Day, 1971), 1:506.

30. These details are from the original French version of the play. The subsequent English text is sparser.

31. *Les Grands Cimetières sous la lune* (Paris: Librairie Plon, 1962), p. 9.

32. Günter Grass, *Die Blechtrommel* (Frankfurt on the Main: Fischer Bücherei, 1963), p. 37.

Chapter Two

1. *Oliver Twist* (London: Oxford University Press, 1974), p. 4.

2. *Great Expectations* (London: Oxford University Press, 1975), pp. 377–78.

3. At the urging of Bulwer Lytton, Dickens changed this ending to an even more optimistic one in which, after the death of "the Spider," Estella and Pip are forever reunited.

4. *The Way of All Flesh* (New York: E. P. Dutton, 1911), p. 26.

5. *Nicholas Nickleby* (London: Oxford University Press, 1974), p. 88.

6. Hieronymus, *The Satirical Letters of Saint Jerome*, trans. Paul Carroll (Chicago: Gateway Editions, 1956), p. 196.

7. The most convincing rationale for this interpretation is that of John Freccero, "Bestial Sign and Bread of Angels (*Inferno* 32–33)," *Yale Italian Studies* 1, no. 1 (Winter 1977), pp. 53–66.

8. Although the account is quite inaccurate as far as names, places, dates and other details are concerned, it is based on historical facts.

9. Antoine de la Salle, *Du Réconfort de Madame du Fresne*, in Joseph Nève, *Antoine de La Salle: Sa Vie et ses ouvrages d'après des documents inédits* (Paris: H. Champion, 1903), p. 134.

10. *Two Spanish Picaresque Novels*, trans. Michael Alpert (Baltimore: Penguin Classics, 1973), p. 27.

11. Ibid., p. 97.

12. Hans Jacob Christoffel von Grimmelshausen, *Die Simplicianischen Schriften*, 2 vols. (Leipzig: F. W. Hendel Verlag, 1939), 1:17–18.

13. *The Painted Bird* (New York: Bantam Books, 1972), p. 8.

14. *Quatre-vingt-treize* (Paris: Hetzel, 1889), pp. 104–11.

15. *Anton Reiser* (Munich: Winkler Verlag, 1971), p. 9.

16. Jeremias Gotthelf, *Werke* (Basel and Stuttgart: Birkhäuer Verlag, 1948), 1:159. The author's assumption of his narrator's name indicates the importance he attaches to it.

17. For a historical treatment of this underlying reality, see John Reed, *Victorian Conventions* (Athens, Ohio: Ohio University Press, 1975), especially chapter 7.

18. *Wuthering Heights* (New York: Harper and Bros., 1848), pp. 22–23.

19. *Jane Eyre* (New York: Macmillan, 1937), p. 10.

20. *Werke*, 1:172.

21. *Sämtliche Werke* (Munich: Winkler Verlag, 1968), 1:286.

22. *Poil de Carotte* (Paris: Flammarion, 1946), p. 354.

23. *Journal*, Bibliothèque de la Pléiade (Paris: Gallimard, 1965), p. 54.

24. S. A. Courtauld, ed., *The Odes and Epodes of Horace*, trans. John Marshall (London: Bickers and Son, 1929), p. 351.

25. *Les Rougon-Macquart*, Bibliothèque de la Pléiade (Paris: Gallimard, 1960), 2:1379.

26. Yukio Mishima, *The Sailor Who Fell from Grace with the Sea* (New York: Berkley Medallion Books, 1971), p. 115.

27. Charles A. Owen, Jr., in his unpublished paper "A Certein Nombre of Conclusiouns: The Nature and Nurture of Children in Chaucer," demonstrates Chaucer's sympathetic attitude toward children.

28. *Oeuvres complètes*, Bibliothèque de la Pléiade (Paris: Gallimard, 1969), 4:419.

29. *Walden Two* (New York: Macmillan, 1962), p. 262.

30. *Paul et Virginie* (Paris: A. Quantin, 1878), pp. 80–81.

31. George Sand, *Histoire de ma vie* (Paris: M. Levy, 1876), 2:151.

32. *Le Grand Meaulnes* (Paris: Librairie Fayard, 1971), p. 72.

33. Cf. Max Primault, Henry Lhong, and Jean Malrieu, *Terres de l'enfance* (Paris: Presses Universitaires de France, 1961). Primault speaks of Alain-Fournier's "ardent quest and ecstatic discovery" (p. 20) and fails to see the destructive nature of Meaulnes's sterile enterprise.

34. *Oeuvres complètes*, Bibliothèque de la Pléiade (Paris: Gallimard, 1968), 2:680.

35. *Point Counter Point* (Harmondsworth, England: Penguin Books, 1976), p. 435.

36. *Les Rougon-Macquart*, 2:809.

37. *Les Plaisirs et les jours* (Paris: Gallimard, 1950), p. 147.

38. *Oeuvres*, Bibliothèque de la Pléiade (Paris: Gallimard, 1958), p. 397.

39. *The Collected Short Stories* (New York: World Publishing Co., 1970), p. 216.

Chapter Three

1. In the following discussion, I use the word *myth* in the sense of a secondary semiological system. Cf. Roland Barthes, *Mythologies* (Paris: Editions du Seuil, 1970), p. 199.

2. Jean Starobinski, *Jean-Jacques Rousseau: La Transparence et l'obstacle* (Paris: Gallimard, 1971), p. 14.

3. *Oeuvres complètes*, 1:20–21.

4. *The Mill on the Floss* (London: Oxford University Press, 1950), p. 205.

5. An unjustly neglected novel that is one of the finest examples of the pattern I am concerned with.

6. *Romans et Nouvelles*, Bibliothèque de la Pléiade (Paris: Gallimard, 1968), 2:59.

7. *The Diary of a Writer*, trans. and ann. Boris Brasol (New York: Charles Scribner's Sons, 1949), 2:590.

8. *Childhood, Boyhood, Youth*, trans. Rosemary Edmonds (Baltimore: Penguin Books, 1964), p. 13.

9. *Les Rougon-Macquart*, 1:1306.

10. Zola insists on this point. Cf. e.g., "He was putting on weight, he was a beautiful child" (p. 1333), "Serge was born into the childhood of morning" (p. 1334), "This was his childhood" (p. 1333).

11. See Emilie Noulet, *Le Premier Visage de Rimbaud* (Brussels: Editions J. Duculot, 1953), in which this thesis is substantially documented.

12. My own analysis is partially based on the brilliant reading of this complex tale in Mark Spilka, "Turning the Freudian Screw: How Not to Do It," *Literature and Psychology* 13, 4 (Fall 1963): 105–11.

13. *The Turn of the Screw* (New York: W. W. Norton, 1966), p. 7.

14. *Les Enfants terribles* (Paris: Grasset, 1929), p. 6.

15. There is a sensitive visual representation of this transmogrification in Cocteau's film *Le Sang d'un poète*. The cinematic version of *Les Enfants terribles* is far less successful in portraying this scene.

16. The famous dancer, whom Cocteau knew, was strangled to death while riding in an open sports car while her flowing scarf caught in one of the wheels. This accident occurred a year before the publication of *Les Enfants terribles*.

17. There is an equally impressive number of recent films based on this pattern. One of the most sensitive is the Spanish *Cria*.

18. As does the film version of the same title.

19. *A High Wind in Jamaica* (New York: Harper & Row, 1972), p. 16.

20. That the death of animals can prove more of a shock for children than that of people is a common phenomenon. It has been beautifully exploited in the opening scene of the film *Les Jeux interdits*. A group of refugees fleeing to unoccupied France is strafed by German planes. Two children survive and, puzzled but emotionless, survey the scene of carnage. When their eyes light upon the bodies of their parents, there is no sign of sorrow, but when they find the remains of their dog they break down in tears, lift up their pet's body, and carry him off in their arms.

21. *Lord of the Flies* (New York: G. P. Putnam's Sons, Capricorn Series, 1959), p. 12.

22. E. T. A. Hoffman, *Sämtliche poetischen Werke*, Die Tempel-Klassiker, 4 vols. (Wiesbaden: Emil Vollmer Verlag, 1976), 2:471.

23. This anti-intellectual image of a deleterious writing fluid is also found throughout the work of Victor Hugo. In *L'Ane*, for example, the poet has a vision of humanity drowned by an inundation of pedants' ink.

24. Thomas Mann, *Gesammelte Werke*, 13 vols. (Frankfurt on the Main: S. Fischer, 1974), 4:485.

25. Mann, *Gesammelte Werke*, 4:582.

26. Mann, *Gesammelte Werke*, 4:668.
27. Mann, *Gesammelte Werke*, 5:1323.
28. Mann, *Gesammelte Werke*, 4:894.
29. Mann, *Gesammelte Werke*, 5:1138.
30. *Sämtliche Werke* (Stuttgart: W. Kohlhammer Verlag, 1958), 3:187.
31. Mann, *Gesammelte Werke*, 5:1329.
32. Ibid., 5:1685.
33. *Gesammelte Werke in zwölf Einzelausgaben: Die Erzählungen* (Stockholm: Bermann-Fischer Verlag, 1945), p. 454.
34. The author refers to it as such in his own notes to the text; ibid., p. 461.

Chapter Four

1. Hieronymus, *Satirical Letters of Saint Jerome*, p. 193.
2. (Darmstadt and Neuwied: Luchterhand, 1977), p. 383.
3. *The Interpretation of Dreams*, p. 215.
4. *La Comédie humaine*, Bibliothèque de la Pléiade (Paris: Gallimard, 1971), 7:1037.
5. *The Writings of George Eliot: Scenes of Clerical Life, Silas Marner* (Boston: Little, Brown, 1900), p. 72.
6. Mann, *Gesammelte Werke*, 4:648.
7. *Oeuvres* (Paris: Mercure de France, 1972), 7:206.
8. For the evolution of reactions to the death of Little Nell, see George H. Ford, *Dickens and His Readers: Aspects of Novel-Criticism since 1836* (Princeton: Princeton University Press, 1955), pp. 55–71. Some recent critics have been more indulgent. Angus Wilson, in his review of Ford's book (*Encounter* 5 (July 1955): 73–76), defends the death of Paul in Dickens's *Dombey and Son*, and Mark Spilka that of Little Nell in his article "Little Nell Revisited" (*Papers of the Michigan Academy of Arts, Science, and Letters* 45 (1960): 427–37).
9. For an analysis of sentimentalism in literature, see Aldous Huxley, "Vulgarity in Literature," in *Music at Night* (London: Chatto & Windus, 1949), pp. 270–336.
10. Gordon Fleming, *The Young Whistler 1834–66* (London: George Allen & Unwin, 1978), p. 34. For other examples of Anna's rejoicing in the deaths of James Whistler's brothers, see pp. 31–32, 35, and 41.
11. *On tue un enfant* (Paris: Editions du Seuil, 1975), p. 12. The opening essay, "Pierre-Marie ou de l'enfant," despite its tortured, Lacanian form of expression, is a psychologist's extraordinary meditation on the death of the child.
12. (New York: Viking Press, 1975), p. 209.
13. D. H. Lawrence, *The Complete Short Stories* (New York: Viking Press, 1975), 3:804.
14. For an extensive discussion of child abuse in the works of Dostoevski, see William W. Rowe, *Dostoievski: Child and Man in His Works* (New York and London: New York University Press and University of London Press, 1968), pp. 3–33.
15. Dostoevski anticipates the contemporary theatre of protest. Cf. Edward Bond's *Saved* (New York: Hill & Wang, 1966). The notorious scene in which an infant, used as a soccer ball, is battered to death, has been condemned as revolting. It is actually a powerful expression of revolt inspired by an unsentimental sense of injustice.

16. For a very subtle and different analysis of this issue, see Mark Spilka, "Human Worth in *The Brothers Karamazov*," *Minnesota Review* 5, no. 1 (1965): 38–49.

17. Albert Camus, *Théâtre—Récits—Nouvelles*, Bibliothèque de la Pléiade (Paris: Gallimard, 1962), p. 1393.

18. Albert Camus, *Essais*, Bibliothèque de la Pléiade (Paris: Gallimard, 1965), p. 466.

19. *Goethes Werke*, Deutsche National-Litteratur, 36 vols. (Stuttgart: Union Deutsche Verlagsgesellschaft, 1882–97), 15, 2:309.

20. Paul Claudel, *Théâtre*, Bibliothèque de la Pléiade, 2 vols. (Paris: Gallimard, 1948), 2:689.

21. Mann, *Gesammelte Werke*, 6:611–12.

22. *Gigi* (Paris: Hachette, 1960), p. 65.

23. *Lolita* (New York: G. P. Putnam's Sons, 1955), p. 23.

Chapter Five

1. *Oeuvres complètes*, 2:601.

2. *Sämtliche Werke* (Stuttgart: W. Kohlhammer, 1957), vol. 3, book I, 3rd letter to Bellarmin, p. 10.

3. Novalis, *Die Dichtungen*, 1:408.

4. *Oeuvres complètes* (Bordeaux: Guy Ducros, 1970), ch. 9:129.

5. Clemens Brentano, *Werke* (Munich: Karl Hanser Verlag, 1968), 1:57–60.

6. Brentano, *Werke*, 1:479.

7. Francis Thompson, *Works of Francis Thompson* (London: Burns and Oates Ltd., 1913), 2:7.

8. Thompson, *Works*, 1:52.

9. Ibid., 1:38.

10. *Oeuvres complètes*, ch. 11:137.

11. I have made no attempt to discuss the development of Wordsworth's thought or to take into account the differences in the two versions of *The Prelude*. This topic has been dealt with extensively, most recently in Robert Pattison, *The Child Figure in English Literature* (Athens, Ga.: University of Georgia Press, 1978), pp. 55–65.

12. Joseph von Eichendorff, *Werke* (Munich: Carl Hanser Verlag, 1959), p. 1061.

13. *My Childhood*, trans. Ronald Wilks (Baltimore: Penguin Books, 1966), p. 234.

14. Heinrich Heine, *Sämtliche Schriften*, ed. Klaus Briegleb, Reihe Hanser 220/1 (Munich/Vienna; Karl Hanser Verlag, 1976), 1:127.

15. *Oeuvres complètes*, Bibliothèque de la Pléiade (Paris: Gallimard, 1972), p. 121.

16. "A Crazed Girl," lines 9–14. See also Yeats's "To a Child Dancing in the Wind."

17. Rainer Maria Rilke, *Sämtliche Werke* (Wiesbaden: Insel-Verlag, 1955), 1–171.

18. This sensation is similar to the dizziness stimulated by Verlaine's "Chevaux de Bois." In both poems the image of faintness suggests the recession of reality.

19. *Oeuvre poétique* (Paris: Gallimard, 1960), 1:51–52.

Conclusion

1. Nathalie Sarraute, *Vous les entendez?* (Paris: Gallimard, Collection Folio, 1976), p. 9.

2. *Collected Plays with Their Prefaces*, 2:29. Shaw's proposals for reform are also far more honest—and radical—than those of Rochefort.

3. *Polylogue* (Paris: Editions du Seuil, 1977), p. 467.

Bibliography

Primary Sources

Agee, James. *A Death in the Family.*
Aicard, François Victor Jean. *La Chanson de l'enfant.*
Aiken, Conrad. "Silent Snow, Secret Snow." In *The Collected Short Stories.*
Alain. *See* Chartier, Emile Auguste.
Alain-Fournier. *See* Fournier, Henri Alain.
Arrabal, Fernando. *Théâtre.*
Ballantyne, R. M. *The Coral Island.*
Balzac, Honoré de. *L'Enfant maudit.*
Barlach, Ernst. *Der Findling.*
Barrie, J. M. *Peter Pan, or the Boy Who Would Not Grow Up.*
Beckett, Samuel. *Endgame.*
———. *Waiting for Godot.*
Benjamin, Walter. *Berliner Kindheit.*
Bernanos, Georges. *Les Enfants humiliés.*
Bernardin de Saint-Pierre, Jacques-Henri. *Paul et Virginie.*
Beyle, Henri-Marie [Stendhal]. *La Vie de Henri Brulard.*
Bitzius, Albert [Jeremias Gotthelf]. *Der Bauernspiegel.*
Blake, William. *Songs of Innocence.*
Bosco, Henri. *L'Ane Culotte.*
Bourget, Paul. *Anomalies.*
Brentano, Clemens. *Gockel, Hinkel, und Gackeleia.*
———. *Romanzen vom Rosenkranz.*
———. *Tagebuch der Ahnfrau.*
Brontë, Charlotte. *Jane Eyre.*
Brontë, Emily. *Wuthering Heights.*
Butler, Samuel. *The Way of All Flesh.*
Campbell, William Edward March [William March]. *The Bad Seed.*
Carroll, Lewis. *See* Dodgson Charles Lutwidge.
Chartier, Emile Auguste [Alain]. *Les Sources de la mythologie enfantine.*
———. *Propos.*
Chaucer, Geoffrey. "The Prioress's Tale." In *The Canterbury Tales.*
Clarke, Arthur C. *Childhood's End.*
Cocteau, Jean. *Les Enfants terribles.*
———. *Les Mariés de la Tour Eiffel.*
Colette, Sidonie-Gabrielle Claudine [Colette] *Claudine à l'école.*
———. "L'Enfant malade." In *Gigi.*

————. *La Maison de Claudine.*

Cortázar, Julio. *Selected Short Stories.*

Daudet, Alphonse. *Jack.*

————. *Le Petit Chose.*

De la Mare, Walter. "The Ideal Craftsman." In *On the Edge.*

D'Houville, Gérard. *L'Enfant.*

Dickens, Charles. *Bleak House.*

————. *David Copperfield.*

————. *Dombey and Son.*

————. *Great Expectations.*

————. *Hard Times.*

————. *Nicholas Nickleby.*

————. *The Old Curiosity Shop.*

————. *Oliver Twist.*

Dodgson, Charles Lutwidge [Lewis Carroll]. *Alice's Adventures in Wonderland.*

————. *Through the Looking Glass.*

Dostoevski, Fëdor. *The Beggar Boy.*

————. *The Brothers Karamazov.*

————. "A Little Boy at Christ's Christmas Tree." In *The Diary of a Writer.*

Drieu La Rochelle, Pierre. *Etat Civil.*

Duhamel, Georges. *Les Plaisirs et les jeux.*

Duvert, Tony. *L'Ile Atlantique.*

Ebner-Eschenbach, Marie von. *Das Gemeindekind.*

Eichendorff, Joseph von. *Aus dem Leben eines Taugenichts.*

————. *Werke,* vol. 1 *Gedichte.*

Eliot, George. *See* Evans, Mary Ann.

————. *Silas Marner.*

Eluard, Paul. *Oeuvres complètes.*

Evans, Mary Ann [George Eliot]. *The Mill on the Floss.*

Fogazzaro, Antonîo. *Piccolo mondo antico.*

Fournier, Henri Alain [Alain-Fournier]. *Le Grand Meaulnes.*

France, Anatole. *See* Thibault, Jacques Anatole François.

Gide, André. *Les Faux-Monnayeurs.*

————. *Si le grain ne meurt.*

————. *Le Voyage d'Urien.*

Giono, Jean. *Jean le bleu.*

Giraudoux, Jean. *Les Aventures de Jérôme Bardini.*

Goethe, J. W. von. *Die Novelle.*

————. *Faust I.*

————. *Wilhelm Meisters Lehrjahre.*

Golding, William. *Lord of the Flies.*

Gorki, Maxim. *My Childhood.*

Gosse, Edmund. *Father and Son.*

Gotthelf, Jeremias. *See* Bitzius, Albert.

Grass, Günter. *Die Blechtrommel.*

————. *Katz und Maus.*

Grimmelshausen, H. J. C. von. *Abenteuerlicher Simplicius Simplicissimus.*

Hardenberg, Friedrich von [Novalis]. *Hymnen an die Nacht.*

————. *Die Lehrlinge zu Sais.*

Hardy, Thomas. *Jude the Obscure.*

Hauptmann, Gerhart. *Bahnwärter Thiel.*

————. *Hanneles Himmelfahrt.*

Hawthorne, Nathaniel. *The Scarlet Letter.*

Hermant, Abel. *Eddy et Paddy.*

Hesse, Hermann. *Demian.*

————. "Kinderseele." In *Klingsor.*

————. *Unterm Rad.*

Hofmannsthal, Hugo von, *Gesammelte Werke: Gedichte und lyrische Dramen.*

Howells, William Dean. *A Boy's Town.*

Hughes, Richard. *A High Wind in Jamaica.*

Hugo, Victor. *L'Homme qui rit.*

————. *Les Misérables.*

————. *Quatre-vingt-treize.*

————. *Selected Poetry.*

James, Henry. *The Awkward Age.*

————. *The Turn of the Screw.*

————. *What Maisie Knew.*

Jammes, Francis. *De l'Âge divin à l'âge ingrat.*

Joyce, James. *A Portrait of the Artist as a Young Man.*

————. *Dubliners.*

Kafka, Franz. "Kinder auf der Landstrasse." In *Erzählungen.*

————. "Ein Landarzt." In *Erzählungen.*

Keller, Gottfried. *Der grüne Heinrich.*

Kipling, Rudyard. "Baa Baa, Black Sheep." In *Wee Willie Winkie.*

————. "Little Tobrah." In *Life's Handicap.*

Kleist, Heinrich von. *Das Erdbeben in Chile.*

————. *Der Findling.*

Kosinski, Jerzy. *The Painted Bird.*

Laforgue, Jules. *Selected Poetry.*

Lane, Harlan. *The Wild Boy of Aveyron.*

Laprade, Victor de. *Le Livre d'un père.*

Larbaud, Valéry. *Enfantines.*

Lawrence, D. H. *The Rainbow.*

————. "The Rocking-Horse Winner." In *The Complete Short Stories,* vol. 3.

Lazarillo de Tormes.

Léger, Alexis Saint-Léger [Saint-John Perse]. *Pour fêter une enfance.*

Leiris, Michel. *La Règle du jeu.*

Loti, Pierre. *See* Viaud, Louis Marie Julien.

Lowell, Robert. *Life Studies.*

Mann, Thomas. *Buddenbrooks: Verfall einer Familie.*

————. *Dr. Faustus.*
————. *Joseph und seine Brüder.*
————. *Tod in Venedig.*
————. *Tristan.*
————. *Das Wunderkind.*
March, William. *See* Campbell, William Edward March.
Mauriac, François. *Le Mystère Frontenac.*
————. *Le Sagouin.*
Mérimée, Prosper. *Mateo Falcone.*
Meyer, Conrad Ferdinand. "Das Leiden eines Knabens." *Sämtliche Werke,*
    vol. 1.
Michelet, Jules. *Ma Jeunesse.*
Millhauser, Steven. *Edwin Mullhouse.*
Mishima, Yukio. *The Sailor Who Fell from Grace with the Sea.*
Montaigne, Michel de. "De l'Institution des enfants." In *Essais* 1 : 26.
Montherlant, Henry de. *La Relève du matin.*
————. *La Ville dont le prince est un enfant.*
Moritz, Karl Philipp. *Anton Reiser.*
Munro, Hector Herbert [Saki]. *The Open Window.*
————. *The Story Teller.*
Nabokov, Vladimir. *Lolita.*
Novalis. *See* Hardenberg, Friedrich von.
Oe, Kenzaburo. *A Personal Matter.*
————. *Teach Us to Outgrow Our Madness.*
Orwell, George. *Coming Up for Air.*
————. *Such, Such Were the Joys.*
Pater, Walter Horatio. *The Child in the House.*
Péguy, Charles. *Le Porche du mystère de la deuxième vertu.*
Perez Galdos, Benito. *Miau.*
————. *Torquemada en el purgatorio.*
————. *Torquemada en la cruz.*
————. *Torquemada en la hoguera.*
————. *Torquemada y San Pedro.*
Perse, Saint-John. *See* Léger, Alexis Saint-Léger.
Proust, Marcel. *A la Recherche du temps perdu.*
————. "Confession d'une jeune fille." In *Les Plaisirs et les jours.*
Quevedo y Villegas, Francisco Gómez de. *The Swindler.* [*La Vida del
    Buscón*].
Rachilde. *See* Vallette, Marguerite.
Racine, Jean. *Athalie.*
Read, Herbert. *The Green Child.*
————. *The Innocent Eye.*
Renan, Ernest. *Souvenirs d'enfance et de jeunesse.*
Renard, Jules. *Poil de Carotte.*
Rilke, Rainer Maria. *Selected Poetry.*
————. "Die Turnstunde." In *Sämtliche Werke,* vol. 4.
————. "Uber Kunst." In *Sämtliche Werke,* vol. 5.

Rochefort, Christiane. *Encore heureux qu'on va vers l'été.*
———. *Les Enfants d'abord.*
Roth, Henry. *Call It Sleep.*
Roth, Phillip. "The Conversion of the Jews." In *Goodbye, Columbus.*
Rousseau, Jean-Jacques. *Emile.*
Saint-Exupéry, Antoine de. *Le Petit Prince.*
Salinger, J. D. *The Catcher in the Rye.*
———. *Nine Stories.*
Sarraute, Nathalie. *Portrait d'un inconnu.*
———. *Vous les entendez?*
Sartre, Jean-Paul. "L'Enfance d'un chef." In *Le Mur.*
———. *Les Mots.*
Saul, John. *Suffer the Children.*
Schwob, Marcel. *La Croisade des enfants.*
Ségur, Sophie, Comtesse de. *Les Malheurs de Sophie.*
Shaw, George Bernard. "Parents and Children." Preface to *Misalliance.*
Sologub, Fëdor. *Lights and Shadows.*
Steinbeck, John. *The Red Pony.*
Stendhal. *See* Beyle, Henri-Marie.
Stifter, Adalbert. *Abdias.*
Strauss, Emil. *Freund Hein.*
Supervielle, Jules. *Le Voleur d'enfants.*
Thackeray, William. *Barry Lyndon.*
Thibault, Jacques Anatole François [Anatole France]. *Le Livre de mon ami.*
———. *Le Petit Pierre.*
Thompson, Francis. *Poems on Children.*
———. *Sister Poems.*
Tieck, Ludwig. "Die Elfen." In *Die Märchen aus dem Phantasus.*
———. *Der gestiefelte Kater.*
Tolstoi, Leo. *Childhood, Boyhood, Youth.*
Traherne, Thomas. *Selected Poetry.*
Vallès, Jules. *L'Enfant.*
Vallette, Marguerite [Rachilde]. *L'Animale.*
Varoujean, Jean-Jacques. *Viendra-t-il un autre été?*
Vaughan, Henry. *Silex Scintillans.*
Viaud, Louis Marie Julien [Pierre Loti]. *Le Roman d'un enfant.*
Vitrac, Roger. *Victor, ou les enfants au pouvoir.*
Watts, Isaac. *Divine and Moral Songs for Children.*
Wharton, Edith. *The Children.*
———. *The Custom of the Country.*
Wittig, Monique. *L'Opoponax.*
Woolf, Virginia. *To the Lighthouse.*
———. *The Years.*
Wordsworth, William. *The Prelude.*
———. *Selected Poetry.*
Zola, Emile. *La Faute de l'Abbé Mouret.*

————. *Germinal.*

————. *Nana.*

————. *Une Page d'amour.*

Secondary Sources

Adelmann, Joseph. "Die Psychologie des Kindes bei Jean Paul und in der romantischen Dichtung." Ph.D. dissertation, University of Würzburg, 1923.

Adler, A. "Children in the 'Juste Milieu' (Comments to the *Journal des Enfans* [1832–1833])." *Romanische Forschungen* 79 (1967): 346–77.

Agamben, Giulio. *Infanzia e storia.* Turin: Einaudi, 1980.

Ahearn, Edward. "The Childlike Sensibility: A Study of Wordsworth and Rimbaud." *Revue de littérature comparée* 42, no. 2 (April–June 1968), pp. 234–56.

Alcorn, Clayton Reed. "The Children in the *Rougon-Macquart.*" Ph.D. dissertation, University of Connecticut, 1968.

Ambs, M. L. "Education of Children in Twentieth Century French Literature." Ph.D. dissertation, Western Reserve University, 1956.

Ariès, Philippe. *Centuries of Childhood: A Social History of Family Life.* Translated by Robert Baldick. New York: Random House, 1965.

Assmann, Aleida. "Werden was wir waren. Anmerkungen zur Geschichte der Kindheitsidee." *Antike und Abendland* 24 (1978): 98–124.

Avery, Gillian. *Childhood's Pattern: A Study of the Heroes and Heroines of Children's Fiction, 1770–1950.* London: Hodder & Stoughton, 1975.

————. *The Echoing Green: Memories of Victorian Youth.* New York: Viking Press, 1974.

————. *Nineteenth Century Children: Heroes and Heroines in English Children's Stories, 1780–1900.* London: Hodder & Stoughton, 1965.

Babenroth, Adolph. *English Childhood: Wordsworth's Treatment of Childhood in the Light of English Poetry prior to Crabbe.* New York: Columbia University Press, 1922.

Bachelard, Gaston. "Les Rêveries vers l'enfance." In *La Poétique de la rêverie.* Paris: Presses Universitaires Françaises, 1961, pp. 84–123.

Bance, A. F. "The Kaspar Hauser Legend and Its Literary Survival." *German Life and Letters* 18, no. 3 (1975), pp. 199–210.

Bäumer, Gertrud, and Droescher, Lili. *Von der Kinderseele.* Leipzig: 1924.

Behler, Wolfgang, ed. *Das Kind: Eine Anthropologie des Kindes.* Freiburg im Breisgau: Herder Verlag, 1971.

Beinlich, Alexander. "Kinder und Kinderseele in der deutschen Dichtung um 1900." Ph.D. dissertation, University of Breslau, 1937.

Bernham, G. F. "A Note on Jean Paul's Attitude to Play." *Neophilologus* 59, no. 2 (1975), pp. 273–76.

Bettelheim, Bruno. *The Empty Fortress*. New York: The Free Press, 1967.
———. *Love Is Not Enough*. Glencoe, Ill.: The Free Press, 1952.
———. *Truants from Life*. Glencoe, Ill.: The Free Press, 1955.
———. *The Uses of Enchantment: The Meaning and Importance of Fairy Tales*. New York: Alfred A. Knopf, 1976.
Bizot, R. "Pater's *The Child in the House* in Perspective." *Papers on Language and Literature* 8, supp. (1972): 79–95.
Blechmann, Wilhelm. "Jules Renard als Dichter der zerstörten Kindheit." *Orbis Litterarum* 1–2 (1963): 172–78.
Boas, George. *The Cult of Childhood*. London: The Warburg Institute, 1966.
Boer, Joseph P. C. de. *Victor Hugo et l'enfant*. Wassenaar: H. J. Dieben, 1933.
Boesch, Hans. *Kinderleben in der deutschen Vergangenheit*. Leipzig: Eugen Diederichs, 1900. Facsimile edition, Düsseldorf and Cologne: Diederichs, 1979.
Bonnefoy, Claude. "Un Thème privilégié: L'Enfance." *Quinzaine littéraire* 83 (16 November 1969): 6–8.
Borgmeier, Raimund. "Welt im Kleinen. Kinder als Zentralcharaktere in der modernen englischen short story." *Poetica* 5, no. 1 (1972), pp. 98–120.
Braunschwig, Marcel. *L'Art et l'enfant*. Paris and Toulouse: Colin, 1910.
Brewer, D. S. "Children in Chaucer." *Review of English Literature* (July 1964).
Bridel, Yves. *L'Esprit d'enfance dans l'oeuvre romanesque de Georges Bernanos*. Collection Lettres Modernes, Thèmes et Mythes, no. 10. Paris: Minard, 1966.
Brooks, Peter, ed. *The Child's Part. Yale French Studies* 43 (1969).
Brown, Diane S. "The Theme of Childhood in Nineteenth Century French Poetry." Ph.D. dissertation, University of Alabama, 1973.
Brown, Norman O. *Life against Death: The Psychoanalytic Meaning of History*. Middletown, Conn.: Wesleyan University Press, 1972.
Calvet, Jean. *L'Enfant dans la littérature française*. 2 vols. Paris: Lanore, 1930.
Carroy, J. R. "De Melville à Lowry, et retour par nos abîmes." *Lettres nouvelles* 2–3 (1974): 123–69.
Cellier, Léon. "Baudelaire et l'enfance." *Annales de la Faculté des Lettres et Sciences humaines de Nice* 2 and 3 (1968): 67–77.
Chamberlain, A. F. *The Child and Childhood in Folk-Thought. The Child in Primitive Culture*. New York: Macmillan, 1896.
———. *The Child: A Study in the Evolution of Man*. London: Walter Scott, 1901.
Charpentreau, Jacques. *Enfance et poésie*. Paris: Editions Ouvrières, Collection Enfance Heureuse, 1972.
Chombart de Lauwe, M. J. *Un Monde autre: L'Enfance, de ses représentations à son mythe*. Paris: Payot, 1971.
Colliot, R. "Perspectives sur la condition familiale de l'enfant dans la lit-

térature." In *Morale pratique et vie quotidienne dans la littérature française du Moyen-âge. Senefiance No. 1 (Cahiers du Cuer Ma).* Aix-en-Provence: Edition Cuer Ma, 1976, pp. 17–33.

———. "Un Thème de la littérature médiévale: 'L'Enfant de la forêt.'" *Annales de la Faculté des Lettres d'Aix* 38 (1964): 137–59.

Coveney, Peter. *The Image of Childhood, the Individual and Society: A Study of the Theme in English Literature.* Baltimore: Penguin Books, 1967.

———. *Poor Monkey: the Child in Literature.* London: Rockliff, 1957.

Cranston, Mechthild. *Enfance mon amour: La Rêverie vers l'enfance dans l'oeuvre de Guillaume Apollinaire, Saint-John Perse et René Char.* Paris: Nouvelles Editions Debresse, 1970.

d'Astorg, Bertrand. "Enfance et littérature." *Esprit* 16 (July 1954): 12–33.

deMause, Lloyd, ed. *The History of Childhood.* New York: Harper & Row, 1975.

Deslandres, Yvonne, and Thibaut, Claude. *L'Enfant et son image.* Paris: Editions Daniel, 1972.

Dupuy, Aimé. *Un Personnage nouveau du roman français: L'Enfant.* Paris: Librairie Hachette, 1931.

Eissler, Ruth S. et al., eds. *The Psychoanalytic Study of the Child.* New York: International Universities Press, 1956.

Empson, William. "Alice in Wonderland: The Child as Swain." In *The Critical Performance.* Edited by Stanley Edgar. Hyman, New York: 1956.

Erikson, Erik H. *Childhood and Society.* New York: W. W. Norton, 1963.

———. *Gandhi's Truth: On the Origins of Militant Nonviolence.* New York: W. W. Norton, 1969.

———. *Identity: Youth and Crisis.* New York: W. W. Norton, 1968.

———. *Young Man Luther. A Study in Psychoanalysis and History.* New York: W. W. Norton, 1958.

Estrin, Barbara, "The Lost Child in Spenser's *The Fairie Queen*, Sidney's "Old Arcadia," and Shakespeare's *The Winter's Tale.*" Ph.D. dissertation, Brown University, 1972.

Evans, J. W. "The Theme of Childhood in Baudelaire." Ph.D. diss., University of Manchester, 1959–60.

Fabre-Dire, Andrée. "Eluard et l'enfant." *Revue des sciences humaines* 36 (1971): 237–60.

Fellinger, Ferdinand. *Das Kind in der altfranzösischen Literatur.* Göttingen: Vandenhoeck & Ruprecht, 1908.

Fiedler, Leslie A. "Boys Will Be Boys!" *New Leader* 41 (1958): 23–26.

———. "The Eye of Innocence: Some Notes on the Role of the Child in Literature." In *The Collected Essays.* Vol. 1. New York: Stein and Day, 1971, pp. 471–511.

———. "From Redemption to Initiation." *New Leader* 41 (1958): 20–23.

————. "Good Good Girl and Good Bad Boy." *New Leader* 41 (1958): 22–25.

————. "The Invention of the Child." *New Leader* 41 (1958): 22–24.

————. *Love and Death in the American Novel.* Rev. ed. New York: Charles Scribner's Sons, 1959.

Fowler, W. Warde. "On the Toga Praetexta of Roman Children." *Classical Review*, October 1896, pp. 317–19.

Fragnière, Sr. Marie-Agnès. *Bernanos, fidèle à l'enfance.* Fribourg: Editions Universitaires, 1963.

Fraiberg, Selma H. *The Magic Years: Understanding and Handling the Problems of Early Childhood.* New York: Charles Scribner's Sons, 1959.

Franz, Marie Louise von. *The Problem of the Puer Aeternus.* New York: Spring Publications, 1970.

Freccero, John. "Bestial Sign and Bread of Angels (*Inferno* 32–33)." *Yale French Studies* 1, no. 1 (Winter, 1977), pp. 53–66.

Freese, Peter. *Die Initiationsreise. Studien zum jugendlichen Helden im modernen amerikanischen Roman* in *Kieler Beiträge zur Anglistik und Amerikanistik,* vol. 9. Neumünster: Karl Wachholtz, 1971.

Freud, Sigmund. *Gesammelte Werke.* Vol. 4: *Zur Psychopathologie des Alltagsleben.* Vol. 5: *Drei Abhandlungen zur Sexualtheorie.* Vol. 7: *Zur sexuellen Aufklärung der Kinder.* Vol. 9: *Eine Kindheitserinnerung des Leonardo da Vinci.* London, 1941.

Garrison, J. M., Jr. "The Adult Consciousness of the Narrator in Joyce's "Araby." *Studies in Short Fiction* 10, no. 4 (1973), pp. 416–17.

George, Jean. "Eluard et l'enfance." *Europe* 525 (January 1973): 132–36.

————. "Quand les poètes font les enfants (*Anthologie permanente de la poésie française*)." *Le Français aujourd'hui* (January 1973): 85–91.

Golda, Edward J. "L'Enfant dans l'oeuvre de Balzac." Ph.D. diss., Laval University, 1969.

Golden, N. M. B. "Enfants et adolescents dans l'oeuvre de Mauriac." Ph.D. dissertation, National University of Ireland, 1957–58.

Goldstein, Laurence. *Ruins and Empire: The Evolution of a Theme in Augustan and Romantic Literature.* Pittsburgh: University of Pittsburgh Press, 1977.

Goodman, Paul. *Growing Up Absurd: Problems of Youth in the Organized System.* New York: Vintage Books, 1960.

Gordon, James. "Demonic Children." *New York Times Book Review,* 11 September 1977, pp. 3, 52–53.

Gorunescu, Elena. "Universul copilariei în romanele lui Cocteau" [*Analele Universitatii Bucuresti Limbi Romanice* 19 (1970): 171–76. Synopsis in French: "L'Univers de l'enfance dans les romans de Cocteau," ["The Universe of Childhood in the Novels of Cocteau"] p. 176.

Gray, Ursula. *Das Bild des Kindes im Spiegel der altdeutschen Dichtung und Literatur. Mit textkritischer Ausgabe von Metlingers "Regiment der jungen Kinder.*" Europäische Hochschuhlschriften, ser. 1, vol. 91. Bern and Frankfurt: Herbert Lang, 1974.

Greene, Graham. "The Burden of Childhood." In *Collected Essays.* London: Bodley Head, 1969, pp. 127–31.

———. "The Lost Childhood." In *Collected Essays.* London: Bodley Head, 1969, pp. 13–19.

Grolman, Adolf von. *Kind und junger Mensch in der Dichtung der Gegenwart.* Berlin: Junker und Dünnhaupt, 1932.

Grützmacher, Curt. *Novalis und Philipp Otto Runge: Drei Zentralmotive und ihre Bedeutungssphäre: Die Blume—Das Kind—Das Licht.* Munich: Eidos Verlag, 1964.

Gutermuth, Else. "Das Kind im englischen Roman von Richardson bis Dickens." In *Giessener Beiträge zur Erforschung der Sprache und Kultur Englands und Nordamerikas.* Edited by Wilhelm Horn. Vol. 2. Giessen: Verlag des Englischen Seminars der Universität Giessen, 1925, pp. 29–60.

Gyurko, L. A. "Cortázar's Fictional Children: Freedom and Its Constraints." *Neophilologus* 57, no. 1 (1973), pp. 24–41.

———. "Fury in Three Short Stories by Julio Cortázar." *Revista de letras* 12 (December 1971).

Hagen, Rainer. *Kinder, wie sie im Buche stehen.* Munich: List, 1967.

———. "Mignon Lebt: Kinder in der deutschen und der französischen Literatur beschrieben und verglichen." *Eckart Jahrbuch* (1966–67): 88–102.

Hagstrun, Jean. "Such, Such Were the Joys: The Childhood of the Man of Feeling." In *Changing Taste in Eighteenth Century Art and Literature.* Edited by E. Minor. Los Angeles: W. A. Clark Memorial Library, 1972, pp. 43–61.

Hamilton, J. W. "Jensen's *Gradiva*: A Further Interpretation." *Imago* 30, no. 4 (1973), pp. 380–412.

Hamilton, Marie Padgett. "Echoes of Childermas in the Tale of the Prioress." In *Chaucer: Modern Essays in Criticism.* Edited by Edward Wagenknecht. New York: Oxford University Press, 1959, pp. 88–97.

Hardach-Pinke, Irene and Hardach, Gerd, eds. *Deutsche Kindheiten. Autobiographische Zeugnisse 1700–1900.* Kronberg: Athenäum Verlag, 1978.

Harder, Richard. Review of R. Kassel, *Quomodo quibus locis . . . . Gnomon* 28 (1956): 306–8.

Harder, W. T. "Crystal Source: Herbert Read's *The Green Child.*" *Sewanee Review* 81, no. 4 (1973), pp. 714–38.

Hartmann, Waltraud. "Das Motiv des Kindertodes in der neueren deutschen Erzählkunst." Ph.D. dissertation, University of Erlangen, 1953.

Hazard, Paul. *Les Livres, les enfants, et les hommes.* Paris: Flammarion, 1932.

Hefting, Victorine. *Kinderportretten*. Rotterdam: Lemniscaat, 1969.

Herter, Hans. "Das Leben ein Kinderspiel." In *Kleine Schriften*. Edited by Ernst Vogt. Studia et Testimonia Antiqua, no. 15. Munich: Wilhelm Fink Verlag, 1975, pp. 586–97.

———. "Das Unschuldige Kind in der antiken Literatur." In *Kleine Schriften*. Edited by Ernst Vogt. Studia et Testimonia Antiqua, no. 15. Munich: Wilhelm Fink Verlag, 1975, pp. 598–619.

Hess, René. "L'Autre." *Esprit* 39 (4 April 1979): 902–4.

Hildick, Wallace. *Children and Fiction. A Critical Study in Depth in the Artistic and Psychological Factors Involved in Writing Fiction for and about Children*. London: Evans, 1970.

Hughes, M. Y. "The Theme of Pre-existence and Infancy in *The Retreate*." *Philological Quarterly* 20 (1941): 484–500.

Hürlimann, Bettina. *Europäische Kinderbücher in drei Jahrhunderten*. Zürich: Siebenstern Taschenbuch Verein, 1959.

Jacobson, I. "The Child as Guilty Witness." *Literature and Psychology* 24, no. 1 (1974), pp. 12–23.

Johansen, Erna M. *Betrogene Kinder: Eine Sozialgeschichte der Kindheit*. Frankfurt on the Main: Fischer Verlag, 1978.

Jones, R. A. H. "The Theme of Childhood Recalled as It Finds Expression in *Sylvie* [Nerval], *Le Grand Meaulnes* [Alain-Fournier], and *Combray* [Proust]." Ph.D. dissertation, King's College (London), 1964–65.

Jung, Carl Gustav, and Kerényi, Karl. *Einführung in das Wesen der Mythologie. Das göttliche Kind. Das göttliche Mädchen*. Zurich: Rhein Verlag, 1951.

Karst, Theodor; Overbeck, Renate; and Tabbert, Reinbert. *Kindheit in der modernen Literatur. Interpretations- und Unterrichtsmodelle zur deutsch-, englisch-, und französischsprachigen Prosa*. Kronberg: Scriptor Verlag, 1976.

Kassel, Rudolfus. *Quomodo quibus locis apud veteres scriptores Graecos infantes atque parvuli pueri inducantur describantur commemorentur*. Meinsenheim on the Glan: Westkulturverlag, 1954.

Kay, Helen. *Picasso's World of Children*. Garden City, N.Y.: Doubleday, n.d.

Kazin, Alfred. "A Procession of Children." *American Scholar* (Spring 1964): 173.

Kempton, Adrian L. P. "Education and the Child in Eighteenth Century French Fiction." *Studies on Voltaire and the Eighteenth Century* 124 (1974): 299–362.

Key, Ellen. *The Century of the Child*. New York and London: G. P. Putnam's Sons, 1909.

Kiell, Norman. *The Adolescent through Fiction: A Psychological Approach*. New York: International Universities Press, 1974.

Kind, Hansgeorg. *Das Kind in der Ideologie und der Dichtung der deutschen Romantik*. Dresden: M. Dittert, 1936.

Klein, Anita E. *Child Life in Greek Art*. New York: Columbia University Press, 1932.

Koch, Willi A. "Das Kind in der Dichtung." *Eckart Jahrbuch* (1938), 6–.

Kohler, Janine. "Thématique et signification de l'enfance dans l'oeuvre poétique de Milosz-Milasius." Ph.D. dissertation, University of Paris (Vincennes), 1971. Abstract: "La Maison de jadis, le jardin de là-bas: Deux Lieux de l'enfance dans la poésie de Milosz." *Cahiers de L'Association des Amis de Milosz* 7 (1972), 21–36.

Kristeva, Julia. "Noms de lieu." In *Polylogue*. Paris: Editions de Seuil, 1977, pp. 467–91.

Kuhn, Reinhard. "The Massacre of the Innocents: Mortality among Fictional Children." *Michigan Quarterly Review*, 5th ser., vol. 19, no. 2 (Spring 1980), pp. 171–92.

———. "Traces in the Sand: Gide and Novalis with the Enigmatic Child." In *Intertextuality: New Perspectives in Criticism*. New York Literary Forum, vol. 2. New York: 1978, pp. 77–86.

Kushnir, Slava M. "L'Archetype de l'enfant dans l'oeuvre de Brasillach." *Revue de l'Université Laurentienne* 3 (2 November 1970): 38–47.

Labrusse, Rita. "Le Thème de l'enfance dans l'oeuvre de Colette." Ph.D. dissertation, University of Nice, 1968.

Lancier, Elisabeth. "Kind und junger Mensch in den Werken Alphonse Daudets." Ph.D. dissertation, Münster, 1935.

Leclaire, Serge. *On tue un enfant: Un Essai sur le narcissisme primaire et la compulsion de mort*. Paris: Editions du Seuil, 1975.

Leulliette, Pierre. *Les Enfants martyrs*. Paris: Editions du Seuil, 1978.

Levin, Harry. "Wonderland Revisited." *Kenyon Review* 27, no. 4 (Autumn 1965), pp. 591–616.

Lewis, R. W. B. *The American Adam: Innocence, Tragedy, and Tradition in the Nineteenth Century*. Chicago: University of Chicago Press, 1955.

Lods, J. "Le Thème de l'enfance dans l'épopée française." *Cahiers de civilisation médiévale* 3 (1960): 58–62.

Madeheim, Helmuth. "Kindheitserinnerungen französischer Dichter (Marcel Pagnol, Julien Green, Simone de Beauvoir)." *Die Neuren Sprachen* 15 (1966): 30–37.

Mannheim, Leonard. "The Dickens Hero as Child." *Studies in the Novel* 1 (Summer 1969): 189–95.

Marcus, Leah Sinanoglou. *Childhood and Cultural Despair: A Theme and Variations in Seventeenth-Century Literature*. Pittsburgh: University of Pittsburgh Press, 1978.

Martin, L. C. "Henry Vaughan and the Theme of Infancy." In *Seventeenth Century Studies Presented to Sir Herbert Grierson*. 1938, pp. 243–55.

Matheson, Annie. "George Eliot's Children." *Macmillan's Magazine* 46 (October 1882): 488–97.

Mercier, R. *L'Enfant dans la société du XVIIIème siècle (avant l'Emile)*. University of Dakar, Publications de la Section de Langues et Littératures, no. 6. Dakar, 1961.

Merleau-Ponty, Maurice. "Méthode en psychologie de l'enfant." *Bulletin de psychologie* 18 (3–6) (1964) pp. 109–40.

Mettra, C. "Le Ventre et son royaume." *L'Arc* 52 (1973): 36–39.

Meyers, J. "Orwell's Apocalypse: *Coming Up for Air*." *Modern Fiction Studies* 21, no. 1 (1975), pp. 69–80.

Micmacker, Ulrike. "Studie über die Darstellung des unglücklichen Kindes im französischen Roman." Ph.D. dissertation, University of Graz, 1971.

Minoque, Valerie. "The Imagery of Childhood in Sarraute's *Portrait d'un inconnu*." *French Studies* 27 (1973): 177–86.

Moorman, Mary. "Wordsworth and his Children." In *Bicentenery Wordsworth Studies in Memory of John Alban Finch*. Edited by Jonathan Wordsworth. Ithaca, N.Y.: Cornell University Press, 1970, pp. 111–41.

Nelson, Kenneth M. "A Religious Metaphor." *Reconstructionist* 31 (26 November 1965): 7–16.

Neumann, Erik. *The Child: Structure and Dynamics of the Nascent Personality*. Translated by Ralph Manheim. New York: G. P. Putnam's Sons, 1973.

Norden, Eduard. *Die Geburt des Kindes: Geschichte einer religiösen Idee*. Darmstadt: Wissenschaftliche Buchgesellschaft, 1958.

Orlando, Fr. *Infanzia, memoria, e storia da Rousseau ai Romantici*. Padua: 1966.

Parker, Clifford S. *The Defense of the Child by French Novelists*. Menasha, Wis.: Banta, 1925.

Pattison, Robert. *The Child Figure in English Literature*. Athens, Ga.: University of Georgia Press, 1978.

Peterson, Virgilia. "Re-entry into Childhood." *New York Times Book Review*, 26 June 1966, p. 4.

Piaget, Jean. *The Child's Conception of the World*. Translated by Joan Tomlinson and Andrew Tomlinson. New York: Harcourt, Brace, 1929.

———. *The Construction of Reality in the Child*. Translated by Margaret Cook. New York: Basic Books, 1955.

Plotnikoff, Natacha. "Les Thèmes de l'enfance chez Proust, Sartre, et Saint-Exupéry." Ph.D. dissertation, Brown University, 1970.

Pons, Roger. "Bernanos, héraut de l'enfance." *Terre humaine* (November 1956): 48–64.

Preyer, George. *Mental Development in the Child*, New York: 1895.

Primault, Max; Lhong, Henry; and Malrieu, Jean. *Terres de l'enfance: Le Mythe de l'enfance dans la littérature contemporaine*. Paris: Presses Universitaires de France, 1961.

Rameckers, Jan Matthias. *Der Kindesmord in der Literatur der Sturm-*

und-Drang-Periode: Ein Beitrag zur Kultur- und Literatur-Geschichte des 18. Jahrhunderts. Rotterdam: Nijgh & Van Ditmar's Uitgevers-Maatschappij, 1927.

Riesz, A. "Die Darstellung des unglücklichen Kindes in der französischen Literatur." Ph.D. dissertation, University of Graz, 1961.

Robichon, J. "Quelques écrivains contemporains et la notion de l'enfance." *La Table ronde* 114 (June 1957): 165–69.

Rowe, William W. *Dostoievsky: Child and Man in His Works.* New York and London: New York University Press and London University Press, 1968.

Santucci, Luigi. *Das Kind, sein Mythos und sein Märchen.* Hannover: 1964.

Saulnier, A.-H. "L'Esprit d'enfance dans la vie et la poésie de Mme Guyon." Ph.D. dissertation, Paris, 1958.

Schaub, Gerhard. *Le Génie enfant: Die Kategorie des Kindlichen bei Clemens Brentano.* Berlin and New York: Walter de Gruyter, 1973.

Scherf, Walter. *Strukturanalyse der Kinder- und Jugendliteratur. Bauelemente und ihre Psychologische Funktion.* Bad Heilbrunn: Verlag Julius Klinkhardt, 1978.

Schorsch, Anita. *Images of Childhood: An Illustrated Social History.* New York: Mayflower, Main Street, 1979.

Schrammen, Gerd. "Die Kinderfiguren im Werk Valery Larbauds." Ph.D. dissertation, Munich, 1967.

Sebbar, Leïla. *On tue les petites filles.* Paris: Stock, 1978.

Shine, Muriel G. *The Fictional Children of Henry James.* Chapel Hill: University of North Carolina Press, 1969.

Sion, Margareta. "Tema copilulvi in opera lui Hugo". *Analele Universitatii Bucuresti Limbi Romanice* 21 (1972): 101–08. Synopsis in French: "L'Enfant dans l'oeuvre de Hugo" ["The Child in the Work of Victor Hugo"], p. 108.

Söntgerath, Alfred. *Pädagogik und Dichtung: Das Kind in der Literatur des 20. Jahrhunderts.* Stuttgart: W. Kohlhammer, 1967.

Spann, Ekkehard. "Problemkinder" in der englischen Erzählkunst der Gegenwart." Ph.D. dissertation, Tübingen: 1970.

Speyer, W. "Das entdeckte heilige Buch in Novalis' Gedicht *An Tieck.*" *Arcadia* 9, no. 1 (1974), pp. 39–47.

Spilka, Mark. *Dickens and Kafka: A Mutual Interpretation.* Bloomington: Indiana University Press, 1963.

Steel, David A. "Le Thème de l'enfance dans l'oeuvre de Gide." Ph.D. dissertation, University of Paris, 1974.

Steinman, Theo. "Der Hang zum Bösen: Kinder im Spiegel neuerer Literatur." *Neues Hochland* 64 (1972): 227–41.

Stewart, Philip. "The Child Comes of Age." *Yale French Studies* 40 (1968): 134–41.

———. "Toward a History of Childhood." *History of Education Quarterly* 12, no. 2 (Summer 1972), pp. 198–209.

Stockmeyer, Clara. "Aufklärung und Sturm und Drang im Spiegel der

Kinderrolle: Eine Basler Doktorrede." *Zeitschrift für Deutschkunde* 37 (1923): 169.

Stoffer, Hellmut. *Die Bedeutung der Kindlichkeit in der modernen Welt.* Munich and Basel: E. Reinhardt, 1964.

Stone, Albert E. *The Innocent Eve: Childhood in Mark Twain's Imagination.* New Haven: Yale University Press, 1961.

Subrenat, Jean. "La Place de quelques petits enfants dans la littérature médiévale." *Mélanges de littérature du moyen âge au XXe siècle, offerts à Mademoiselle Jeanne Lods. . . , par ses collègues, ses élèves et ses amis.* (Paris: École Normale Supérieure de Jeunes Filles, 1978), 21:547−57.

Sully, James. *Studies of Childhood.* New York: D. Appleton & Co., 1895.

Süssmuth, Rita. "Studien zur Anthropologie des Kindes in der französischen Literatur der Gegenwart unter besonderer Berücksichtigung Mauriacs." Ph..D. dissertation, University of Münster, 1964.

Talbot, Toby, ed. *The World of the Child: Birth to Adolescence from the Child's Viewpoint.* New York: Doubleday, Anchor Books, 1968.

Tauber, Christian. *Le Thème de l'enfance dans la littérature actuelle.* Zurich: Juris-Verlag, 1971.

Taylor, Marissa G. "The Theme of Childhood Recollections in the Poetry of Hugo." Ph.D. dissertation, Wayne State University, 1973.

Tedder, James D. "On the Palingenetic Aesthetic: A Suggested Term for Critical Theory." *Journal of Aesthetics and Art Criticism* (Summer 1972): 507−17.

Thiher, Allen. "Vigo's *Zéro de conduite*: Surrealism and the Myth of Childhood." *Dada/Surrealism* 7 (1977): 99−108.

Trudel, Louise. "L'Enfance dans les contes de Schwob." *Revue de l'Université d'Ottawa* 38 (1968): 561−87.

Turner, Alison Mary. "The Motif of the Prodigal Son in French and German Literature to 1910." Ph.D. dissertation, University of North Carolina, 1966.

Vadin, Béatrix. "L'Absence de représentation de l'enfant et/ou du sentiment de l'enfance dans la littérature médiévale." In *Exclus et systèmes d'exclusion dans la littérature et la civilisation médiévale.* Senefiance no. 5, Cahiers Cuer Ma. Aix-en-Provence: Edition Cuer Ma, 1978, pp. 365−84.

Walsh, William. "Coleridge's Vision of Childhood." *Listener,* no. 53, February 1955, pp. 336−40.

Weber-Kellermann, Ingeborg. *Die Kindheit. Kleidung und Wohnen. Arbeit und Spiel: Eine Kulturgeschichte.* Frankfurt on the Main: Insel Verlag, 1979.

Wetherill, A. "The Significance of the Child in the Works of Flaubert, Zola, and Maupassant. Ph.D. dissertation, University of Sheffield, 1955−56.

Wickes, Frances G. *The Inner World of Childhood.* New York: Appleton, 1929.

Wicksteed, Joseph H. *Blake's Innocence and Experience*. New York: E. P. Dutton & Co., 1928.

Wilson, Angus. "Dickens on Children and Childhood." In *Dickens 1970*. Edited by Michael Slater. New York: Stein and Day, 1970, pp. 195–227.

Wind, Edgar. "Humanitätsidee und heroisiertes Porträt in der Englischen Kultur des 18. Jahrhunderts." *Vorträge der Bibliothek Warburg 9* (1930–31): 156–229.

Winterholer, Hans. *Eltern und Kinder in der deutschen Literatur des 18. Jahrhunderts*. Giessener Beiträge zur deutschen Literatur. Giessen: Münchow'sche University Press O. Kindt, 1924.

Wolff, Hilde. "Die Darstellung des Kindes in der deutschen Dichtung des ausgehenden 18. Jahrhunderts." Ph.D. dissertation, University of Cologne, 1924.

Wolfzettel, Friedrich. "Zur Stellung und Bedeutung der 'Enfances' in der altfranzösischen Epik." *Zeitschrift für französische Sprache und Literatur* 83 (1973): 317–48 and 84 (1974): 1–34.

Zwerdling, A. "Esther Summerson Rehabilitated." *PMLA* 88, no. 3 (1973), pp. 429–39.

In addition to the items above, it is useful to consult the four volumes of the *History of Childhood Quarterly*, which appeared between 1973 and 1977, and the subsequent issues of *The Journal of Psychohistory*, which replaced it. Although neither of these periodicals contains articles dealing directly with literature, many have important implications for a study of the child in literature.

Index

Corruption in Paradise
THE CHILD IN WESTERN LITERATURE

Reinhard Kuhn

"We do not know childhood," Rousseau once said, and two centuries and hundreds of books later the child is still an enigma. Picking up on the ground-breaking work done by Philippe Ariès in *Centuries of Childhood* (1960), Reinhard Kuhn turns in another direction to search for a comprehension of the real child through a study of his fictional counterpart. This is not a straightforward history of the appearance of the child in literature, but rather an inter-textual approach. By juxtaposing the work of such writers as Chrétien de Troyes and Henry James, for instance, the author facilitates new readings of familiar texts and detects common threads among them.

Literary children have traditionally evoked messages from mysterious worlds in ineffective yet tantalizing ways. Although exaggerated worship of the child may be a modern phenomenon, throughout Western literature writers have been intrigued by the earliest phases of development and the enigmas surrounding those worlds. In some sense the lost realities of childhood are akin to a forgotten dream world and the Freudian concept of "childhood amnesia." Kuhn's concept of the child is broad enough to embrace not only Blake's innocent two-day-old infant but also Proust's not-so-dutiful daughter well past her adolescence. He seeks to illuminate the fictional child, and in the process casts light upon the flesh-and-blood child of today, a child that is an assertive presence in his own right and also deep within each adult.